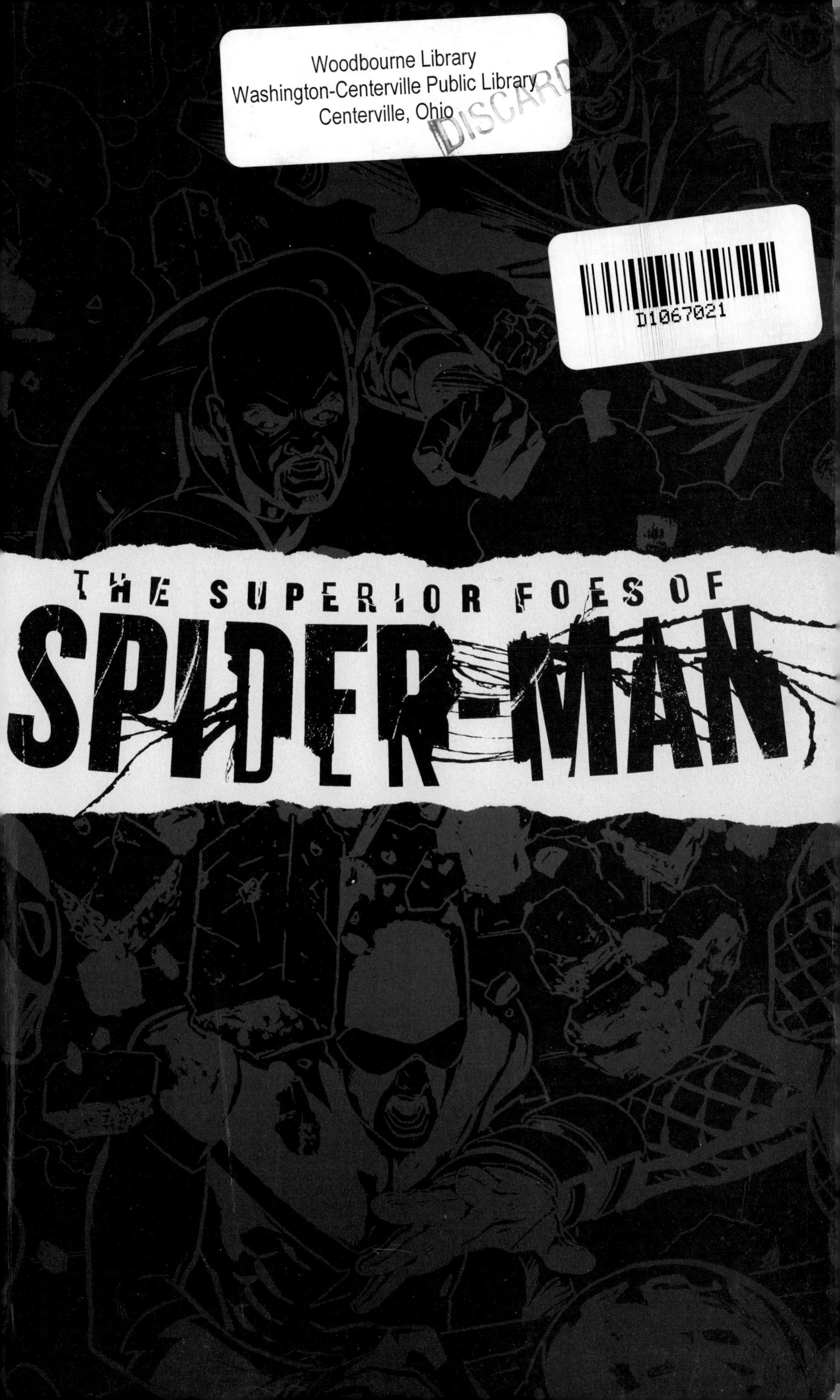
THE SUPERIOR FOES OF
SPIDER-MAN

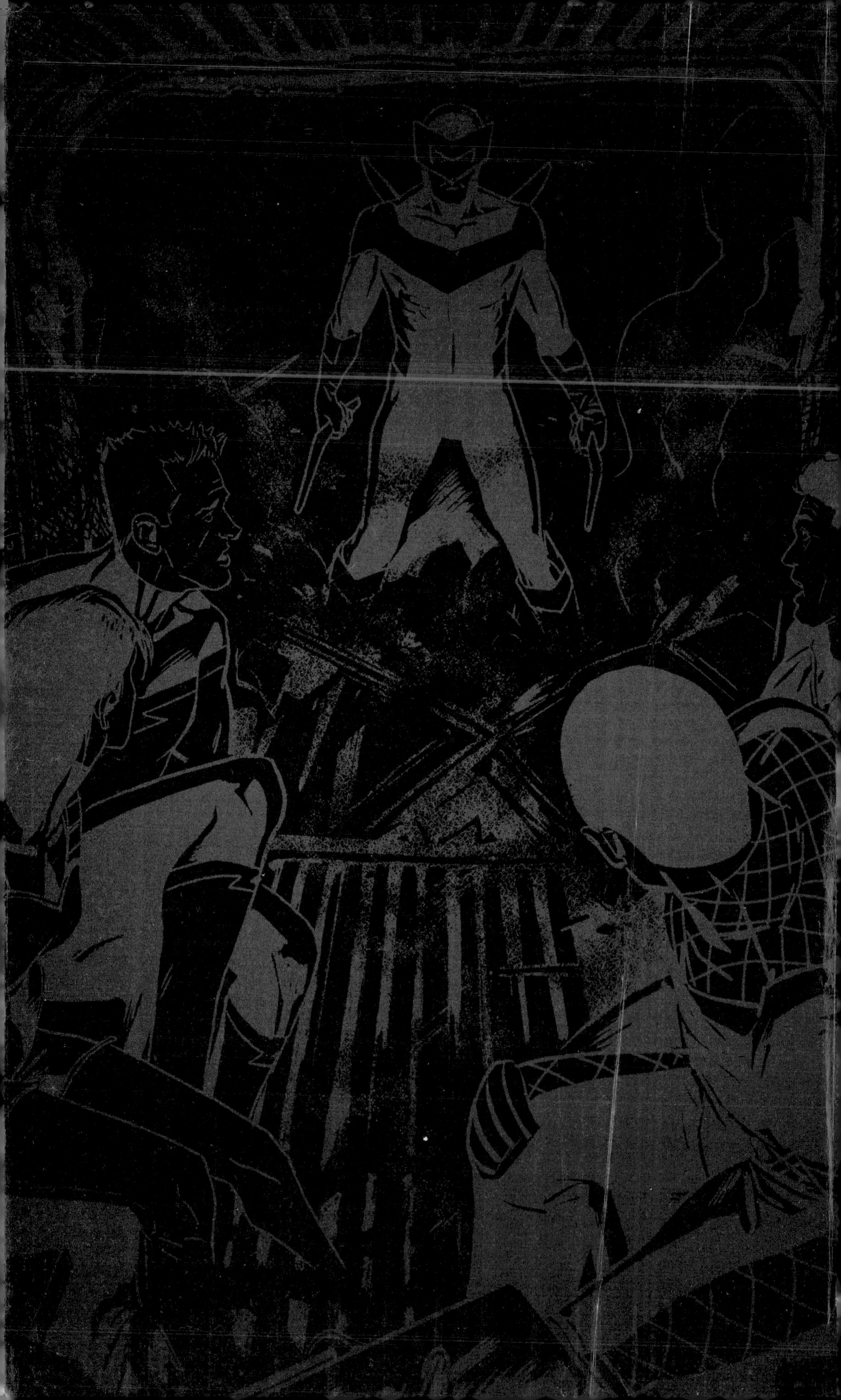

THE SUPERIOR FOES OF SPIDER-MAN

GETTING THE BAND BACK TOGETHER

WRITER
NICK SPENCER

ARTIST
STEVE LIEBER

COLOR ARTIST
RACHELLE ROSENBERG

LETTERER
VC'S JOE CARAMAGNA

COVER ART
MARCOS MARTIN (#1); **ED McGUINNESS & MORRY HOLLOWELL** (#2);
MICHAEL DEL MUNDO (#3); **PAULO SIQUEIRA & MARTE GRACIA** (#4);
STEVE LIEBER (#5); AND **STEVE LIEBER & RACHELLE ROSENBERG** (#6)

EDITOR
TOM BRENNAN

SENIOR EDITOR
STEPHEN WACKER

Collection Editor: **Jennifer Grünwald** • Assistant Editor: **Sarah Brunstad** • Associate Managing Editor: **Alex Starbuck**
Editor, Special Projects: **Mark D. Beazley** Senior Editor, Special Projects: **Jeff Youngquist** SVP Print, Sales & Marketing: **David Gabriel**

Editor in Chief: **Axel Alonso** • Chief Creative Officer: **Joe Quesada** • Publisher: **Dan Buckley** • Executive Producer: **Alan Fine**

E SUPERIOR FOES OF SPIDER-MAN VOL. 1: GETTING THE BAND BACK TOGETHER. Contains material originally published in magazine form as THE SUPERIOR FOES OF SPIDER-MAN #1-6. First printing 4. ISBN# 978-0-7851-8494-2. Published by MARVEL WORLDWIDE, INC., a subsidiary of MARVEL ENTERTAINMENT, LLC. OFFICE OF PUBLICATION: 135 West 50th Street, New York, NY 10020. **Printed in Canada.** ALAN FINE, EVP - Office of the President, Marvel Worldwide, Inc. and EVP & CMO Marvel Characters B.V.; DAN BUCKLEY, Publisher & President - Print, Animation & ital Divisions; JOE QUESADA, Chief Creative Officer; TOM BREVOORT, SVP of Publishing; DAVID BOGART, SVP of Operations & Procurement, Publishing; C.B. CEBULSKI, SVP of Creator & Content Development; VID GABRIEL, SVP of Print & Digital Publishing Sales; JIM O'KEEFE, VP of Operations & Logistics; DAN CARR, Executive Director of Publishing Technology; SUSAN CRESPI, Editorial Operations Manager; EX MORALES, Publishing Operations Manager; STAN LEE, Chairman Emeritus. For information regarding advertising in Marvel Comics or on Marvel.com, please contact Niza Disla, Director of Marvel tnerships, at ndisla@marvel.com. For Marvel subscription inquiries, please call 800-217-9158. **Manufactured between 1/3/2014 and 2/10/2014 by SOLISCO PRINTERS, SCOTT, QC, CANADA.**

987654321

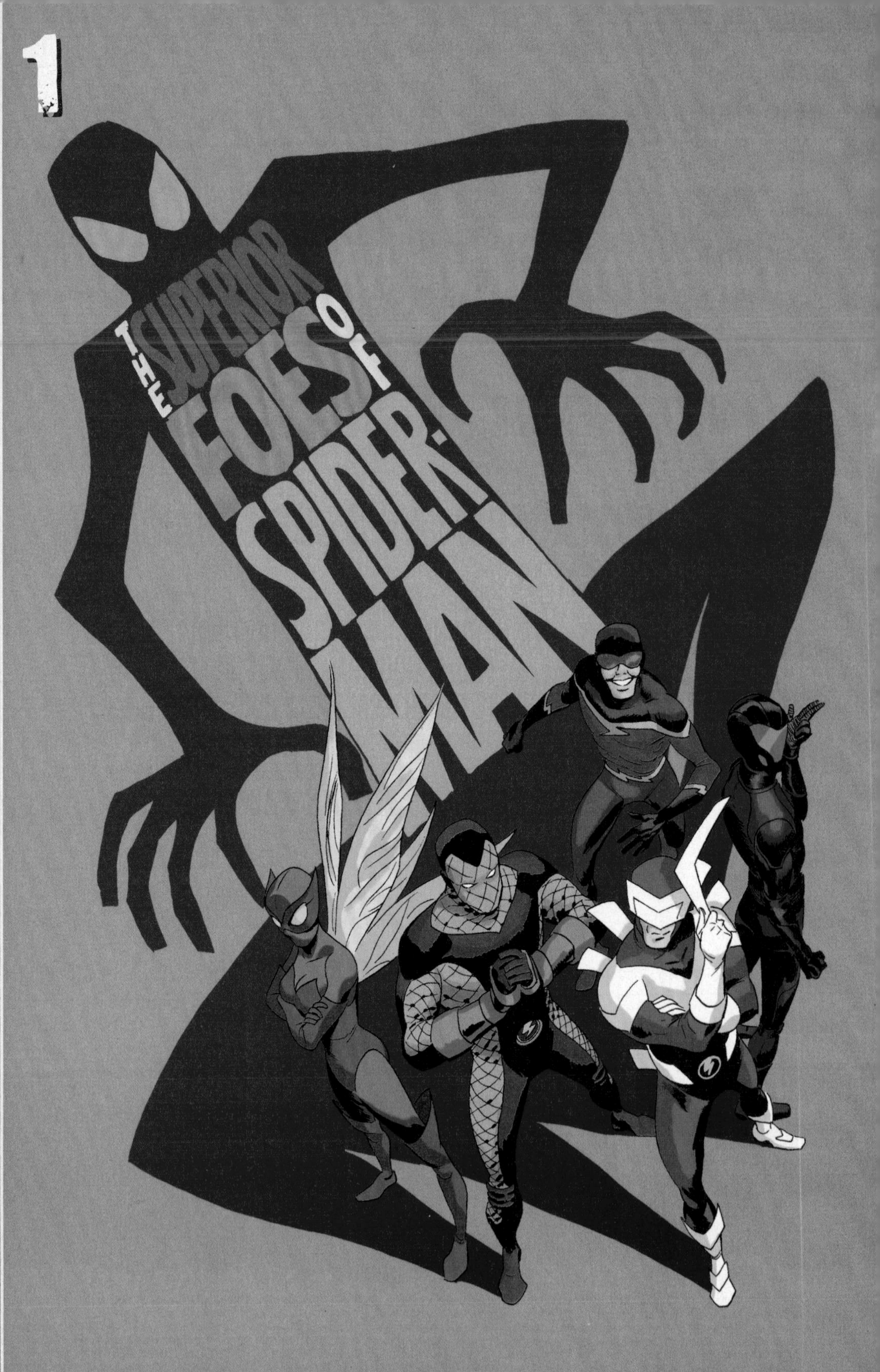
1
THE SUPERIOR FOES OF SPIDER-MAN

BOOMERANG, **SHOCKER**, **OVERDRIVE**, **SPEED DEMON**, AND **BEETLE** ARE NOT HEROES. THEY'RE NOT LOVEABLE ROGUES, AND THEY'RE NOT REBELS WITH A CAUSE. MAKE NO MISTAKE, THE NEW **SINISTER SIX** ARE VILLAINS, PLAIN AND SIMPLE. THEY'RE LIARS, CHEATERS AND THIEVES. THEY DON'T LIKE YOU. THEY DON'T EVEN LIKE EACH OTHER THAT MUCH. THE ONE THING THEY HAVE IN COMMON IS A SHARED HATRED FOR THEIR NEMESIS, THE **SUPERIOR SPIDER-MAN** — EVEN IF HE'S POSSESSED BY THEIR OLD BOSS **DOCTOR OCTOPUS** AT THE MOMENT. SOMETIMES THAT MUTUAL DISDAIN FORCES THEM TO SUCK IT UP AND JOIN FORCES.

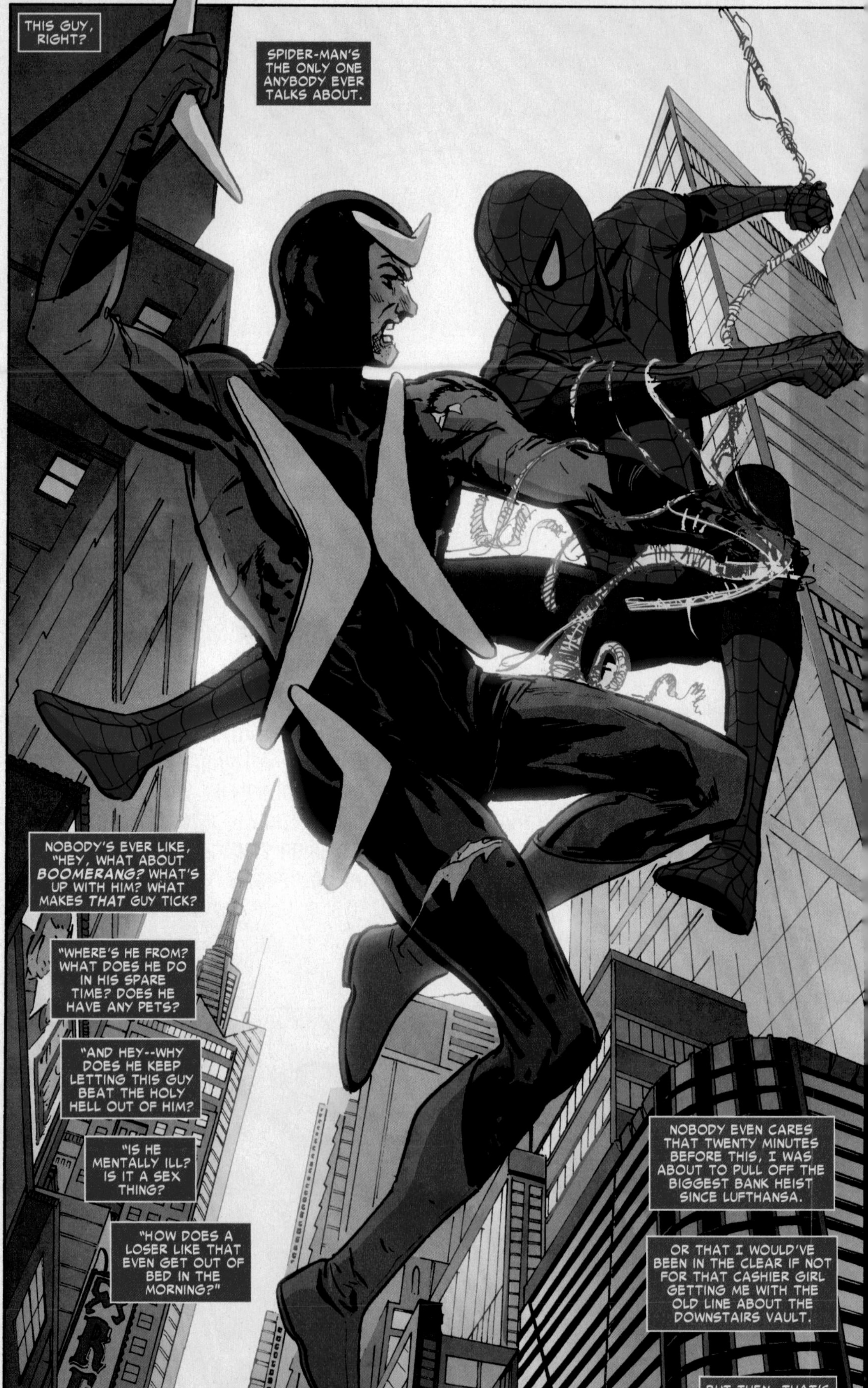
THIS GUY, RIGHT?
SPIDER-MAN'S THE ONLY ONE ANYBODY EVER TALKS ABOUT.
NOBODY'S EVER LIKE, "HEY, WHAT ABOUT *BOOMERANG?* WHAT'S UP WITH HIM? WHAT MAKES *THAT* GUY TICK?
"WHERE'S HE FROM? WHAT DOES HE DO IN HIS SPARE TIME? DOES HE HAVE ANY PETS?
"AND HEY--WHY DOES HE KEEP LETTING THIS GUY BEAT THE HOLY HELL OUT OF HIM?
"IS HE MENTALLY ILL? IS IT A SEX THING?
"HOW DOES A LOSER LIKE THAT EVEN GET OUT OF BED IN THE MORNING?"
NOBODY EVEN CARES THAT TWENTY MINUTES BEFORE THIS, I WAS ABOUT TO PULL OFF THE BIGGEST BANK HEIST SINCE LUFTHANSA.
OR THAT I WOULD'VE BEEN IN THE CLEAR IF NOT FOR THAT CASHIER GIRL GETTING ME WITH THE OLD LINE ABOUT THE DOWNSTAIRS VAULT.
BUT THEN, THAT'S THE THING ABOUT GUYS LIKE ME--

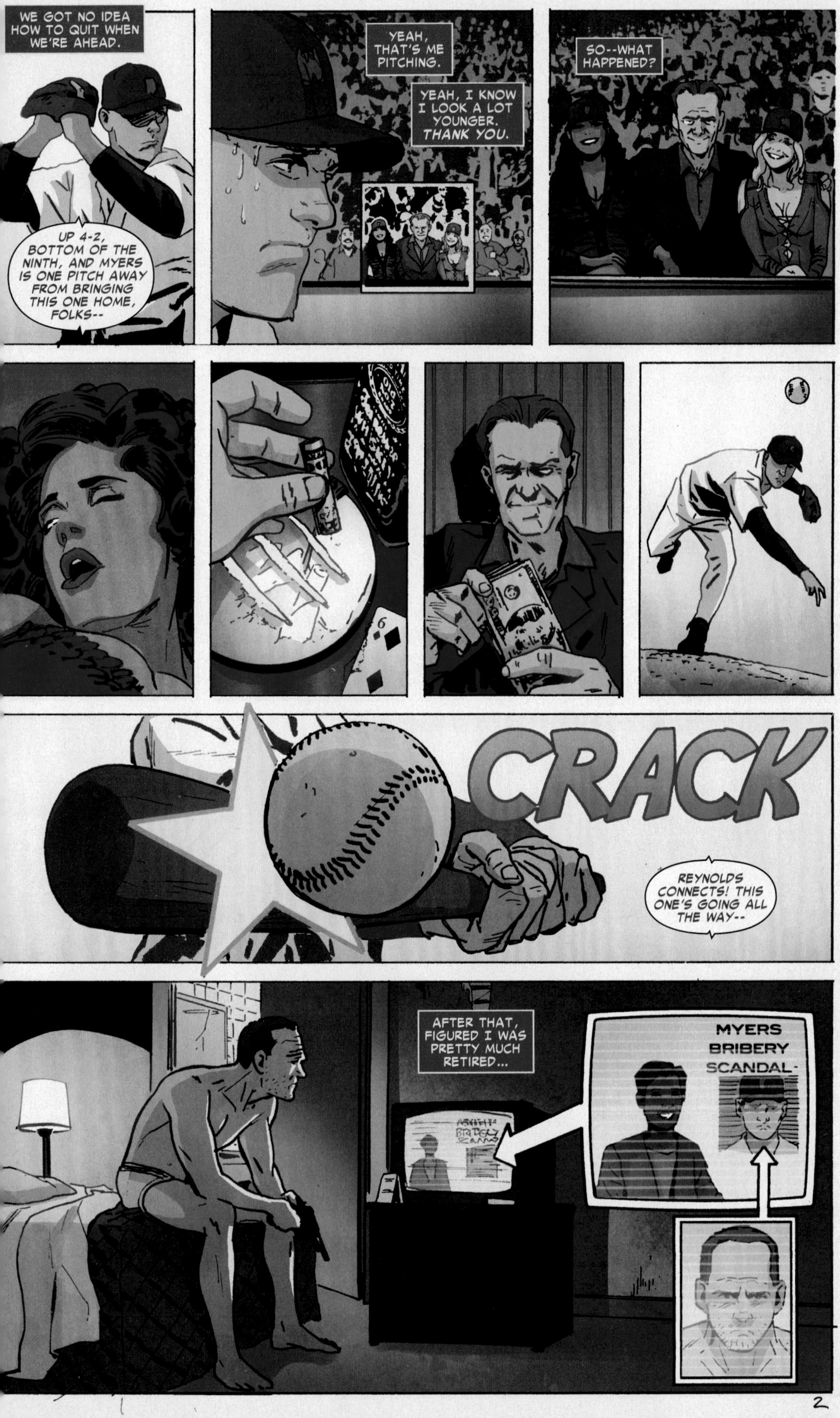
WE GOT NO IDEA HOW TO QUIT WHEN WE'RE AHEAD.
UP 4-2, BOTTOM OF THE NINTH, AND MYERS IS ONE PITCH AWAY FROM BRINGING THIS ONE HOME, FOLKS--
YEAH, THAT'S ME PITCHING.
YEAH, I KNOW I LOOK A LOT YOUNGER. THANK YOU.
SO--WHAT HAPPENED?
CRACK
REYNOLDS CONNECTS! THIS ONE'S GOING ALL THE WAY--
AFTER THAT, FIGURED I WAS PRETTY MUCH RETIRED...
MYERS
BRIBERY
SCANDAL-

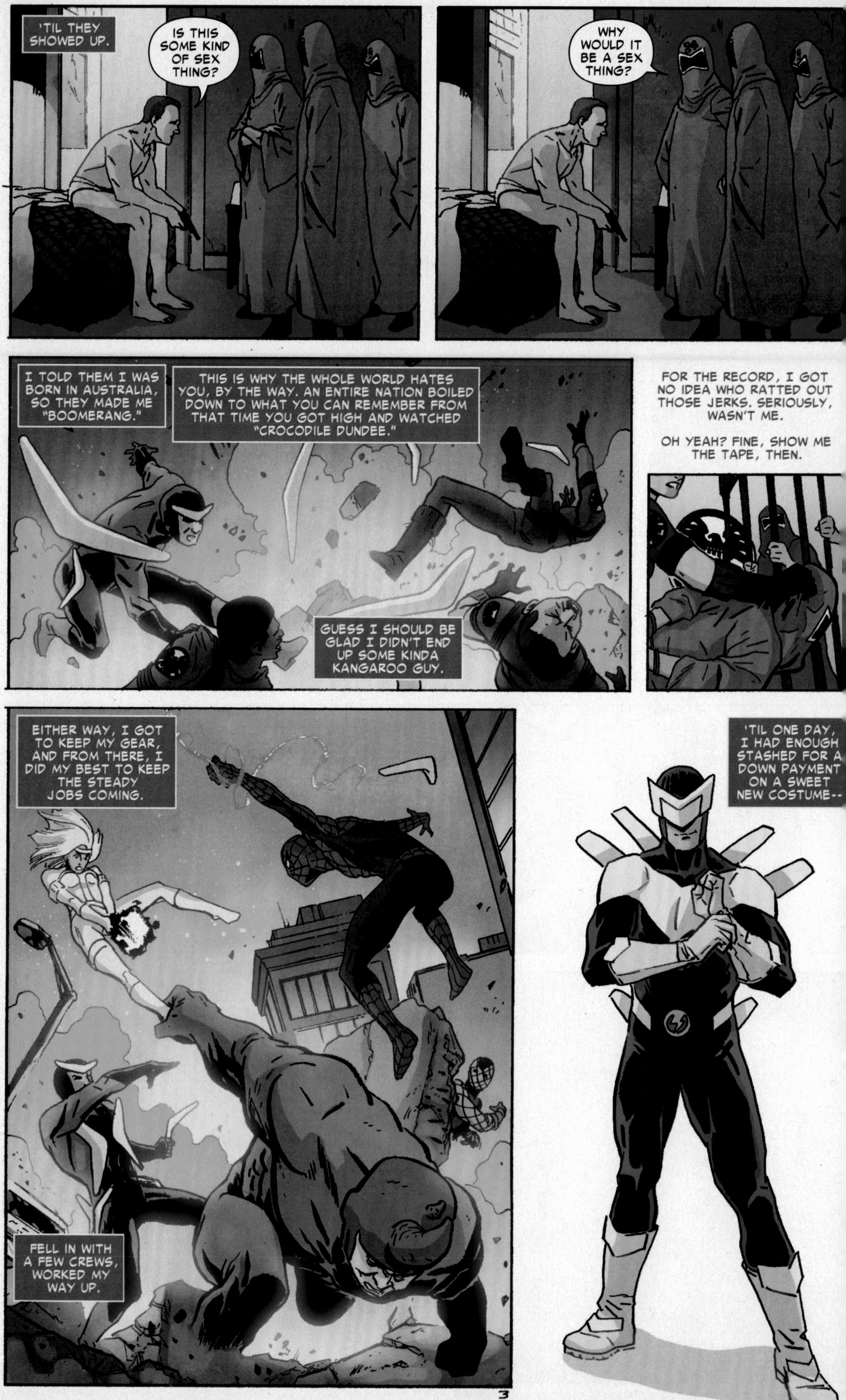

'TIL THEY SHOWED UP.
IS THIS SOME KIND OF SEX THING?
WHY WOULD IT BE A SEX THING?
I TOLD THEM I WAS BORN IN AUSTRALIA, SO THEY MADE ME "BOOMERANG."
THIS IS WHY THE WHOLE WORLD HATES YOU, BY THE WAY. AN ENTIRE NATION BOILED DOWN TO WHAT YOU CAN REMEMBER FROM THAT TIME YOU GOT HIGH AND WATCHED "CROCODILE DUNDEE."
GUESS I SHOULD BE GLAD I DIDN'T END UP SOME KINDA KANGAROO GUY.
FOR THE RECORD, I GOT NO IDEA WHO RATTED OUT THOSE JERKS. SERIOUSLY, WASN'T ME.
OH YEAH? FINE, SHOW ME THE TAPE, THEN.
EITHER WAY, I GOT TO KEEP MY GEAR, AND FROM THERE, I DID MY BEST TO KEEP THE STEADY JOBS COMING.
FELL IN WITH A FEW CREWS, WORKED MY WAY UP.
'TIL ONE DAY, I HAD ENOUGH STASHED FOR A DOWN PAYMENT ON A SWEET NEW COSTUME--

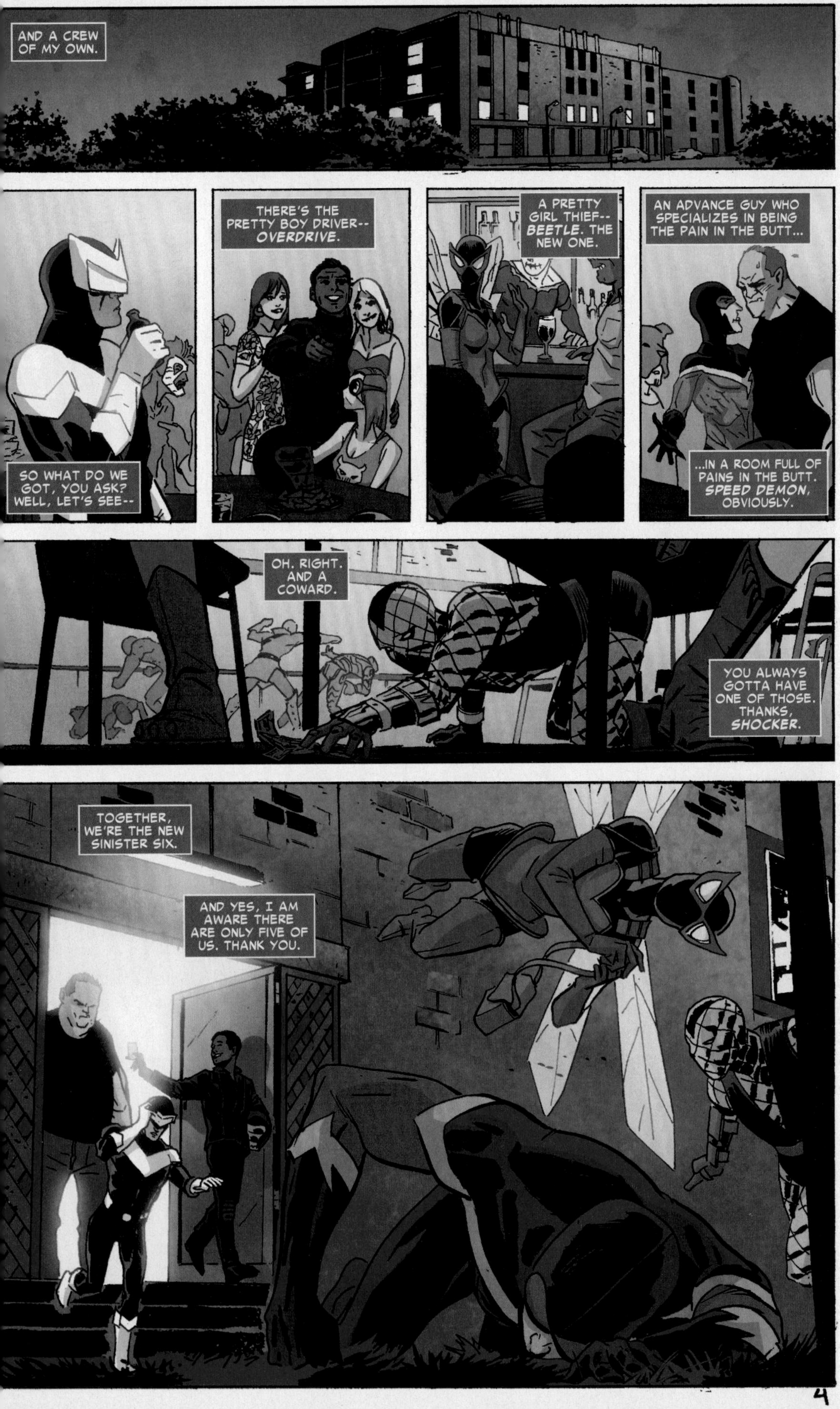

AND A CREW OF MY OWN.
SO WHAT DO WE GOT, YOU ASK? WELL, LET'S SEE--
THERE'S THE PRETTY BOY DRIVER-- OVERDRIVE.
A PRETTY GIRL THIEF-- BEETLE. THE NEW ONE.
AN ADVANCE GUY WHO SPECIALIZES IN BEING THE PAIN IN THE BUTT...
...IN A ROOM FULL OF PAINS IN THE BUTT. SPEED DEMON, OBVIOUSLY.
OH. RIGHT. AND A COWARD.
YOU ALWAYS GOTTA HAVE ONE OF THOSE. THANKS, SHOCKER.
TOGETHER, WE'RE THE NEW SINISTER SIX.
AND YES, I AM AWARE THERE ARE ONLY FIVE OF US. THANK YOU.

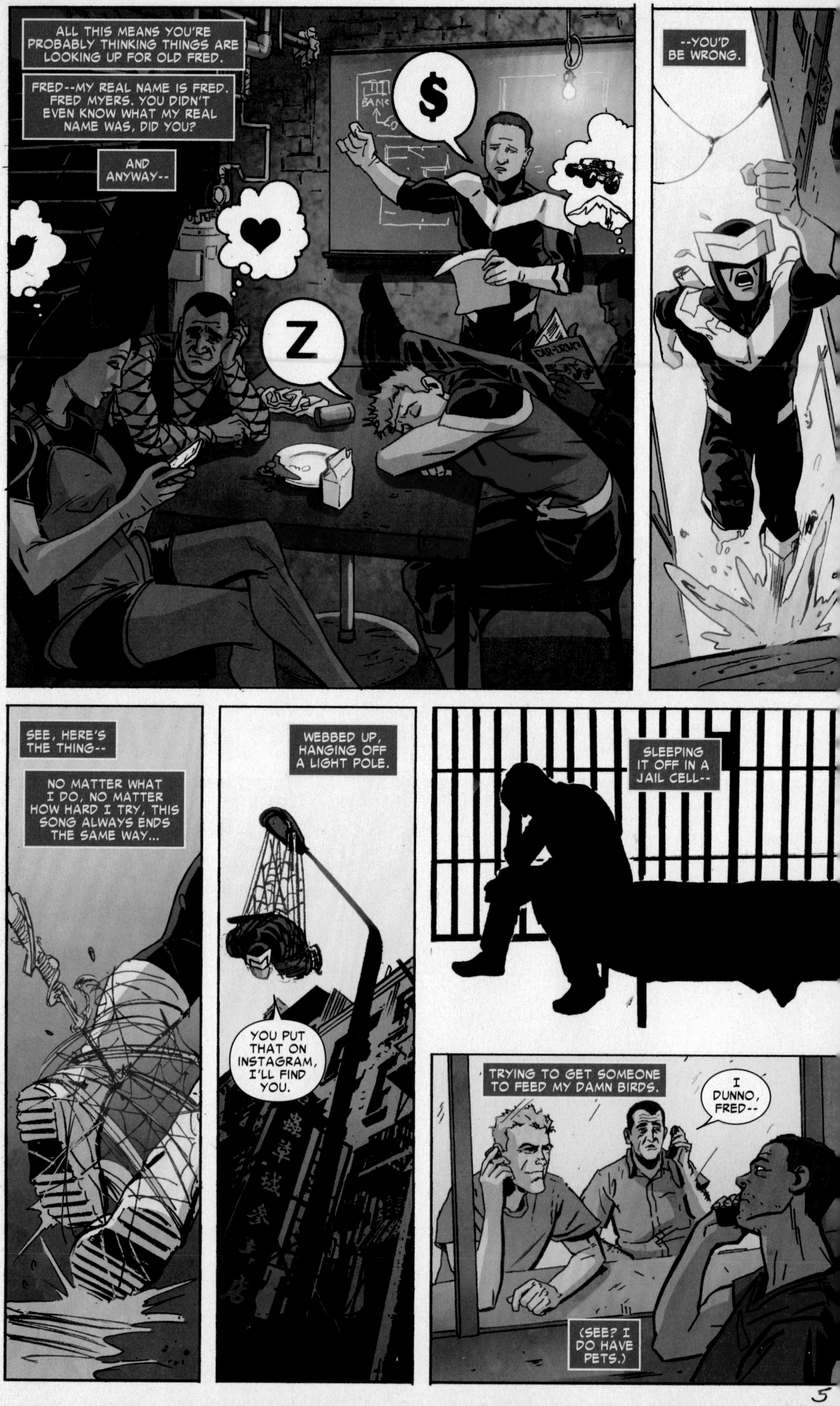
ALL THIS MEANS YOU'RE PROBABLY THINKING THINGS ARE LOOKING UP FOR OLD FRED.
FRED--MY REAL NAME IS FRED. FRED MYERS. YOU DIDN'T EVEN KNOW WHAT MY REAL NAME WAS, DID YOU?
AND ANYWAY--
$
Z
--YOU'D BE WRONG.
SEE, HERE'S THE THING--
NO MATTER WHAT I DO, NO MATTER HOW HARD I TRY, THIS SONG ALWAYS ENDS THE SAME WAY...
WEBBED UP, HANGING OFF A LIGHT POLE.
YOU PUT THAT ON INSTAGRAM, I'LL FIND YOU.
SLEEPING IT OFF IN A JAIL CELL--
TRYING TO GET SOMEONE TO FEED MY DAMN BIRDS.
I DUNNO, FRED--
(SEE? I DO HAVE PETS.)

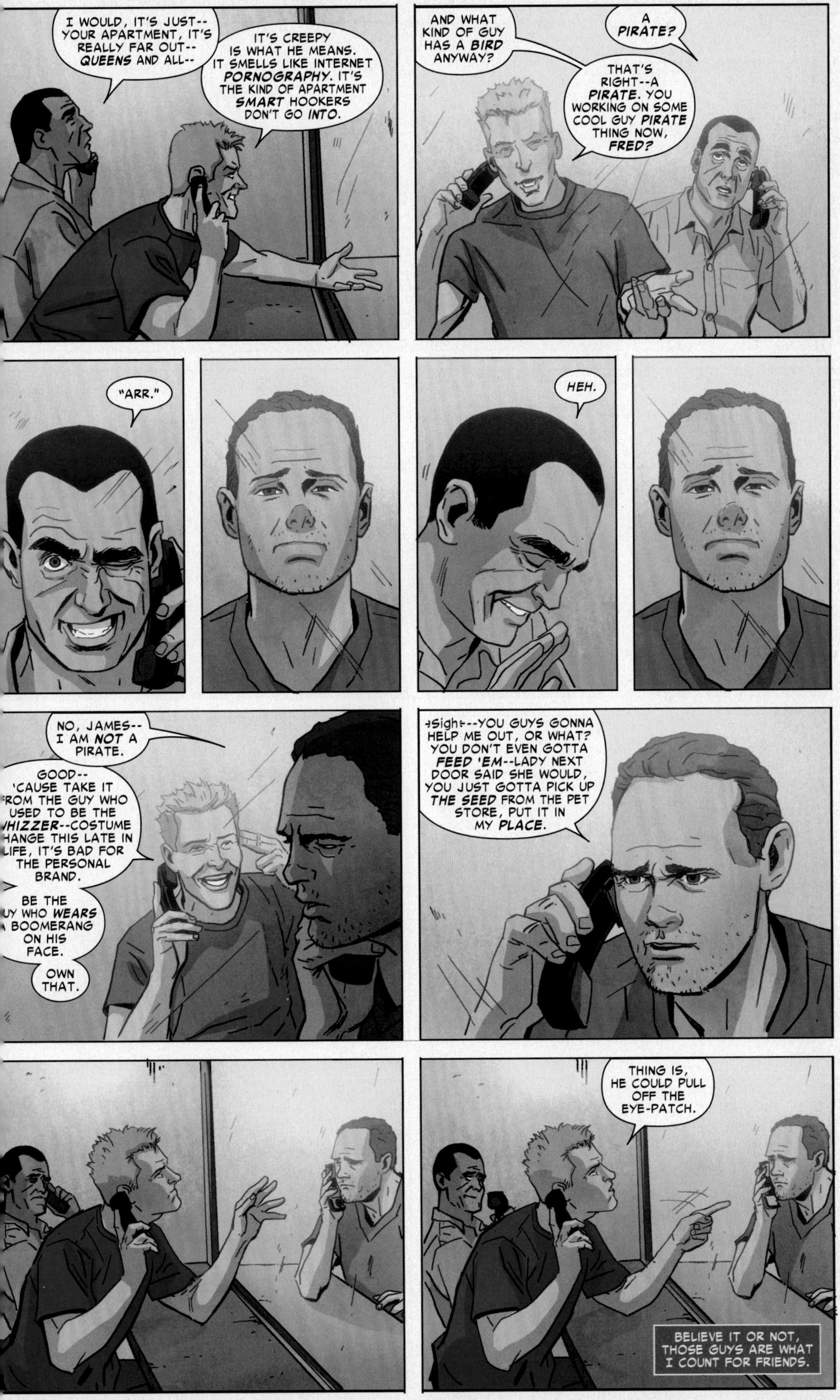

I WOULD, IT'S JUST-- YOUR APARTMENT, IT'S REALLY FAR OUT-- QUEENS AND ALL--
IT'S CREEPY IS WHAT HE MEANS. IT SMELLS LIKE INTERNET PORNOGRAPHY. IT'S THE KIND OF APARTMENT SMART HOOKERS DON'T GO INTO.
AND WHAT KIND OF GUY HAS A BIRD ANYWAY?
A PIRATE?
THAT'S RIGHT--A PIRATE. YOU WORKING ON SOME COOL GUY PIRATE THING NOW, FRED?
"ARR."
HEH.
NO, JAMES-- I AM NOT A PIRATE.
GOOD-- 'CAUSE TAKE IT FROM THE GUY WHO USED TO BE THE WHIZZER--COSTUME CHANGE THIS LATE IN LIFE, IT'S BAD FOR THE PERSONAL BRAND.
BE THE GUY WHO WEARS A BOOMERANG ON HIS FACE.
OWN THAT.
=Sigh=--YOU GUYS GONNA HELP ME OUT, OR WHAT? YOU DON'T EVEN GOTTA FEED 'EM--LADY NEXT DOOR SAID SHE WOULD, YOU JUST GOTTA PICK UP THE SEED FROM THE PET STORE, PUT IT IN MY PLACE.
THING IS, HE COULD PULL OFF THE EYE-PATCH.
BELIEVE IT OR NOT, THOSE GUYS ARE WHAT I COUNT FOR FRIENDS.

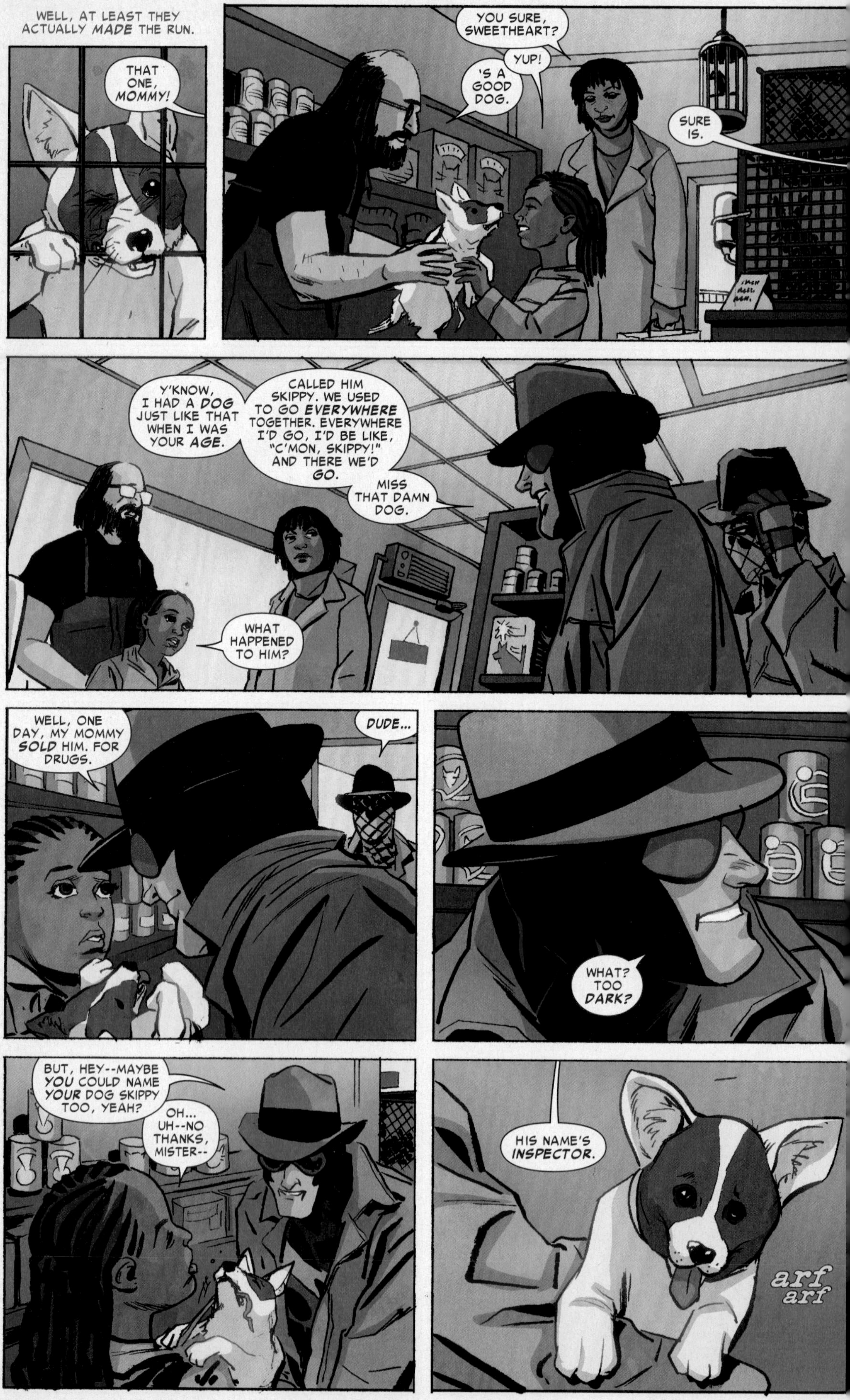
WELL, AT LEAST THEY ACTUALLY MADE THE RUN.
THAT ONE, MOMMY!
YOU SURE, SWEETHEART?
YUP!
'S A GOOD DOG.
SURE IS.
Y'KNOW, I HAD A DOG JUST LIKE THAT WHEN I WAS YOUR AGE.
CALLED HIM SKIPPY. WE USED TO GO EVERYWHERE TOGETHER. EVERYWHERE I'D GO, I'D BE LIKE, "C'MON, SKIPPY!" AND THERE WE'D GO.
MISS THAT DAMN DOG.
WHAT HAPPENED TO HIM?
WELL, ONE DAY, MY MOMMY SOLD HIM. FOR DRUGS.
DUDE...
WHAT? TOO DARK?
BUT, HEY--MAYBE YOU COULD NAME YOUR DOG SKIPPY TOO, YEAH?
OH... UH--NO THANKS, MISTER--
HIS NAME'S INSPECTOR.
arf arf

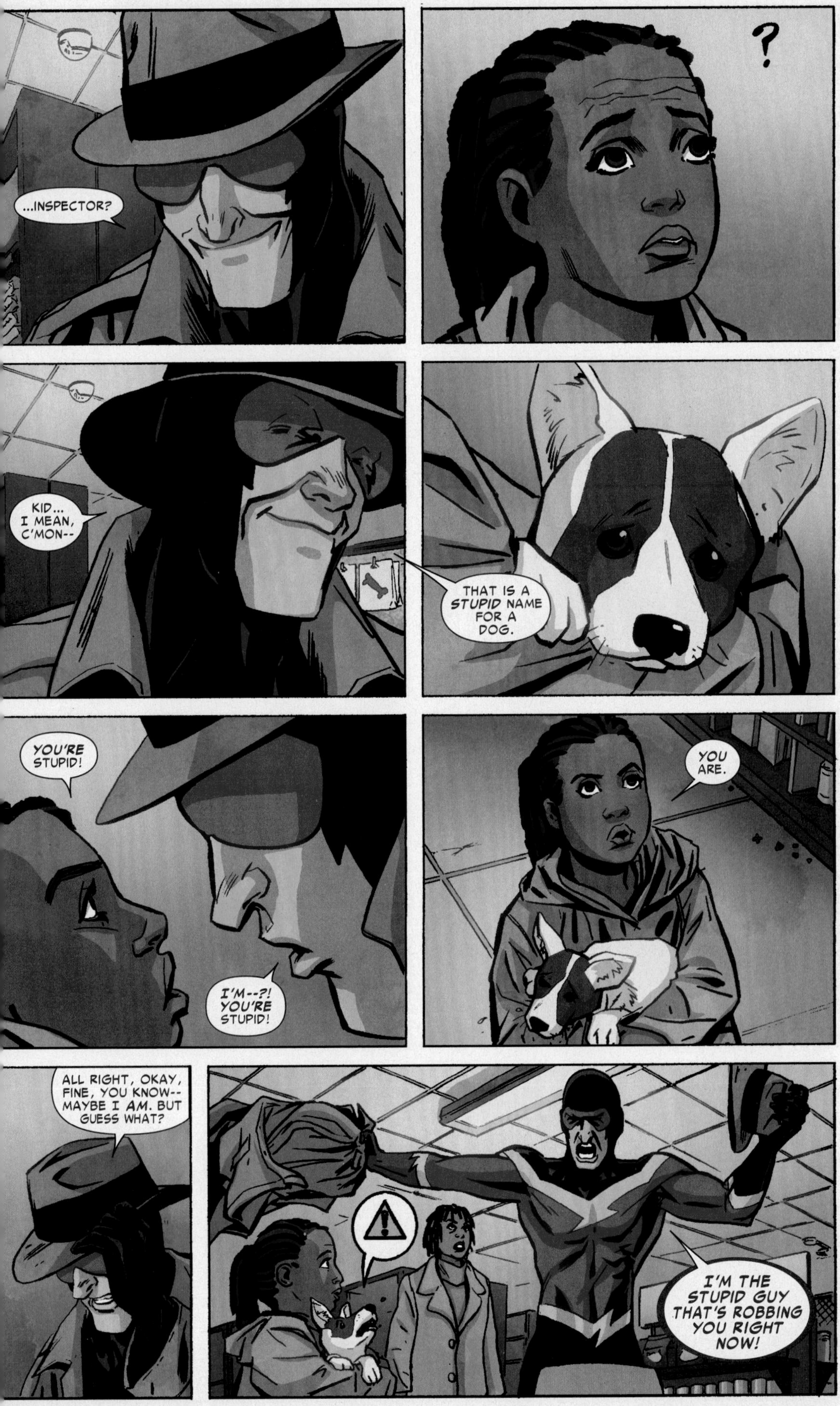
...INSPECTOR?
?
KID... I MEAN, C'MON--
THAT IS A STUPID NAME FOR A DOG.
YOU'RE STUPID!
I'M--?! YOU'RE STUPID!
YOU ARE.
ALL RIGHT, OKAY, FINE, YOU KNOW-- MAYBE I AM. BUT GUESS WHAT?
I'M THE STUPID GUY THAT'S ROBBING YOU RIGHT NOW!

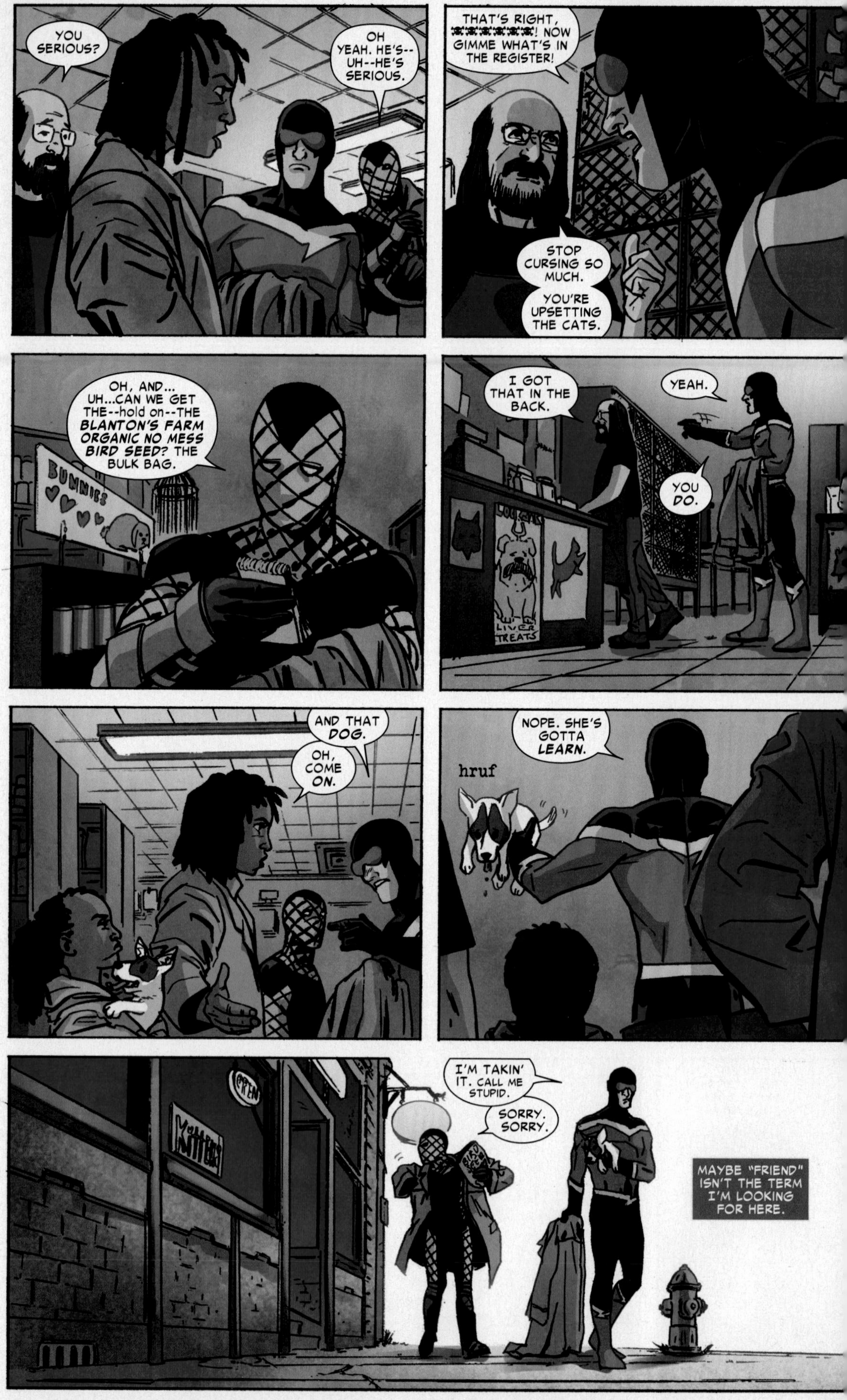
YOU SERIOUS?
OH YEAH. HE'S-- UH--HE'S SERIOUS.
THAT'S RIGHT, ☠☠☠☠☠! NOW GIMME WHAT'S IN THE REGISTER!
STOP CURSING SO MUCH.
YOU'RE UPSETTING THE CATS.
OH, AND... UH...CAN WE GET THE--hold on--THE BLANTON'S FARM ORGANIC NO MESS BIRD SEED? THE BULK BAG.
BUNNIES
I GOT THAT IN THE BACK.
YEAH.
YOU DO.
LIVER TREATS
AND THAT DOG.
OH, COME ON.
NOPE. SHE'S GOTTA LEARN.
hruf
OPEN
I'M TAKIN' IT. CALL ME STUPID.
SORRY. SORRY.
MAYBE "FRIEND" ISN'T THE TERM I'M LOOKING FOR HERE.

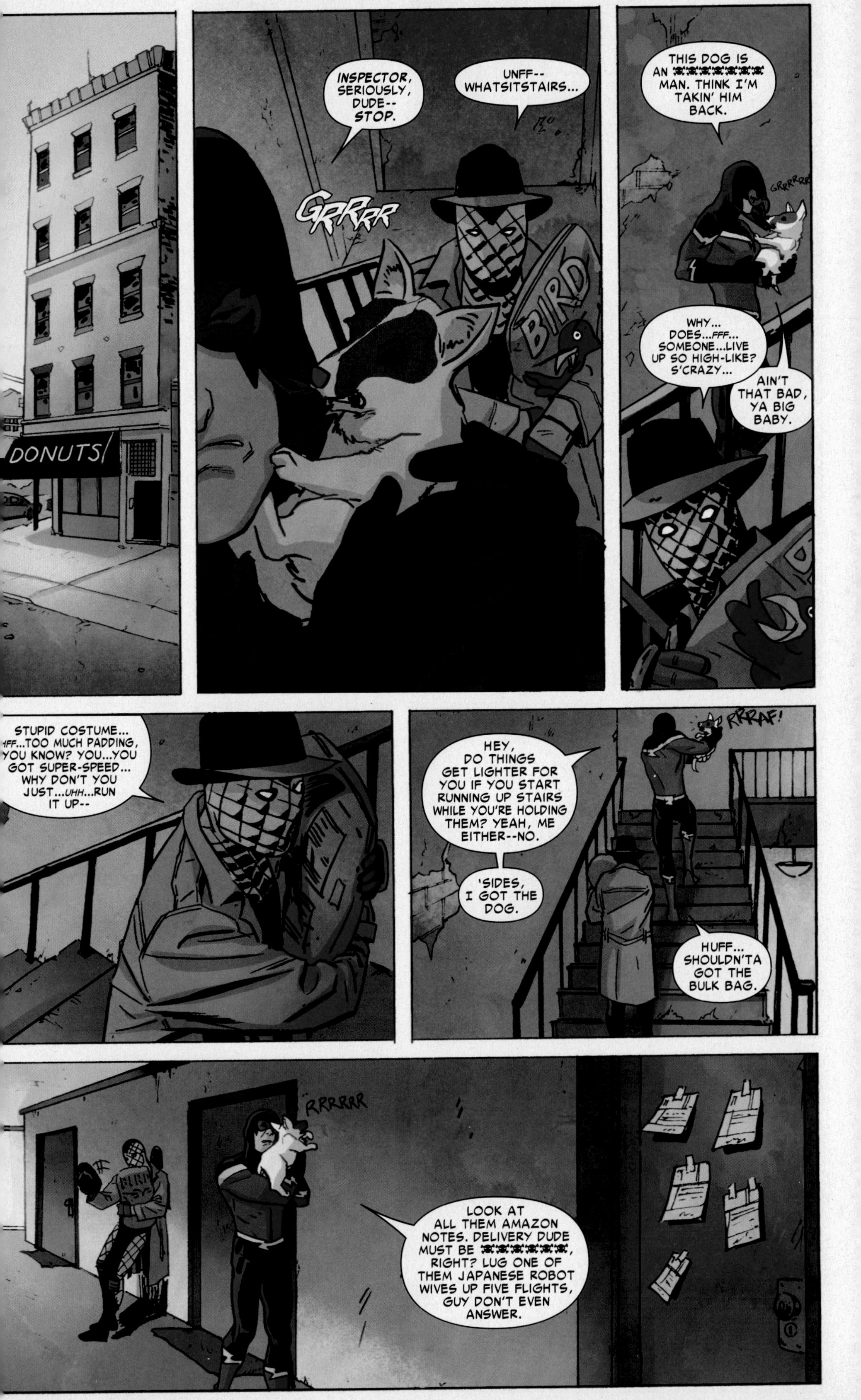
INSPECTOR, SERIOUSLY, DUDE-- STOP.
UNFF-- WHATSITSTAIRS...
GRRRR
THIS DOG IS AN ☠✱☠✱☠✱ MAN. THINK I'M TAKIN' HIM BACK.
GRRRRR
WHY... DOES...FFF... SOMEONE...LIVE UP SO HIGH-LIKE? S'CRAZY...
AIN'T THAT BAD, YA BIG BABY.
DONUTS
STUPID COSTUME... HFF...TOO MUCH PADDING, YOU KNOW? YOU...YOU GOT SUPER-SPEED... WHY DON'T YOU JUST...UHH...RUN IT UP--
RRRAF!
HEY, DO THINGS GET LIGHTER FOR YOU IF YOU START RUNNING UP STAIRS WHILE YOU'RE HOLDING THEM? YEAH, ME EITHER--NO.
'SIDES, I GOT THE DOG.
HUFF... SHOULDN'TA GOT THE BULK BAG.
RRRRRR
LOOK AT ALL THEM AMAZON NOTES. DELIVERY DUDE MUST BE ☠✱☠✱☠✱, RIGHT? LUG ONE OF THEM JAPANESE ROBOT WIVES UP FIVE FLIGHTS, GUY DON'T EVEN ANSWER.

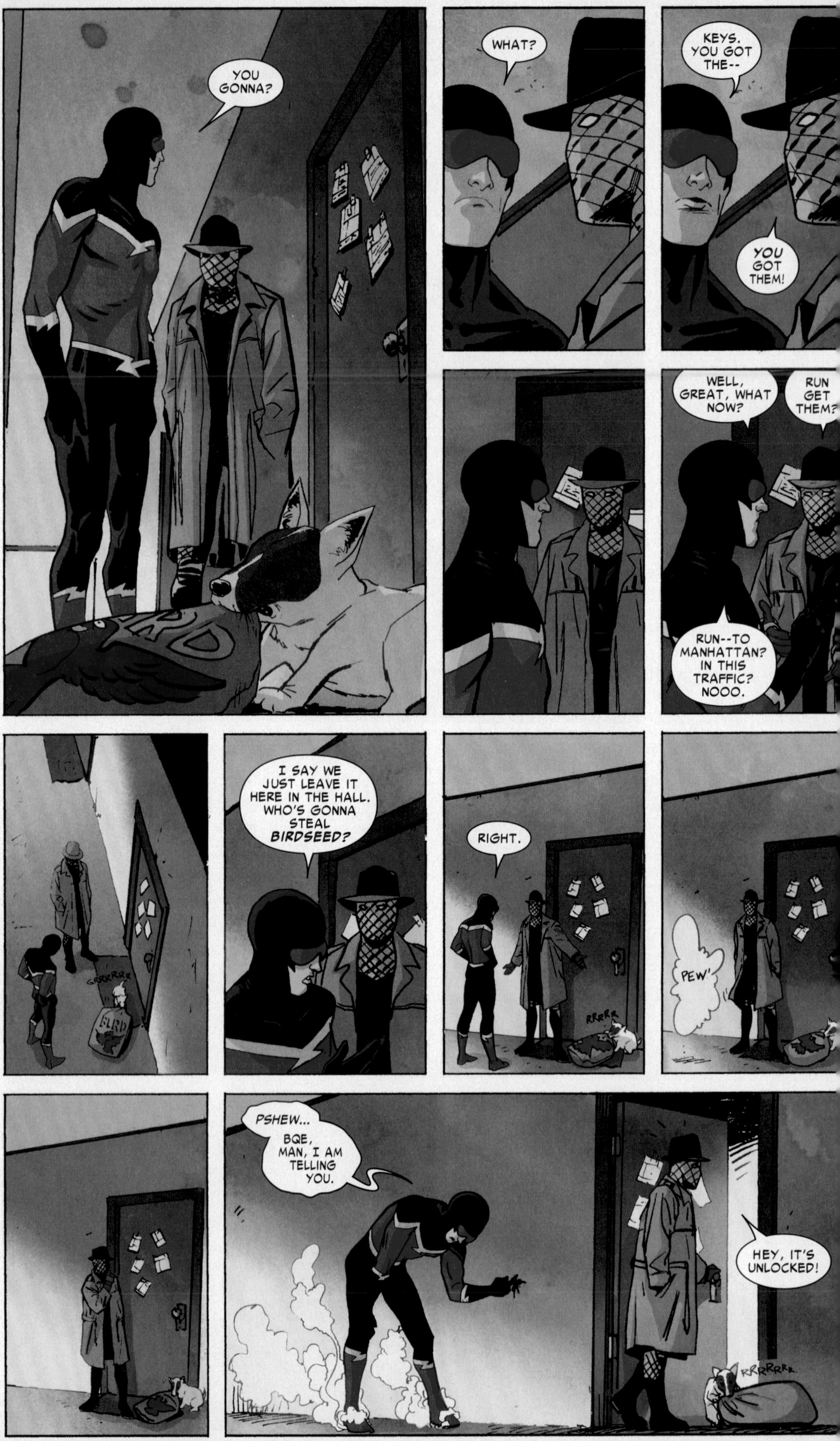

YOU GONNA?
WHAT?
KEYS. YOU GOT THE--
YOU GOT THEM!
WELL, GREAT, WHAT NOW?
RUN GET THEM?
RUN--TO MANHATTAN? IN THIS TRAFFIC? NOOO.
GRRRRRRR
I SAY WE JUST LEAVE IT HERE IN THE HALL. WHO'S GONNA STEAL BIRDSEED?
RIGHT.
RRRRR
PEW'
PSHEW... BQE, MAN, I AM TELLING YOU.
HEY, IT'S UNLOCKED!
RRRRRRR

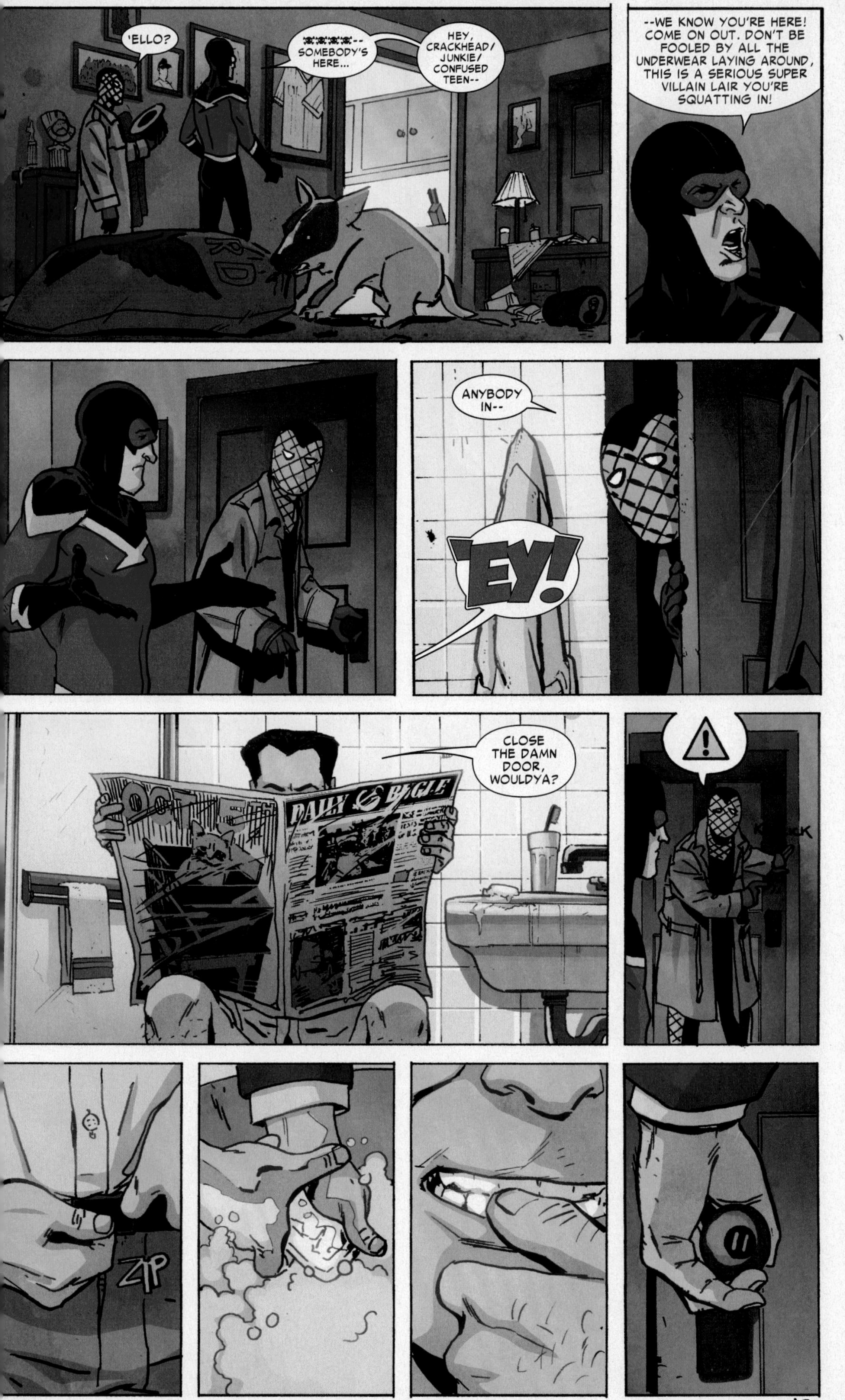
'ELLO?
--SOMEBODY'S HERE...
HEY, CRACKHEAD/ JUNKIE/ CONFUSED TEEN--
--WE KNOW YOU'RE HERE! COME ON OUT. DON'T BE FOOLED BY ALL THE UNDERWEAR LAYING AROUND, THIS IS A SERIOUS SUPER VILLAIN LAIR YOU'RE SQUATTING IN!
ANYBODY IN--
'EY!
DAILY BUGLE
CLOSE THE DAMN DOOR, WOULDYA?
ZIP

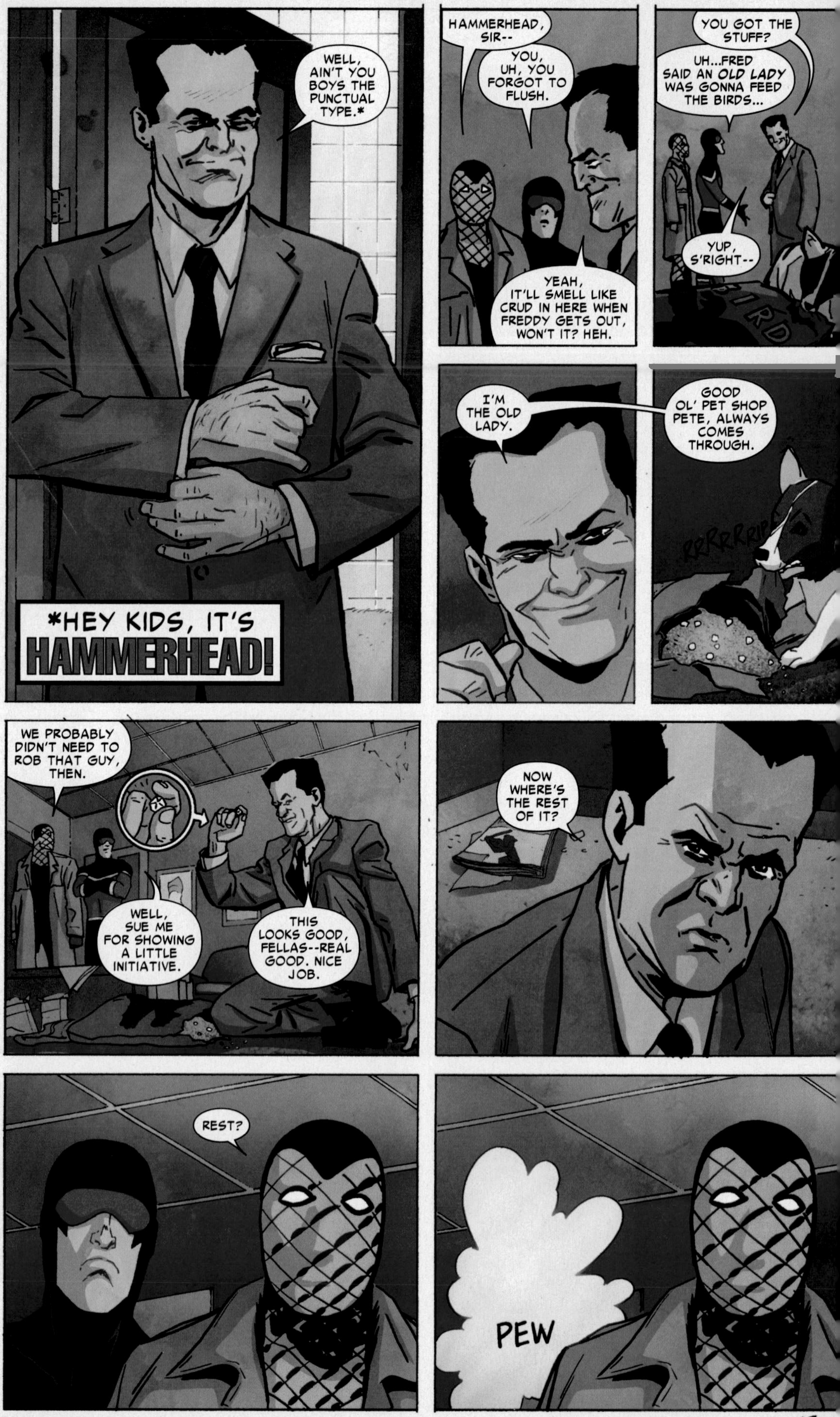

WELL, AIN'T YOU BOYS THE PUNCTUAL TYPE.*
*HEY KIDS, IT'S HAMMERHEAD!
HAMMERHEAD, SIR--
YOU, UH, YOU FORGOT TO FLUSH.
YEAH, IT'LL SMELL LIKE CRUD IN HERE WHEN FREDDY GETS OUT, WON'T IT? HEH.
YOU GOT THE STUFF?
UH...FRED SAID AN OLD LADY WAS GONNA FEED THE BIRDS...
YUP, S'RIGHT--
BIRD
I'M THE OLD LADY.
GOOD OL' PET SHOP PETE, ALWAYS COMES THROUGH.
RRRRRRIP
WE PROBABLY DIDN'T NEED TO ROB THAT GUY, THEN.
WELL, SUE ME FOR SHOWING A LITTLE INITIATIVE.
THIS LOOKS GOOD, FELLAS--REAL GOOD. NICE JOB.
NOW WHERE'S THE REST OF IT?
REST?
PEW

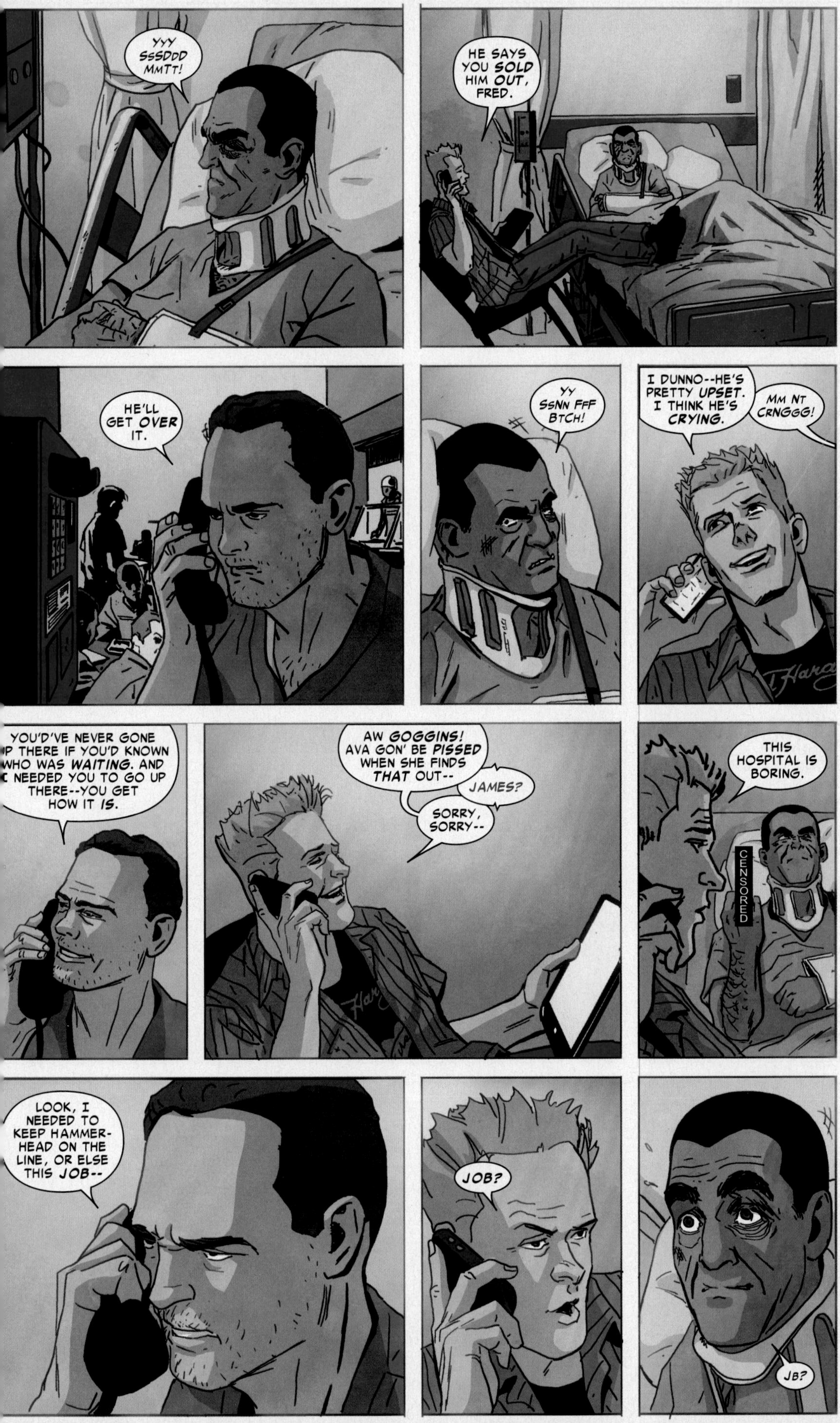
YYY SSSDDD MMTT!
HE SAYS YOU SOLD HIM OUT, FRED.
HE'LL GET OVER IT.
YY SSNN FFF BTCH!
I DUNNO--HE'S PRETTY UPSET. I THINK HE'S CRYING.
MM NT CRNGGG!
YOU'D'VE NEVER GONE UP THERE IF YOU'D KNOWN WHO WAS WAITING. AND I NEEDED YOU TO GO UP THERE--YOU GET HOW IT IS.
AW GOGGINS! AVA GON' BE PISSED WHEN SHE FINDS THAT OUT--
JAMES?
SORRY, SORRY--
THIS HOSPITAL IS BORING.
CENSORED
LOOK, I NEEDED TO KEEP HAMMER-HEAD ON THE LINE, OR ELSE THIS JOB--
JOB?
JB?

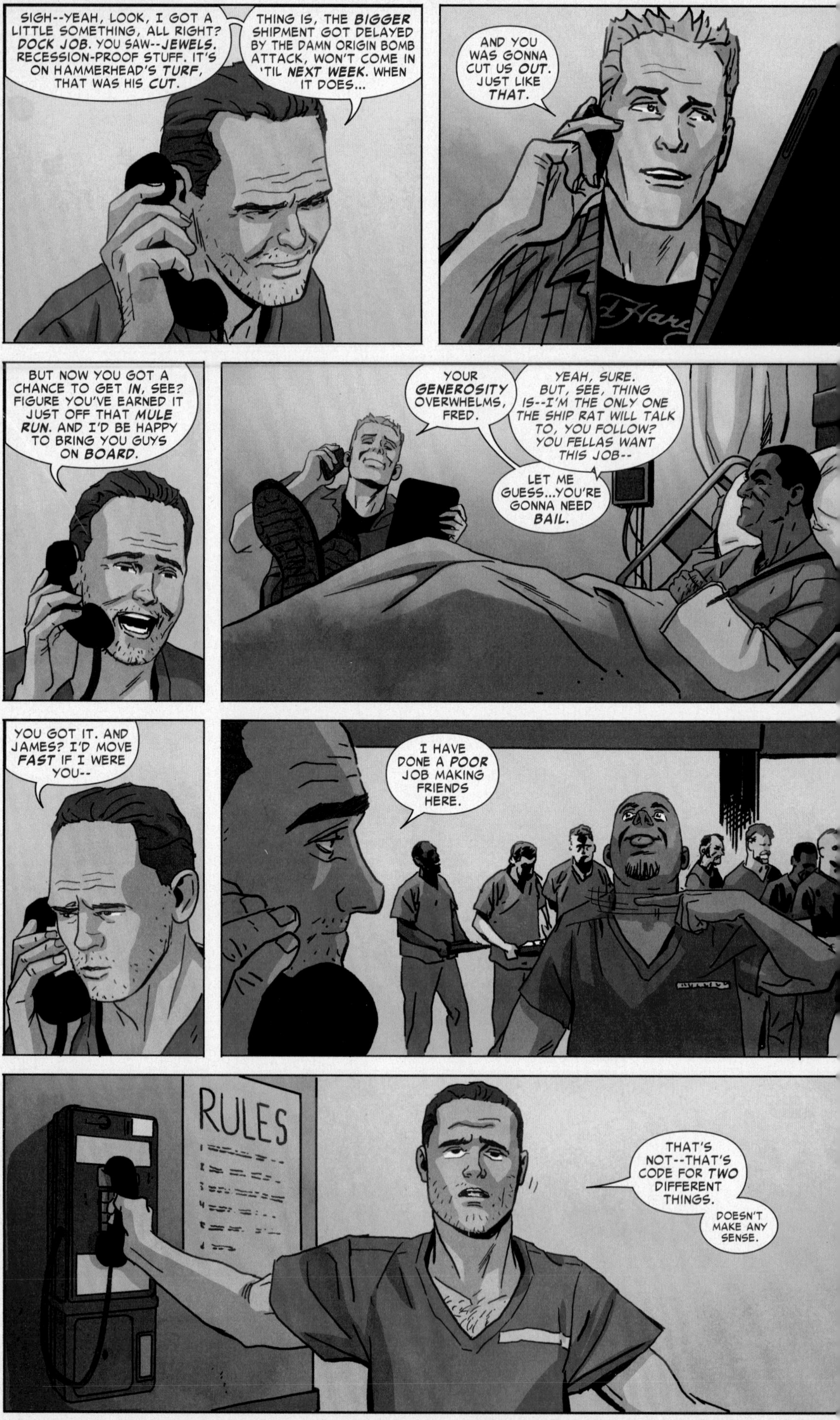

SIGH--YEAH, LOOK, I GOT A LITTLE SOMETHING, ALL RIGHT? DOCK JOB. YOU SAW--JEWELS. RECESSION-PROOF STUFF. IT'S ON HAMMERHEAD'S TURF, THAT WAS HIS CUT.
THING IS, THE BIGGER SHIPMENT GOT DELAYED BY THE DAMN ORIGIN BOMB ATTACK, WON'T COME IN 'TIL NEXT WEEK. WHEN IT DOES...
AND YOU WAS GONNA CUT US OUT. JUST LIKE THAT.
BUT NOW YOU GOT A CHANCE TO GET IN, SEE? FIGURE YOU'VE EARNED IT JUST OFF THAT MULE RUN. AND I'D BE HAPPY TO BRING YOU GUYS ON BOARD.
YOUR GENEROSITY OVERWHELMS, FRED.
YEAH, SURE. BUT, SEE, THING IS--I'M THE ONLY ONE THE SHIP RAT WILL TALK TO, YOU FOLLOW? YOU FELLAS WANT THIS JOB--
LET ME GUESS...YOU'RE GONNA NEED BAIL.
YOU GOT IT. AND JAMES? I'D MOVE FAST IF I WERE YOU--
I HAVE DONE A POOR JOB MAKING FRIENDS HERE.
RULES
THAT'S NOT--THAT'S CODE FOR TWO DIFFERENT THINGS.
DOESN'T MAKE ANY SENSE.

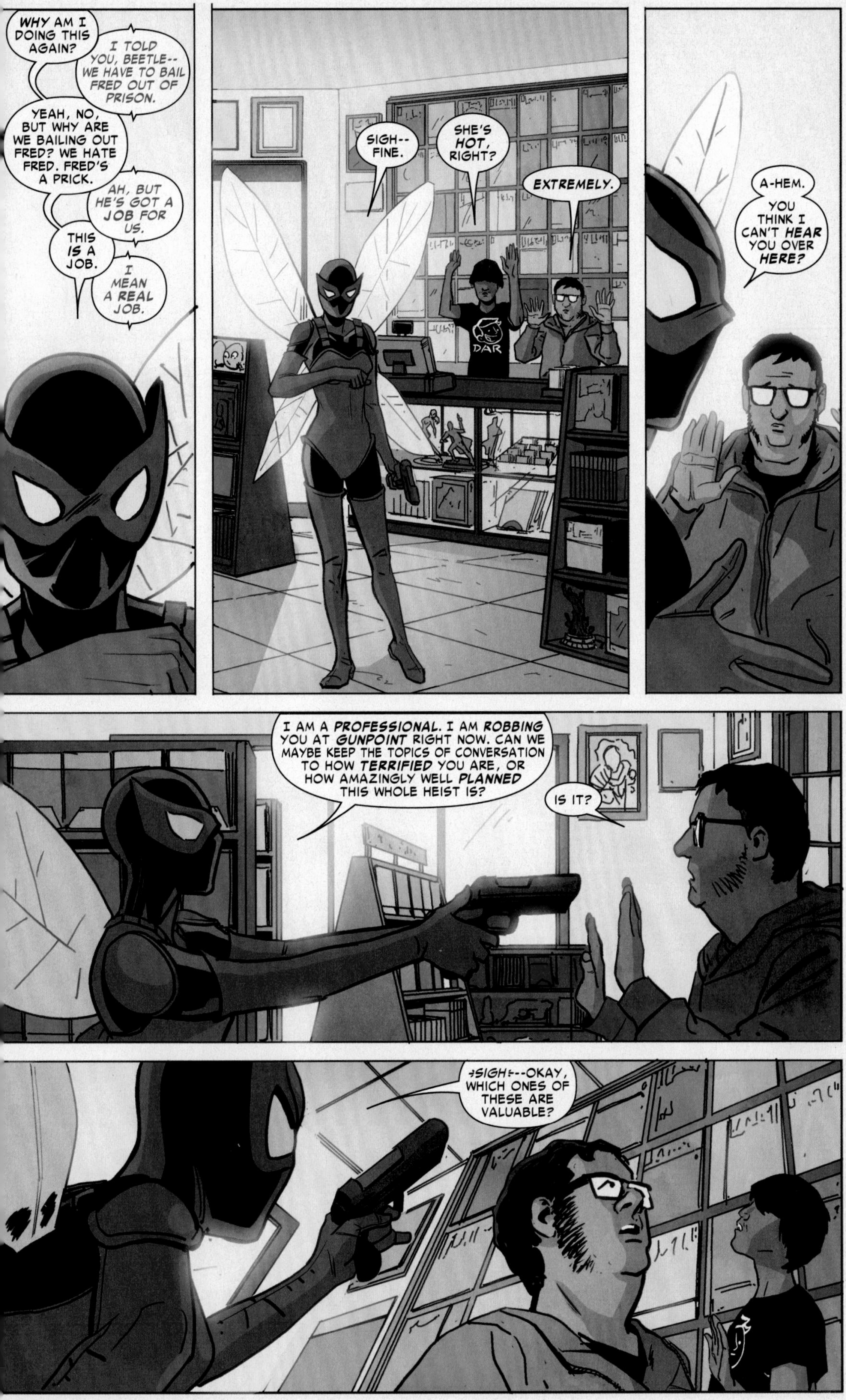
WHY AM I DOING THIS AGAIN?
I TOLD YOU, BEETLE-- WE HAVE TO BAIL FRED OUT OF PRISON.
YEAH, NO, BUT WHY ARE WE BAILING OUT FRED? WE HATE FRED. FRED'S A PRICK.
AH, BUT HE'S GOT A JOB FOR US.
THIS IS A JOB.
I MEAN A REAL JOB.
SIGH-- FINE.
SHE'S HOT, RIGHT?
EXTREMELY.
DAR
A-HEM. YOU THINK I CAN'T HEAR YOU OVER HERE?
I AM A PROFESSIONAL. I AM ROBBING YOU AT GUNPOINT RIGHT NOW. CAN WE MAYBE KEEP THE TOPICS OF CONVERSATION TO HOW TERRIFIED YOU ARE, OR HOW AMAZINGLY WELL PLANNED THIS WHOLE HEIST IS?
IS IT?
-SIGH---OKAY, WHICH ONES OF THESE ARE VALUABLE?

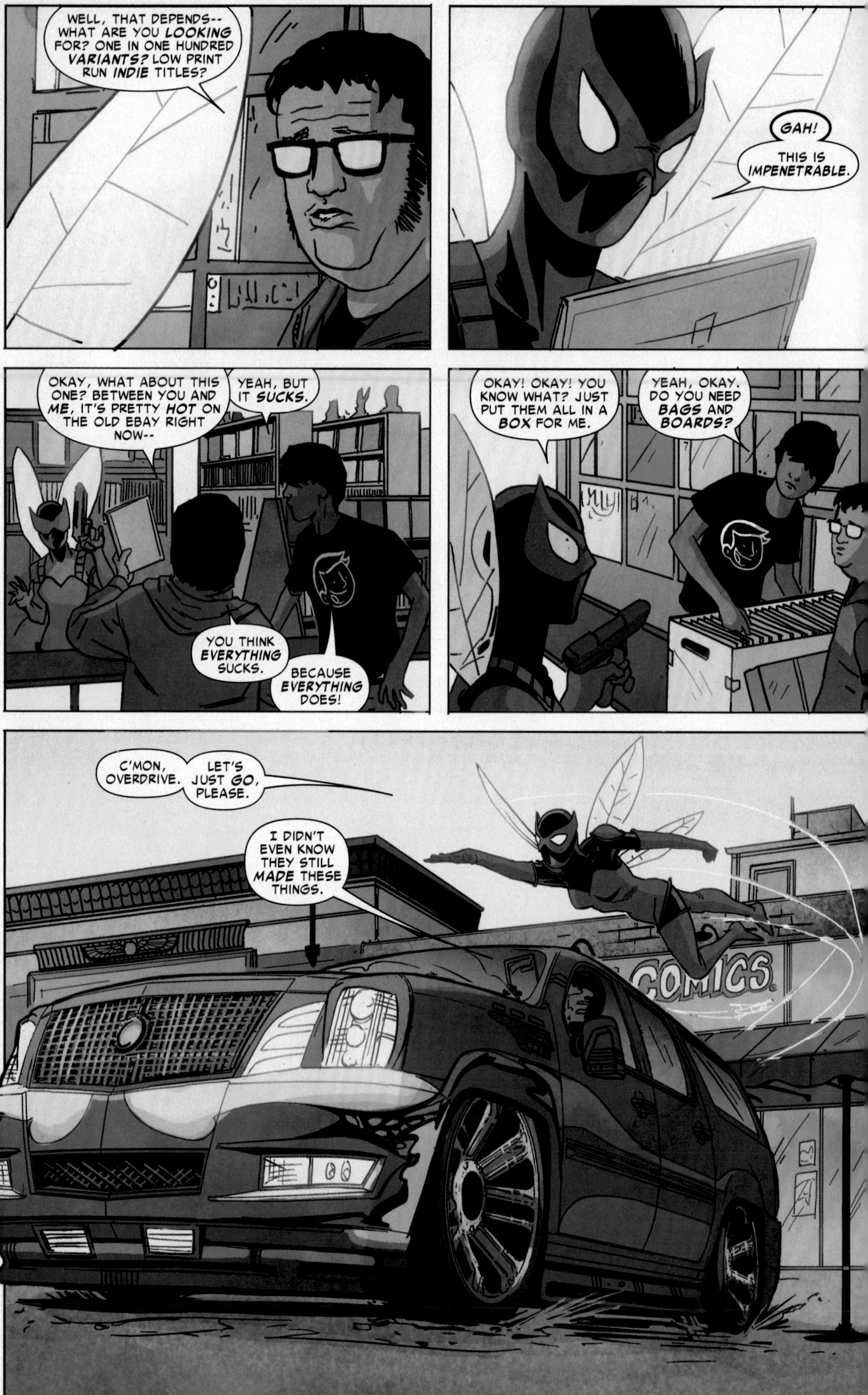

WELL, THAT DEPENDS-- WHAT ARE YOU LOOKING FOR? ONE IN ONE HUNDRED VARIANTS? LOW PRINT RUN INDIE TITLES?
GAH!
THIS IS IMPENETRABLE.
OKAY, WHAT ABOUT THIS ONE? BETWEEN YOU AND ME, IT'S PRETTY HOT ON THE OLD EBAY RIGHT NOW--
YEAH, BUT IT SUCKS.
YOU THINK EVERYTHING SUCKS.
BECAUSE EVERYTHING DOES!
OKAY! OKAY! YOU KNOW WHAT? JUST PUT THEM ALL IN A BOX FOR ME.
YEAH, OKAY. DO YOU NEED BAGS AND BOARDS?
C'MON, OVERDRIVE.
LET'S JUST GO, PLEASE.
I DIDN'T EVEN KNOW THEY STILL MADE THESE THINGS.
COMICS

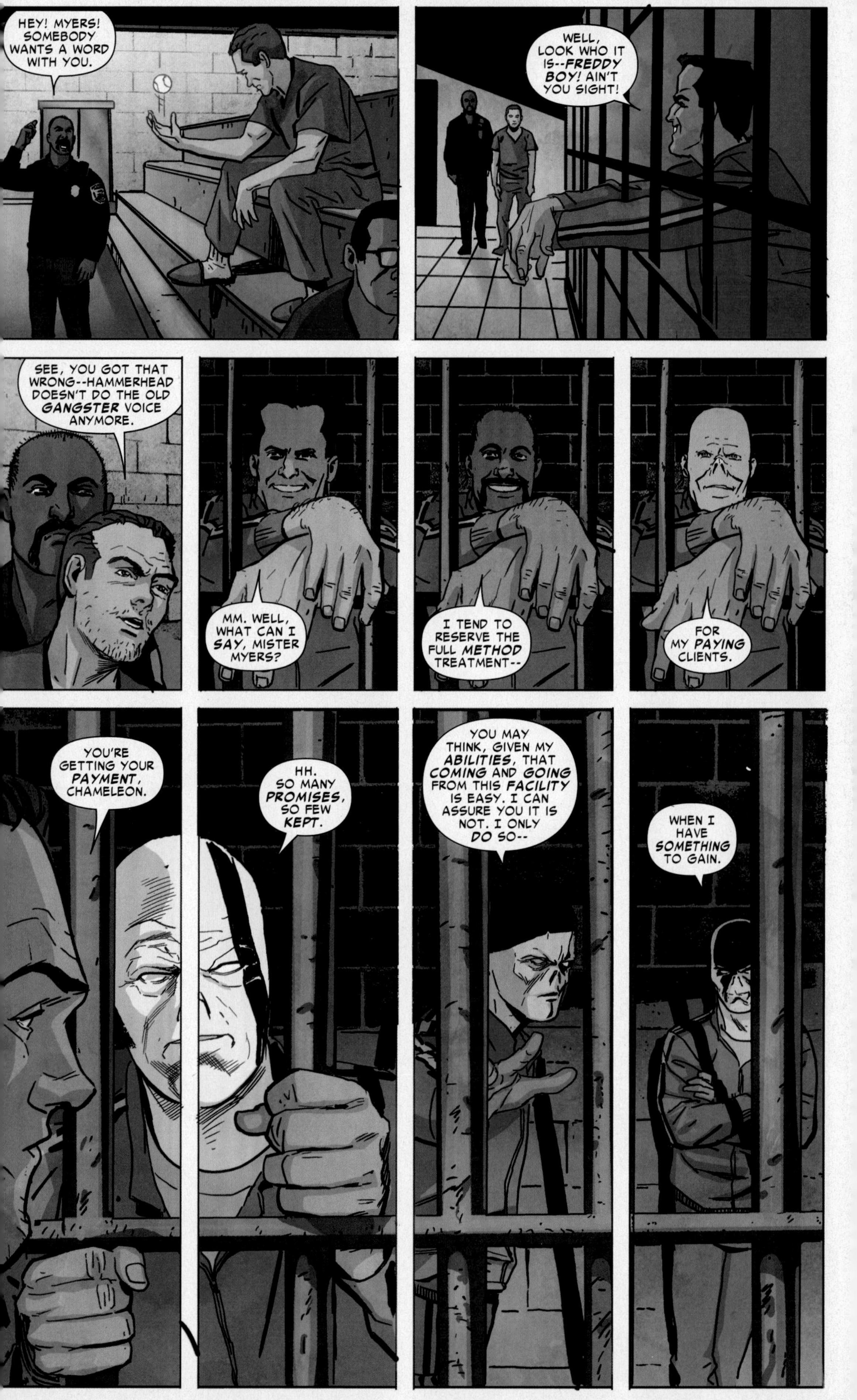
HEY! MYERS! SOMEBODY WANTS A WORD WITH YOU.
WELL, LOOK WHO IT IS--FREDDY BOY! AIN'T YOU SIGHT!
SEE, YOU GOT THAT WRONG--HAMMERHEAD DOESN'T DO THE OLD GANGSTER VOICE ANYMORE.
MM. WELL, WHAT CAN I SAY, MISTER MYERS?
I TEND TO RESERVE THE FULL METHOD TREATMENT--
FOR MY PAYING CLIENTS.
YOU'RE GETTING YOUR PAYMENT, CHAMELEON.
HH. SO MANY PROMISES, SO FEW KEPT.
YOU MAY THINK, GIVEN MY ABILITIES, THAT COMING AND GOING FROM THIS FACILITY IS EASY. I CAN ASSURE YOU IT IS NOT. I ONLY DO SO--
WHEN I HAVE SOMETHING TO GAIN.

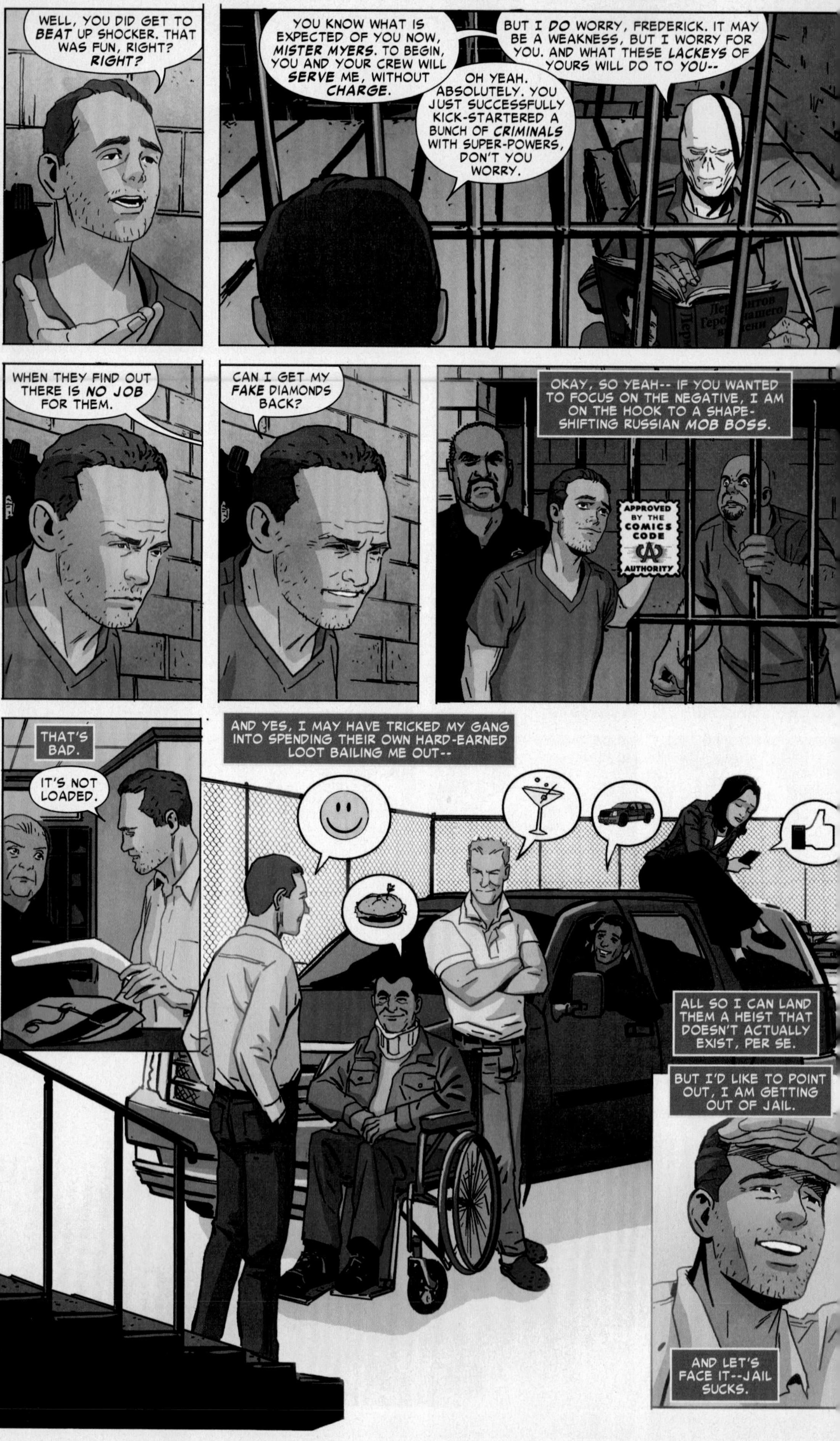
WELL, YOU DID GET TO BEAT UP SHOCKER. THAT WAS FUN, RIGHT? RIGHT?
YOU KNOW WHAT IS EXPECTED OF YOU NOW, MISTER MYERS. TO BEGIN, YOU AND YOUR CREW WILL SERVE ME, WITHOUT CHARGE.
OH YEAH. ABSOLUTELY. YOU JUST SUCCESSFULLY KICK-STARTERED A BUNCH OF CRIMINALS WITH SUPER-POWERS, DON'T YOU WORRY.
BUT I DO WORRY, FREDERICK. IT MAY BE A WEAKNESS, BUT I WORRY FOR YOU. AND WHAT THESE LACKEYS OF YOURS WILL DO TO YOU--
WHEN THEY FIND OUT THERE IS NO JOB FOR THEM.
CAN I GET MY FAKE DIAMONDS BACK?
OKAY, SO YEAH-- IF YOU WANTED TO FOCUS ON THE NEGATIVE, I AM ON THE HOOK TO A SHAPE-SHIFTING RUSSIAN MOB BOSS.
APPROVED BY THE COMICS CODE AUTHORITY
THAT'S BAD.
IT'S NOT LOADED.
AND YES, I MAY HAVE TRICKED MY GANG INTO SPENDING THEIR OWN HARD-EARNED LOOT BAILING ME OUT--
ALL SO I CAN LAND THEM A HEIST THAT DOESN'T ACTUALLY EXIST, PER SE.
BUT I'D LIKE TO POINT OUT, I AM GETTING OUT OF JAIL.
AND LET'S FACE IT--JAIL SUCKS.

SO THE QUESTION WAS, HOW DO I GET *OUT OF BED* IN THE MORNING?

WELL, YOUR *WIFE* DON'T MAKE IT *EASY*, I'LL SAY THAT MUCH. *HEY-O.*

BUT REALLY, THE THING IS-- CALL ME *NUTS*, CALL ME AN IDIOT, BUT I KNOW--I KNOW IN MY DAMN *HEART OF HEARTS*-- THAT ONE OF THESE DAYS, IT'S GONNA *HAPPEN* FOR ME.

I'M GONNA GET THE DROP ON HIM.

I'M GONNA BEAT THE RAP.

ACQUITTED

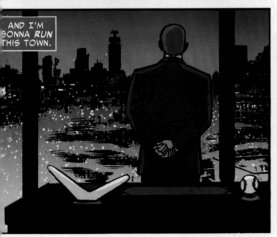

AND I'M GONNA *RUN* THIS TOWN.

LAW OF ODDS *ALONE* SAYS ONE OF THESE DAYS, IT'S *GOTTA* HAPPEN, RIGHT?

MY ONLY PROBLEM *BEING--*

EARLY RELEASE

IT SURE AS HELL AIN'T *TODAY.*

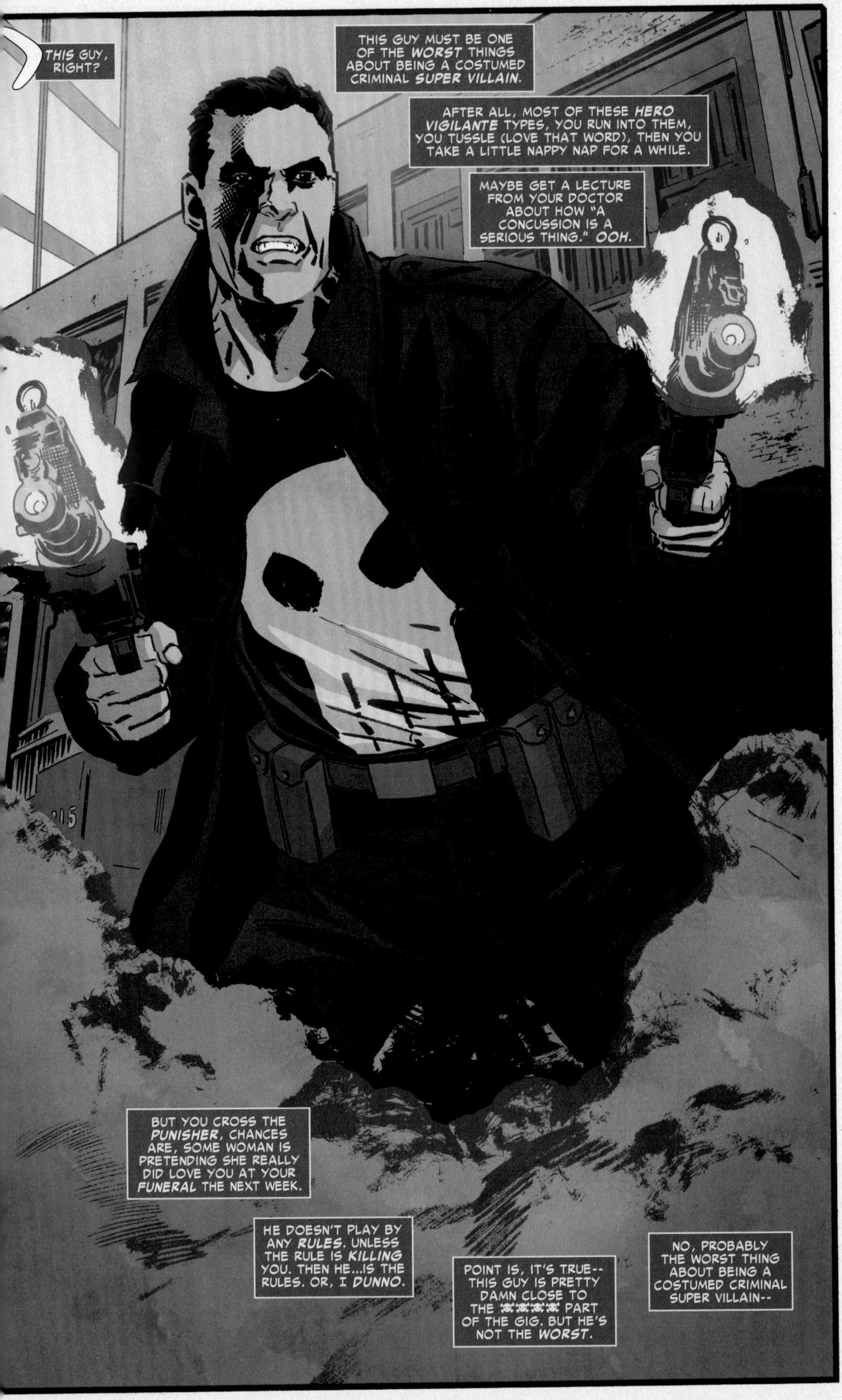

THIS GUY, RIGHT?
THIS GUY MUST BE ONE OF THE WORST THINGS ABOUT BEING A COSTUMED CRIMINAL SUPER VILLAIN.
AFTER ALL, MOST OF THESE HERO VIGILANTE TYPES, YOU RUN INTO THEM, YOU TUSSLE (LOVE THAT WORD), THEN YOU TAKE A LITTLE NAPPY NAP FOR A WHILE.
MAYBE GET A LECTURE FROM YOUR DOCTOR ABOUT HOW "A CONCUSSION IS A SERIOUS THING." OOH.
BUT YOU CROSS THE PUNISHER, CHANCES ARE, SOME WOMAN IS PRETENDING SHE REALLY DID LOVE YOU AT YOUR FUNERAL THE NEXT WEEK.
HE DOESN'T PLAY BY ANY RULES. UNLESS THE RULE IS KILLING YOU. THEN HE...IS THE RULES. OR, I DUNNO.
POINT IS, IT'S TRUE-- THIS GUY IS PRETTY DAMN CLOSE TO THE ☠☠☠☠ PART OF THE GIG. BUT HE'S NOT THE WORST.
NO, PROBABLY THE WORST THING ABOUT BEING A COSTUMED CRIMINAL SUPER VILLAIN--

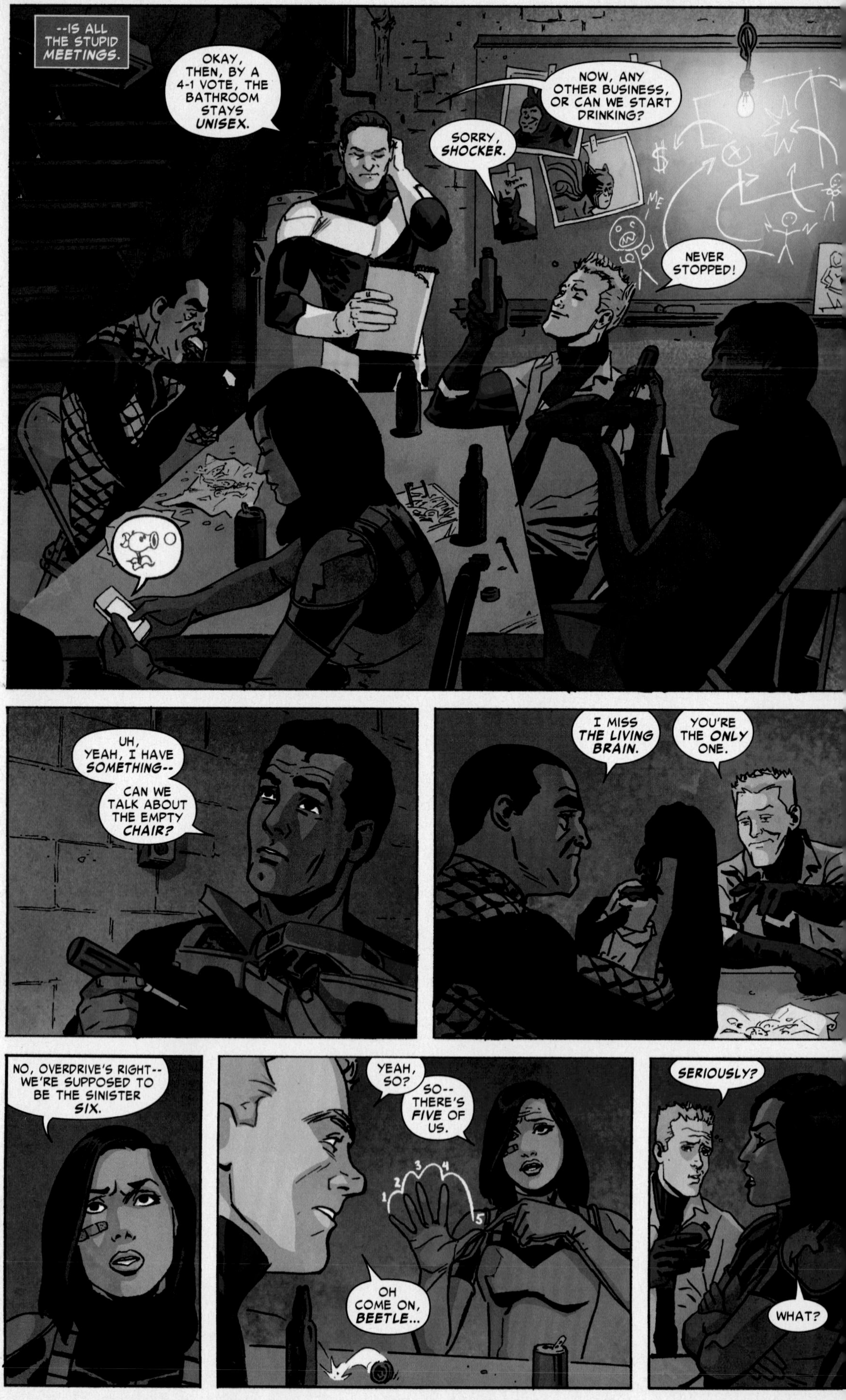

2

--IS ALL THE STUPID MEETINGS.
OKAY, THEN, BY A 4-1 VOTE, THE BATHROOM STAYS UNISEX.
NOW, ANY OTHER BUSINESS, OR CAN WE START DRINKING?
SORRY, SHOCKER.
NEVER STOPPED!
ME
UH, YEAH, I HAVE SOMETHING--
CAN WE TALK ABOUT THE EMPTY CHAIR?
I MISS THE LIVING BRAIN.
YOU'RE THE ONLY ONE.
NO, OVERDRIVE'S RIGHT--WE'RE SUPPOSED TO BE THE SINISTER SIX.
YEAH, SO?
SO--THERE'S FIVE OF US.
1 2 3 4 5
OH COME ON, BEETLE...
SERIOUSLY?
WHAT?

LOOK, WHAT'S A BETTER DEAL THAN BEING THE *SINISTER SIX,* BUT ONLY SPLITTING THE MONEY *FIVE* WAYS? HUH? HUH?

PLUS, *OBAMACARE,* YOU GO TO *SIX* EMPLOYEES-- IT'S *TRICKY.*

PEOPLE ARE GOING TO BE *CONFUSED.*

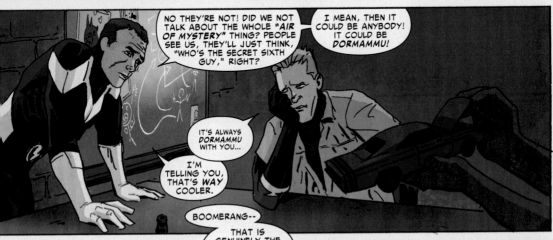

NO THEY'RE NOT! DID WE NOT TALK ABOUT THE WHOLE "*AIR OF MYSTERY*" THING? PEOPLE SEE US, THEY'LL JUST THINK, "WHO'S THE SECRET SIXTH GUY," RIGHT?

I MEAN, THEN IT COULD BE ANYBODY! IT COULD BE *DORMAMMU!*

IT'S ALWAYS *DORMAMMU* WITH YOU...

I'M TELLING YOU, THAT'S *WAY* COOLER.

BOOMERANG--

THAT IS GENUINELY THE *STUPIDEST* THING I HAVE EVER HEARD A REAL *PERSON* SAY.

YOU'RE STUPID!

SORRY.

WE UH--WE COULD ALWAYS GO WITH "THE *SINISTER SYNDICATE*..."

NO!

BOO! SHUT UP!

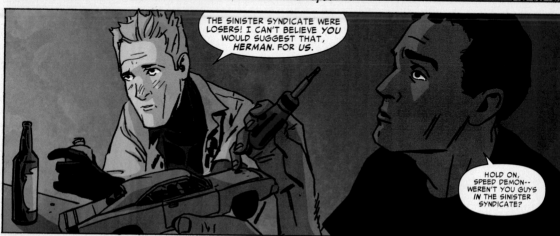

THE SINISTER SYNDICATE WERE *LOSERS!* I CAN'T BELIEVE *YOU* WOULD SUGGEST THAT, *HERMAN.* FOR *US.*

HOLD ON, SPEED DEMON-- WEREN'T YOU GUYS *IN* THE SINISTER SYNDICATE?

WELL, *YEAH,* RIGHT, SURE-- BUT NOW WE'RE *THE SINISTER SIX!*

HOW DO YOU PEOPLE NOT *GET* THIS?

BEING AN EXECUTIVE IS *HARD.*

BUT YOU KNOW, I TAKE IT *BACK.* THAT'S NOT THE *WORST* PART OF BEING A COSTUMED SUPER VILLAIN. NO, *WORST* PART, MAYBE--

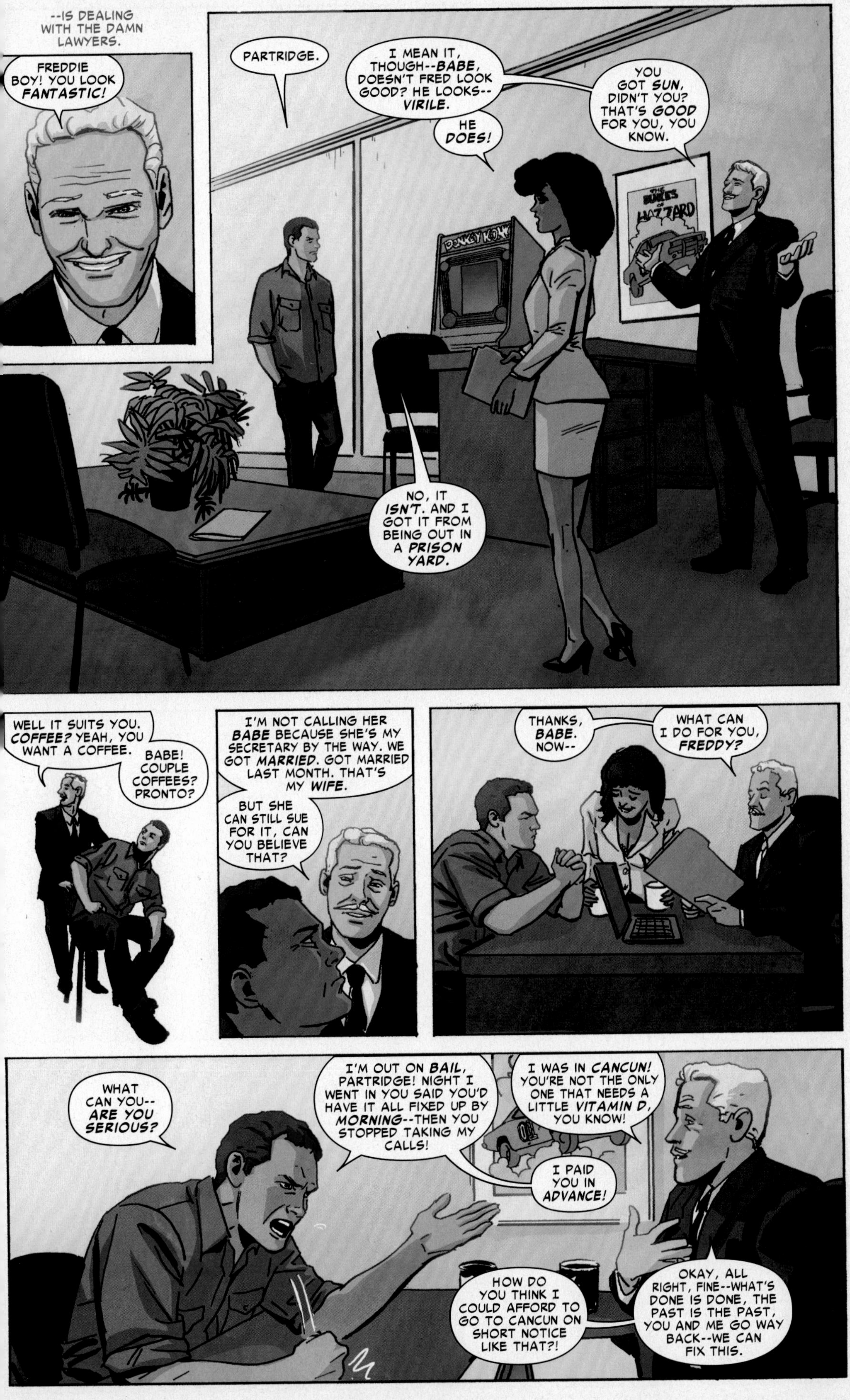
--IS DEALING WITH THE DAMN LAWYERS.
FREDDIE BOY! YOU LOOK *FANTASTIC!*
PARTRIDGE.
I MEAN IT, THOUGH--*BABE*, DOESN'T FRED LOOK GOOD? HE LOOKS-- *VIRILE*.
HE *DOES!*
YOU GOT *SUN*, DIDN'T YOU? THAT'S *GOOD* FOR YOU, YOU KNOW.
DONKEY KONG
THE DUKES OF HAZZARD
NO, IT *ISN'T*. AND I GOT IT FROM BEING OUT IN A *PRISON YARD*.
WELL IT SUITS YOU. *COFFEE?* YEAH, YOU WANT A COFFEE.
BABE! COUPLE COFFEES? PRONTO?
I'M NOT CALLING HER *BABE* BECAUSE SHE'S MY SECRETARY BY THE WAY. WE GOT *MARRIED*. GOT MARRIED LAST MONTH. THAT'S MY *WIFE*.
BUT SHE CAN STILL SUE FOR IT, CAN YOU BELIEVE THAT?
THANKS, *BABE*. NOW--
WHAT CAN I DO FOR YOU, *FREDDY?*
WHAT CAN YOU-- *ARE YOU SERIOUS?*
I'M OUT ON *BAIL*, PARTRIDGE! NIGHT I WENT IN YOU SAID YOU'D HAVE IT ALL FIXED UP BY *MORNING*--THEN YOU STOPPED TAKING MY CALLS!
I WAS IN *CANCUN!* YOU'RE NOT THE ONLY ONE THAT NEEDS A LITTLE *VITAMIN D*, YOU KNOW!
I PAID YOU IN *ADVANCE!*
HOW DO YOU THINK I COULD AFFORD TO GO TO CANCUN ON SHORT NOTICE LIKE THAT?!
OKAY, ALL RIGHT, FINE--WHAT'S DONE IS DONE, THE PAST IS THE PAST, YOU AND ME GO WAY BACK--WE CAN FIX THIS.

I'M LISTENING.

WELL, THE *GOOD NEWS* IS, I HAD A LUNCH WITH MY FRIEND IN THE DISTRICT ATTORNEY'S OFFICE, AND WE CAN GET THEM TO DROP *MOST* OF THESE CHARGES.

SOME *YUPPY THING*, I DUNNO. JANICE'LL E-MAIL YOU.

WHAT'S THAT GONNA *COST* ME?

FINE.

BUT THERE'S ONE MORE THING--

THERE *ALWAYS* IS.

YOU VIOLATED THE TERMS OF YOUR *PAROLE*, PAL!

I WAS ON *PAROLE*?

YEAH, AND NOTHING I CAN DO ON THAT ONE, OKAY?

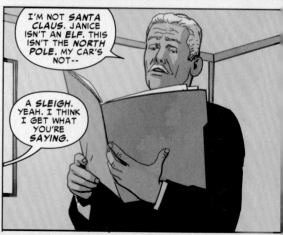

I'M NOT *SANTA CLAUS.* JANICE ISN'T AN *ELF.* THIS ISN'T THE *NORTH POLE.* MY CAR'S NOT--

A *SLEIGH.* YEAH. I THINK I GET WHAT YOU'RE *SAYING.*

BESIDES IT'S AUGUST! CAN'T BE CHRISTMAS, RIGHT? BUT DON'T YOU WORRY--ODDS ARE, THEY JUST GIVE YOU A LITTLE SLAP ON THE WRIST.

HEY, WHERE DO YOU THINK THAT SAYING COMES FROM ANYWAY? I'VE NEVER BEEN SLAPPED ON MY WRIST!

I DON'T KNOW, PARTRIDGE.

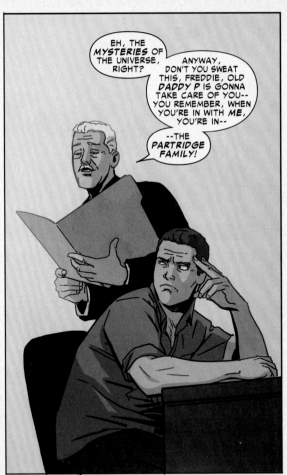

EH, THE MYSTERIES OF THE UNIVERSE, RIGHT?

ANYWAY, DON'T YOU SWEAT THIS, FREDDIE, OLD DADDY P IS GONNA TAKE CARE OF YOU-- YOU REMEMBER, WHEN YOU'RE IN WITH ME, YOU'RE IN--

--THE PARTRIDGE FAMILY!

LOOK, WE'LL GO MEET WITH YOUR PAROLE BOARD, PLAY NICE, AND BEFORE YOU KNOW IT YOU'LL BE ALL GOOD WITH THE CITY OF NEW YORK.

WE'RE A TOWN THAT BELIEVES IN SECOND CHANCES! GOOD FOR US, RIGHT?

BUT ONE THING, FREDDY-- 'TIL THAT MEETING, WHATEVER YOU DO--

YOU KEEP YOUR NOSE CLEAN, YOU HEAR ME?

WHAT?

GIMME EVERYTHING YOU *GOT!*

GUY'S GOTTA EAT.

ZOLAR--

ZAGAT.

RIGHT. ZAGAT CALLS THIS PLACE *"THE ULTIMATE IN ABSURDLY DECADENT MANHATTAN DINING."*

STUFF LIKE THIRTY-FIVE GRAND FOR A *SUNDAE* WITH A *DIAMOND* IN IT. TEN GRAND FOR A *MARTINI* THAT COMES WITH A *DIAMOND NECKLACE.*

KINDA PLACE ALL THE WALL STREET GUYS GO WITH THEIR *NOT-WIVES* TO SHOW OFF THE MONEY THEY *STOLE* FROM THE GOVERNMENT TO MAKE UP FOR THE MONEY THEY LOST STEALING FROM *POOR PEOPLE.*

I MYSELF AM MORE OF A *BURGER AND FRIES* GUY.

BUT IT OPENED *BIG*--THE PLACE IS THE TALK OF THE TOWN. PROBLEM IS, LIKE *EVERYTHING* IN NEW YORK--

SOMEONE GOT HERE BEFORE *YOU DID.*

RESTAURANT ACROSS THE STREET WAS *DEAD AS DISCO,* SO WE WERE ABLE TO WORK OUT A DEAL.

WE COME IN, BUST THE PLACE UP FOR THEM, GET IT SHUT DOWN FOR A *FEW WEEKS*--WHICH IN THIS TOWN IS LONG ENOUGH TO MAKE *YOU OLD NEWS.*

IN EXCHANGE, WE GET OUR *FEE,* PLUS WHATEVER WE WANT--

NO ACCESS

--FROM THE *KITCHEN.*

24K 24K
24K 24K
24K 24K
24K 24K
24K 24K

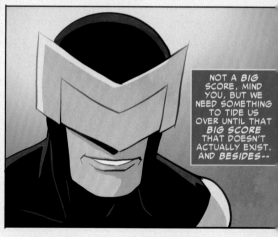

NOT A *BIG* SCORE, MIND YOU, BUT WE NEED SOMETHING TO TIDE US OVER UNTIL THAT *BIG SCORE* THAT DOESN'T ACTUALLY EXIST. AND *BESIDES*--

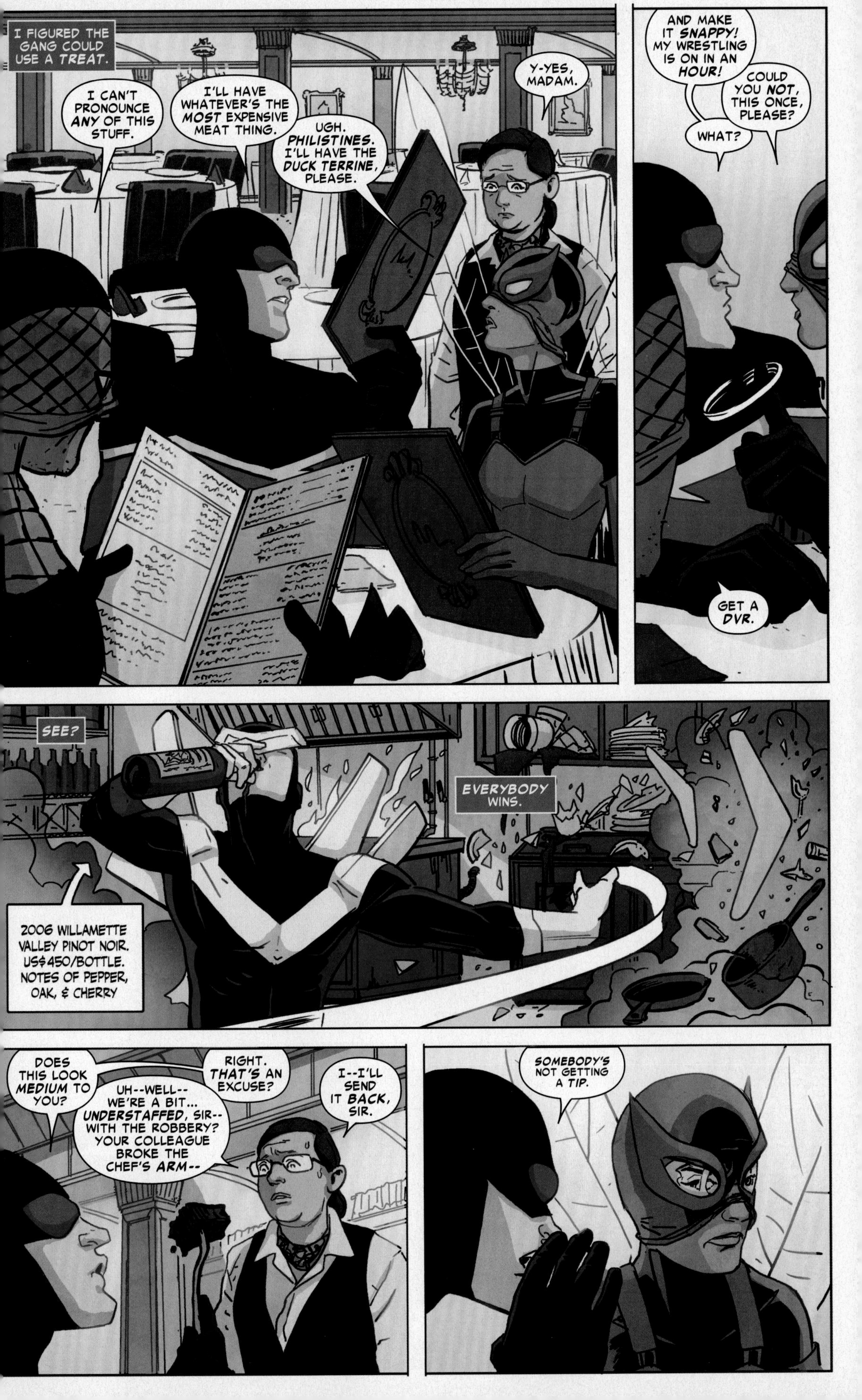
I FIGURED THE GANG COULD USE A TREAT.
I CAN'T PRONOUNCE ANY OF THIS STUFF.
I'LL HAVE WHATEVER'S THE MOST EXPENSIVE MEAT THING.
UGH. PHILISTINES. I'LL HAVE THE DUCK TERRINE, PLEASE.
Y-YES, MADAM.
AND MAKE IT SNAPPY! MY WRESTLING IS ON IN AN HOUR!
WHAT?
COULD YOU NOT, THIS ONCE, PLEASE?
GET A DVR.
SEE?
EVERYBODY WINS.
2006 WILLAMETTE VALLEY PINOT NOIR. US$450/BOTTLE. NOTES OF PEPPER, OAK, & CHERRY
DOES THIS LOOK MEDIUM TO YOU?
UH--WELL-- WE'RE A BIT... UNDERSTAFFED, SIR-- WITH THE ROBBERY? YOUR COLLEAGUE BROKE THE CHEF'S ARM--
RIGHT. THAT'S AN EXCUSE?
I--I'LL SEND IT BACK, SIR.
SOMEBODY'S NOT GETTING A TIP.

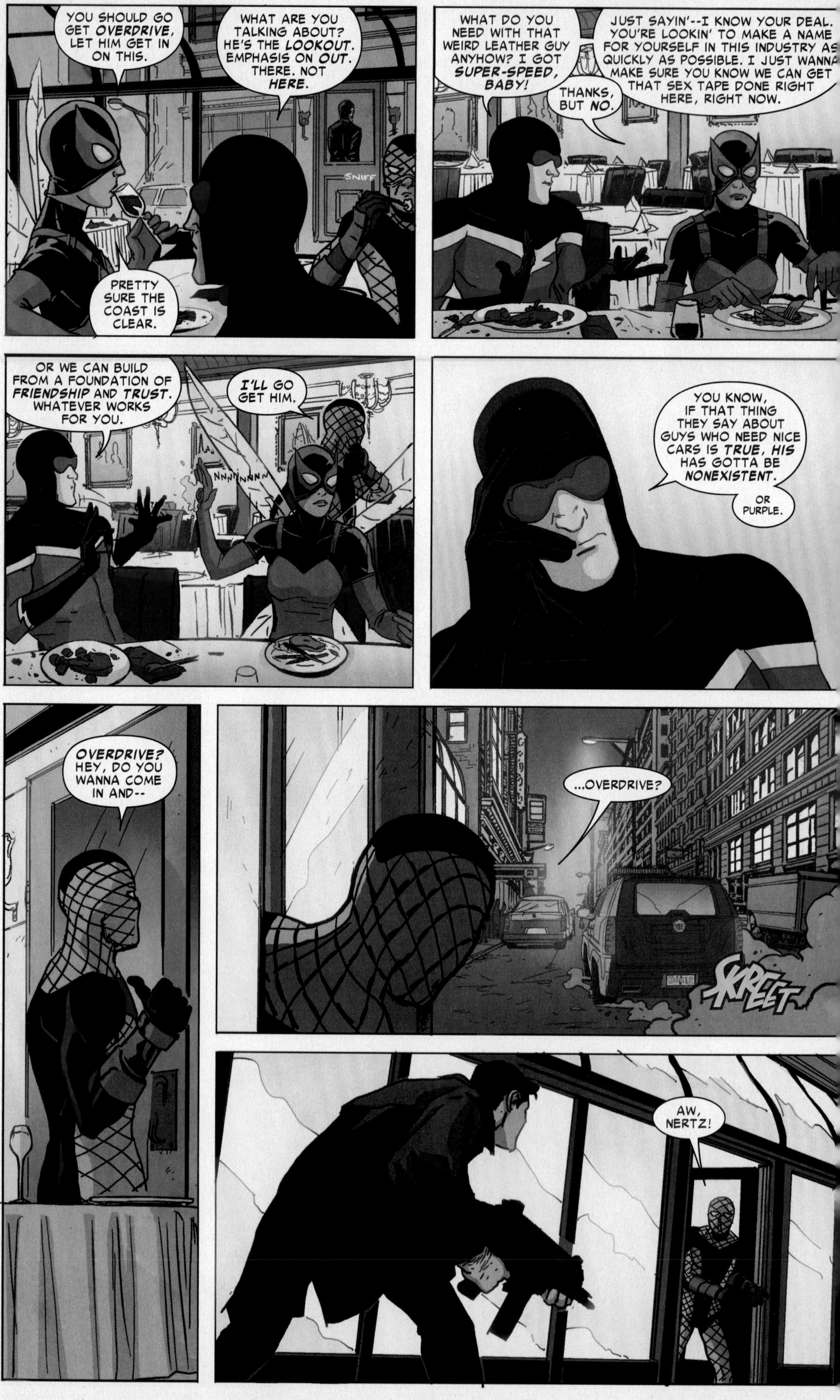
YOU SHOULD GO GET OVERDRIVE, LET HIM GET IN ON THIS.
WHAT ARE YOU TALKING ABOUT? HE'S THE LOOKOUT. EMPHASIS ON OUT. THERE. NOT HERE.
SNIFF
PRETTY SURE THE COAST IS CLEAR.
WHAT DO YOU NEED WITH THAT WEIRD LEATHER GUY ANYHOW? I GOT SUPER-SPEED, BABY!
JUST SAYIN'--I KNOW YOUR DEAL. YOU'RE LOOKIN' TO MAKE A NAME FOR YOURSELF IN THIS INDUSTRY AS QUICKLY AS POSSIBLE. I JUST WANNA MAKE SURE YOU KNOW WE CAN GET THAT SEX TAPE DONE RIGHT HERE, RIGHT NOW.
THANKS, BUT NO.
OR WE CAN BUILD FROM A FOUNDATION OF FRIENDSHIP AND TRUST. WHATEVER WORKS FOR YOU.
I'LL GO GET HIM.
NNNNNNNN
YOU KNOW, IF THAT THING THEY SAY ABOUT GUYS WHO NEED NICE CARS IS TRUE, HIS HAS GOTTA BE NONEXISTENT.
OR PURPLE.
OVERDRIVE? HEY, DO YOU WANNA COME IN AND--
...OVERDRIVE?
SKREEET
AW, NERTZ!

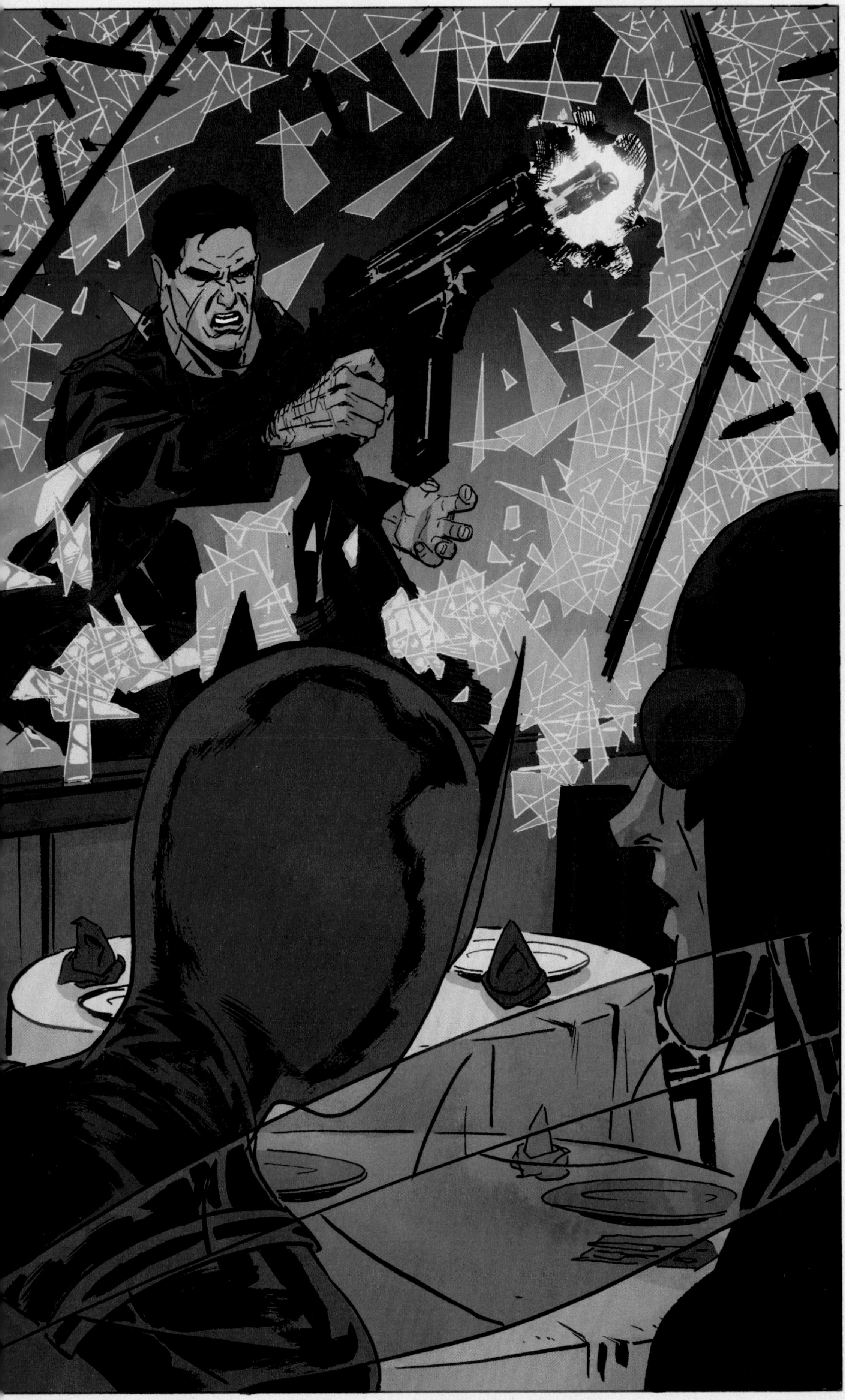

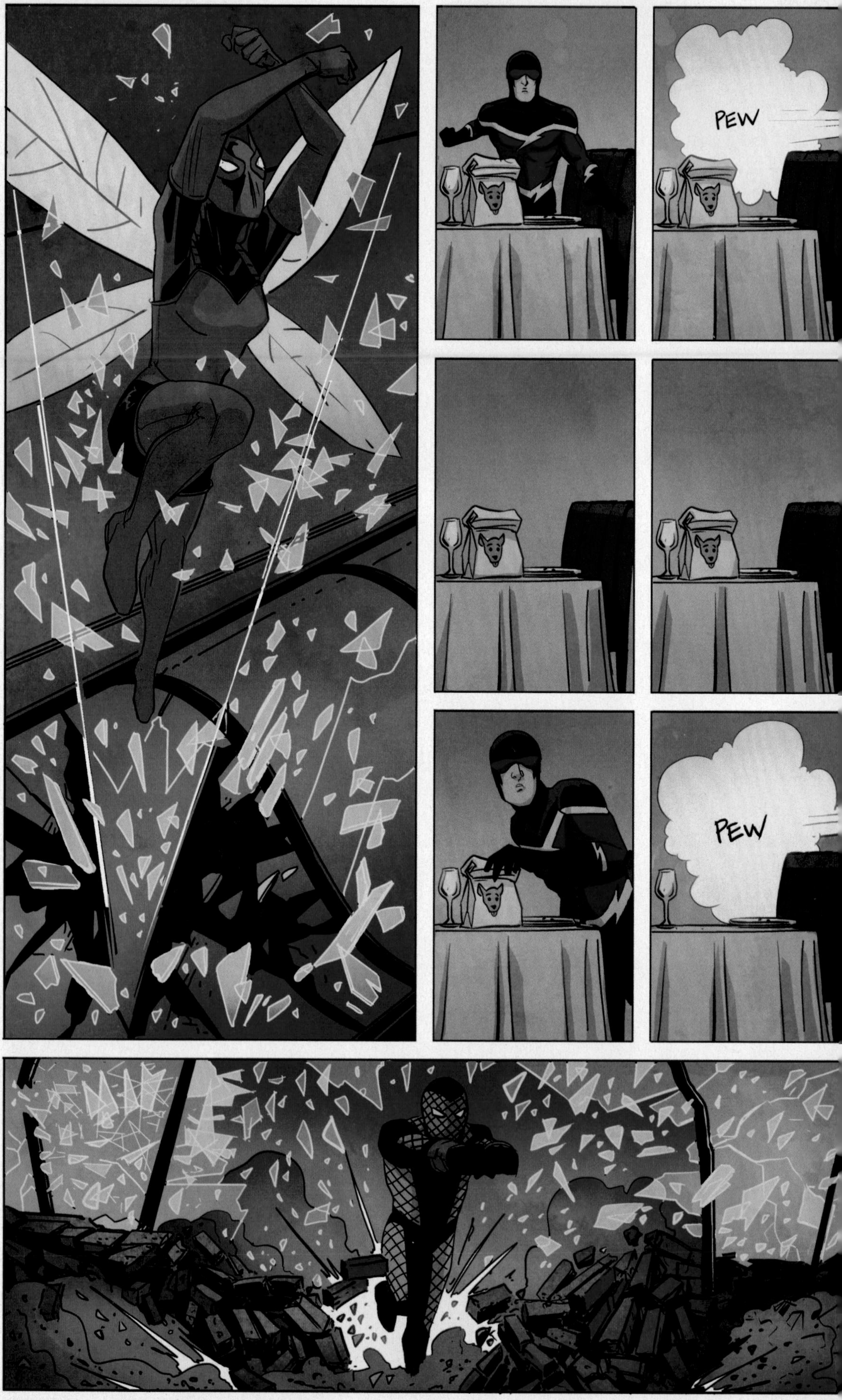
PEW
PEW

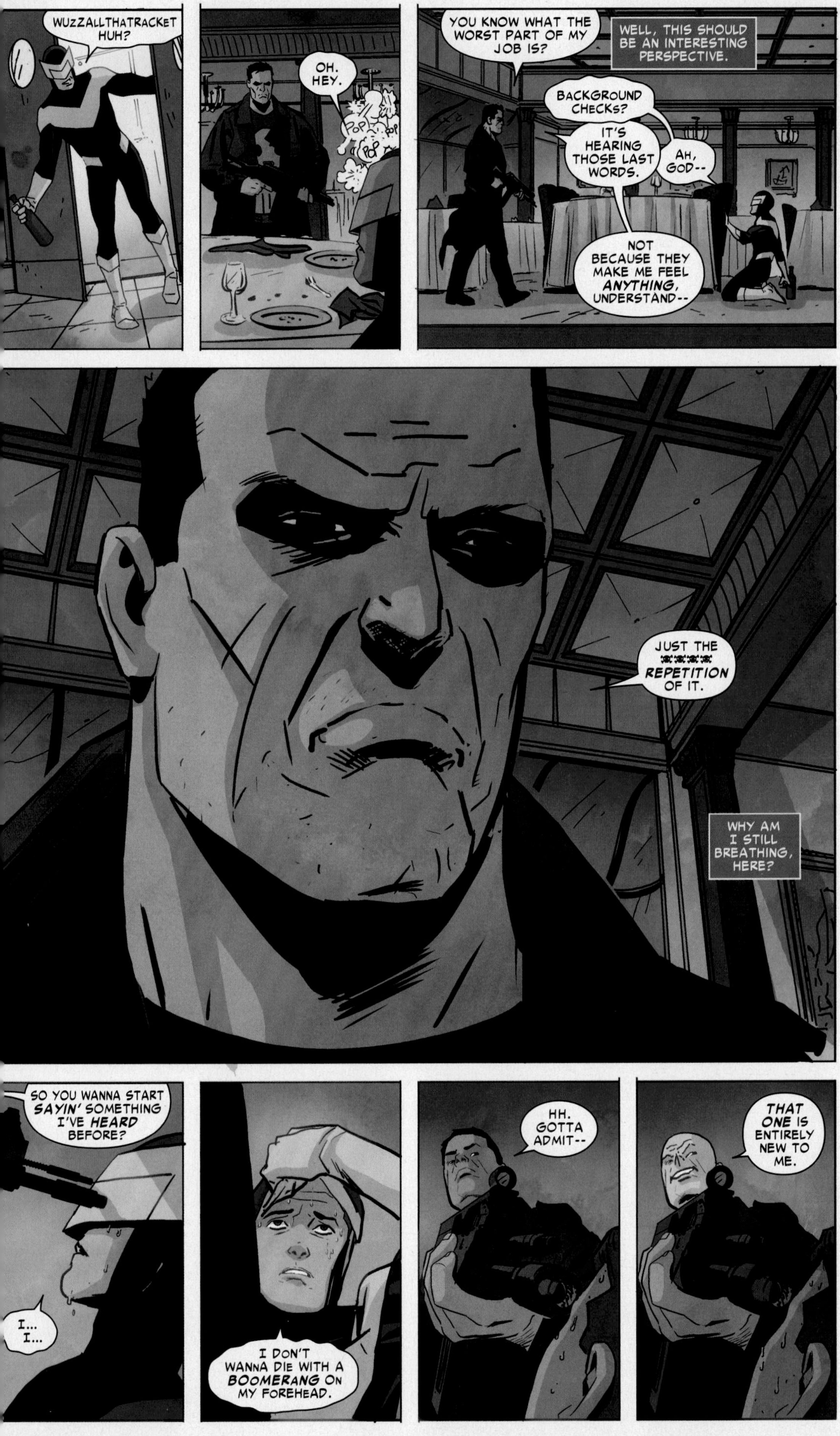
WUZZALLTHATRACKET HUH?
OH. HEY.
YOU KNOW WHAT THE WORST PART OF MY JOB IS?
WELL, THIS SHOULD BE AN INTERESTING PERSPECTIVE.
BACKGROUND CHECKS?
IT'S HEARING THOSE LAST WORDS.
AH, GOD--
NOT BECAUSE THEY MAKE ME FEEL *ANYTHING*, UNDERSTAND--
JUST THE ☠☠☠☠ *REPETITION* OF IT.
WHY AM I STILL BREATHING, HERE?
SO YOU WANNA START *SAYIN'* SOMETHING I'VE *HEARD* BEFORE?
I... I...
I DON'T WANNA DIE WITH A *BOOMERANG* ON MY FOREHEAD.
HH. GOTTA ADMIT--
THAT ONE IS ENTIRELY NEW TO ME.

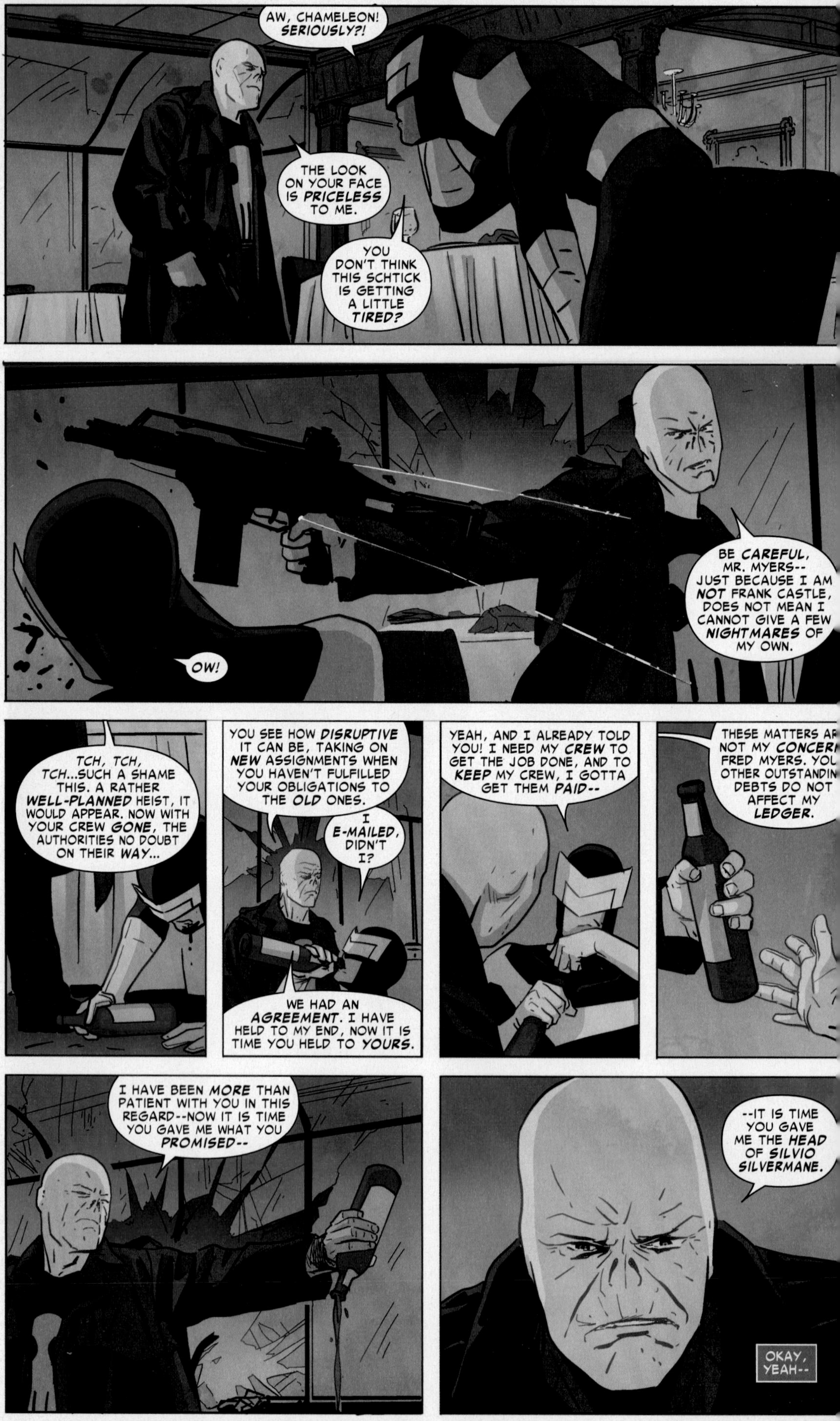
AW, CHAMELEON! SERIOUSLY?!
THE LOOK ON YOUR FACE IS PRICELESS TO ME.
YOU DON'T THINK THIS SCHTICK IS GETTING A LITTLE TIRED?
BE CAREFUL, MR. MYERS-- JUST BECAUSE I AM NOT FRANK CASTLE, DOES NOT MEAN I CANNOT GIVE A FEW NIGHTMARES OF MY OWN.
OW!
TCH, TCH, TCH...SUCH A SHAME THIS. A RATHER WELL-PLANNED HEIST, IT WOULD APPEAR. NOW WITH YOUR CREW GONE, THE AUTHORITIES NO DOUBT ON THEIR WAY...
YOU SEE HOW DISRUPTIVE IT CAN BE, TAKING ON NEW ASSIGNMENTS WHEN YOU HAVEN'T FULFILLED YOUR OBLIGATIONS TO THE OLD ONES.
I E-MAILED, DIDN'T I?
WE HAD AN AGREEMENT. I HAVE HELD TO MY END, NOW IT IS TIME YOU HELD TO YOURS.
YEAH, AND I ALREADY TOLD YOU! I NEED MY CREW TO GET THE JOB DONE, AND TO KEEP MY CREW, I GOTTA GET THEM PAID--
THESE MATTERS AR NOT MY CONCER FRED MYERS. YOU OTHER OUTSTANDIN DEBTS DO NOT AFFECT MY LEDGER.
I HAVE BEEN MORE THAN PATIENT WITH YOU IN THIS REGARD--NOW IT IS TIME YOU GAVE ME WHAT YOU PROMISED--
--IT IS TIME YOU GAVE ME THE HEAD OF SILVIO SILVERMANE.
OKAY, YEAH--

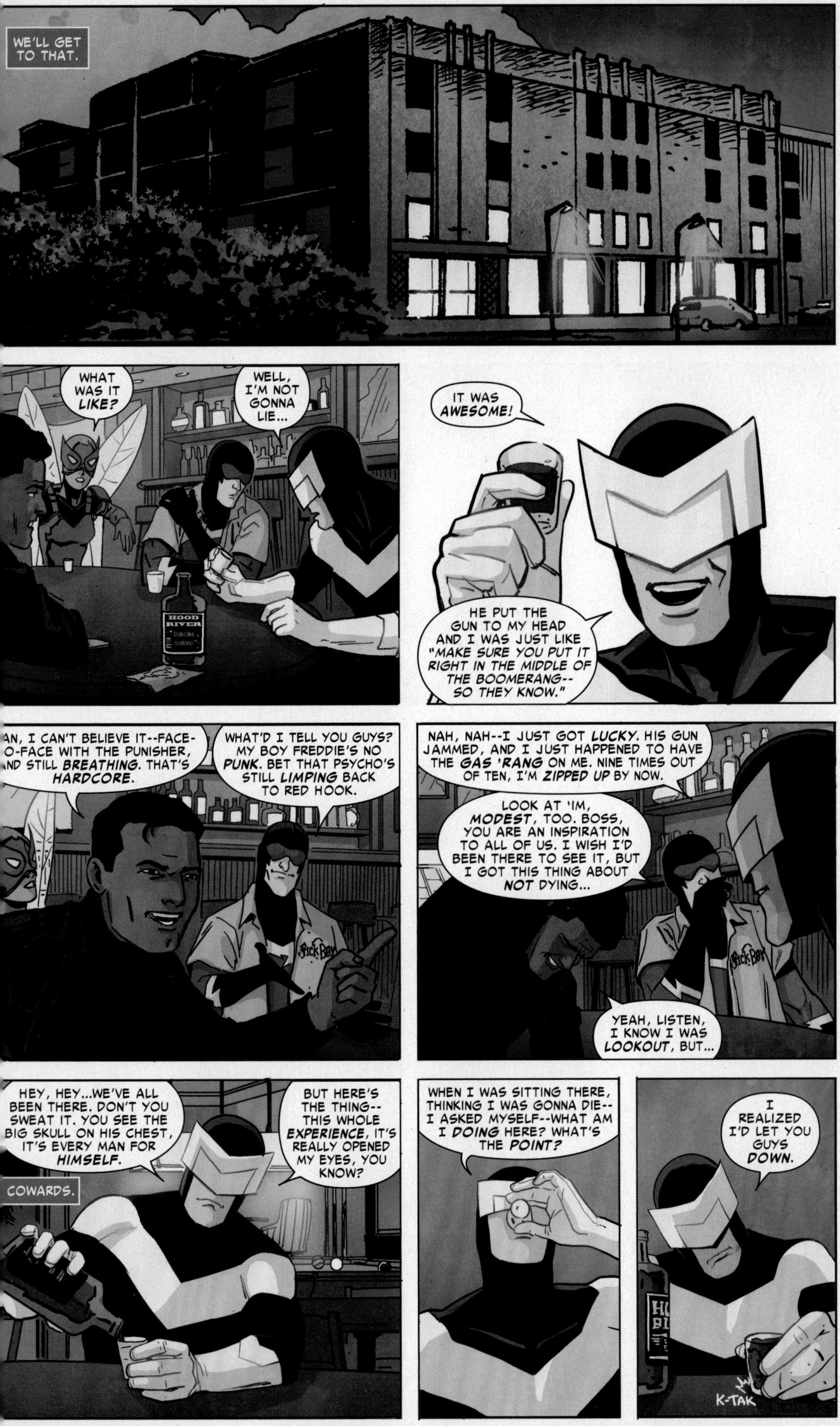
WE'LL GET TO THAT.
WHAT WAS IT LIKE?
WELL, I'M NOT GONNA LIE...
IT WAS AWESOME!
HE PUT THE GUN TO MY HEAD AND I WAS JUST LIKE "MAKE SURE YOU PUT IT RIGHT IN THE MIDDLE OF THE BOOMERANG-- SO THEY KNOW."
HOOD RIVER
AN, I CAN'T BELIEVE IT--FACE-O-FACE WITH THE PUNISHER, AND STILL BREATHING. THAT'S HARDCORE.
WHAT'D I TELL YOU GUYS? MY BOY FREDDIE'S NO PUNK. BET THAT PSYCHO'S STILL LIMPING BACK TO RED HOOK.
NAH, NAH--I JUST GOT LUCKY. HIS GUN JAMMED, AND I JUST HAPPENED TO HAVE THE GAS 'RANG ON ME. NINE TIMES OUT OF TEN, I'M ZIPPED UP BY NOW.
LOOK AT 'IM, MODEST, TOO. BOSS, YOU ARE AN INSPIRATION TO ALL OF US. I WISH I'D BEEN THERE TO SEE IT, BUT I GOT THIS THING ABOUT NOT DYING...
YEAH, LISTEN, I KNOW I WAS LOOKOUT, BUT...
HEY, HEY...WE'VE ALL BEEN THERE. DON'T YOU SWEAT IT. YOU SEE THE BIG SKULL ON HIS CHEST, IT'S EVERY MAN FOR HIMSELF.
COWARDS.
BUT HERE'S THE THING-- THIS WHOLE EXPERIENCE, IT'S REALLY OPENED MY EYES, YOU KNOW?
WHEN I WAS SITTING THERE, THINKING I WAS GONNA DIE-- I ASKED MYSELF--WHAT AM I DOING HERE? WHAT'S THE POINT?
I REALIZED I'D LET YOU GUYS DOWN.
K-TAK

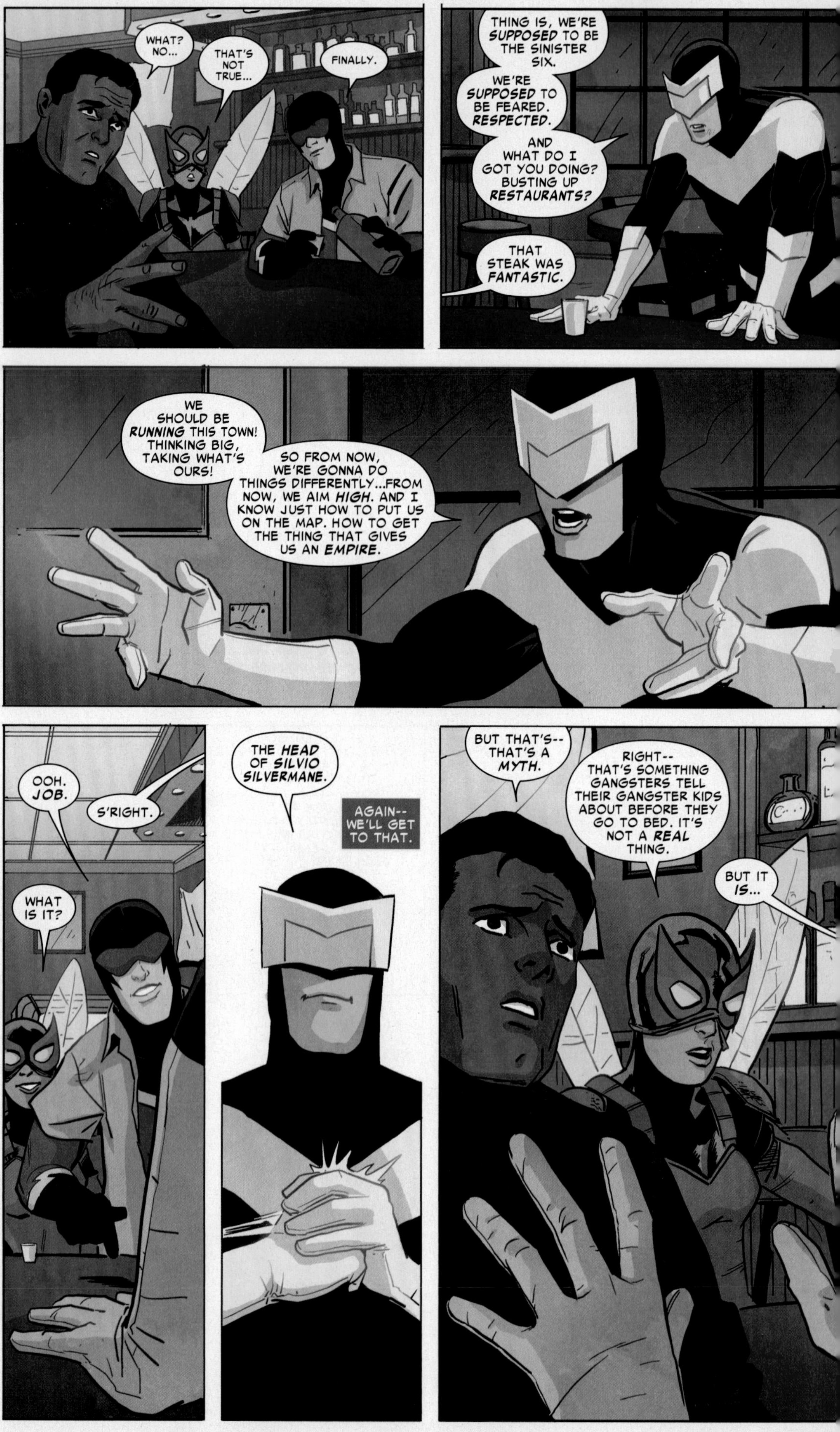

WHAT? NO...
THAT'S NOT TRUE...
FINALLY.
THING IS, WE'RE SUPPOSED TO BE THE SINISTER SIX.
WE'RE SUPPOSED TO BE FEARED. RESPECTED.
AND WHAT DO I GOT YOU DOING? BUSTING UP RESTAURANTS?
THAT STEAK WAS FANTASTIC.
WE SHOULD BE RUNNING THIS TOWN! THINKING BIG, TAKING WHAT'S OURS!
SO FROM NOW, WE'RE GONNA DO THINGS DIFFERENTLY...FROM NOW, WE AIM HIGH. AND I KNOW JUST HOW TO PUT US ON THE MAP. HOW TO GET THE THING THAT GIVES US AN EMPIRE.
OOH. JOB.
S'RIGHT.
WHAT IS IT?
THE HEAD OF SILVIO SILVERMANE.
AGAIN-- WE'LL GET TO THAT.
BUT THAT'S-- THAT'S A MYTH.
RIGHT-- THAT'S SOMETHING GANGSTERS TELL THEIR GANGSTER KIDS ABOUT BEFORE THEY GO TO BED. IT'S NOT A REAL THING.
BUT IT IS...

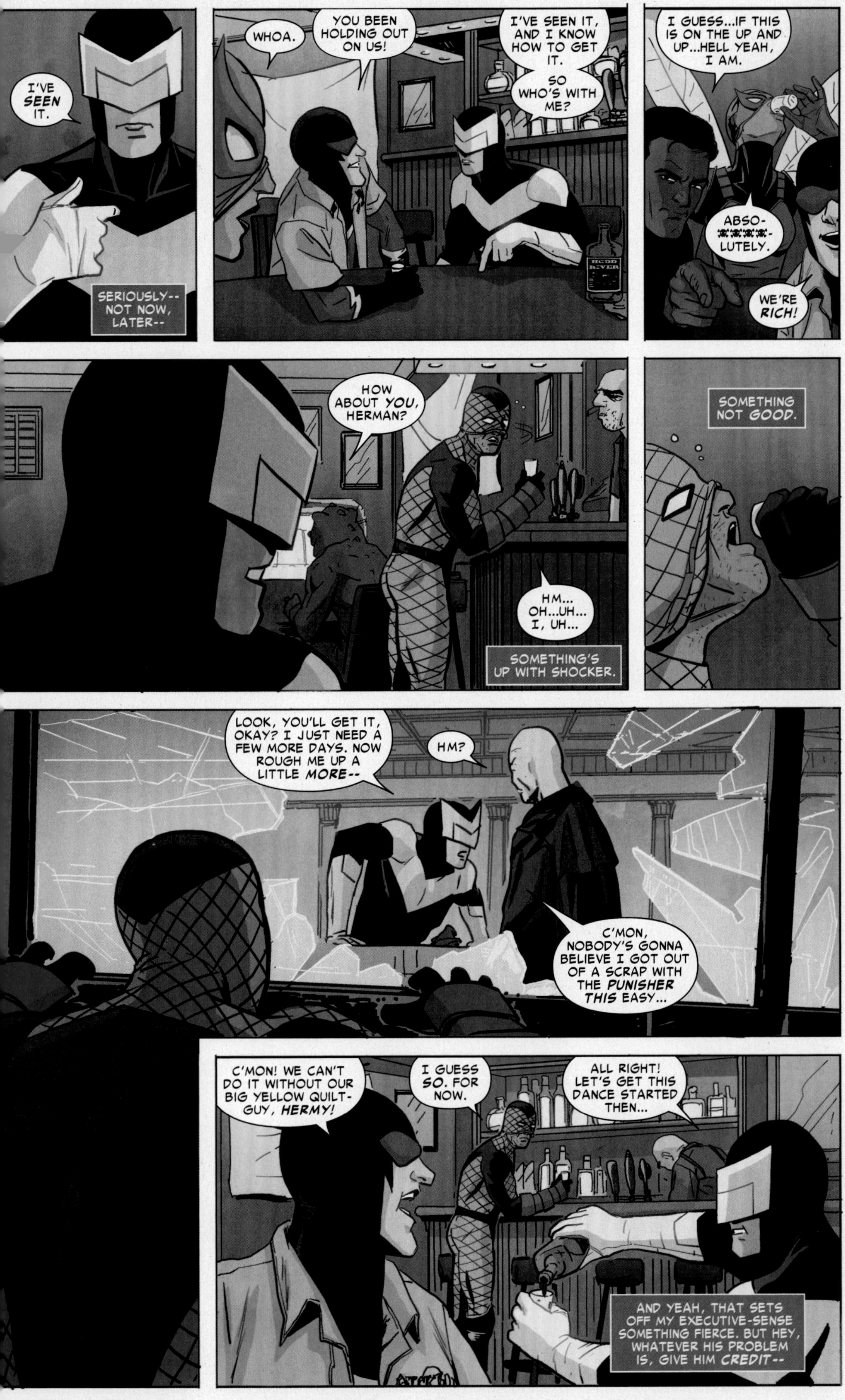
I'VE SEEN IT.
SERIOUSLY--NOT NOW, LATER--
WHOA.
YOU BEEN HOLDING OUT ON US!
I'VE SEEN IT, AND I KNOW HOW TO GET IT.
SO WHO'S WITH ME?
I GUESS...IF THIS IS ON THE UP AND UP...HELL YEAH, I AM.
ABSO-☠☠☠-LUTELY.
WE'RE RICH!
HOW ABOUT YOU, HERMAN?
HM... OH...UH... I, UH...
SOMETHING'S UP WITH SHOCKER.
SOMETHING NOT GOOD.
LOOK, YOU'LL GET IT, OKAY? I JUST NEED A FEW MORE DAYS. NOW ROUGH ME UP A LITTLE MORE--
HM?
C'MON, NOBODY'S GONNA BELIEVE I GOT OUT OF A SCRAP WITH THE PUNISHER THIS EASY...
C'MON! WE CAN'T DO IT WITHOUT OUR BIG YELLOW QUILT-GUY, HERMY!
I GUESS SO. FOR NOW.
ALL RIGHT! LET'S GET THIS DANCE STARTED THEN...
AND YEAH, THAT SETS OFF MY EXECUTIVE-SENSE SOMETHING FIERCE. BUT HEY, WHATEVER HIS PROBLEM IS, GIVE HIM CREDIT--

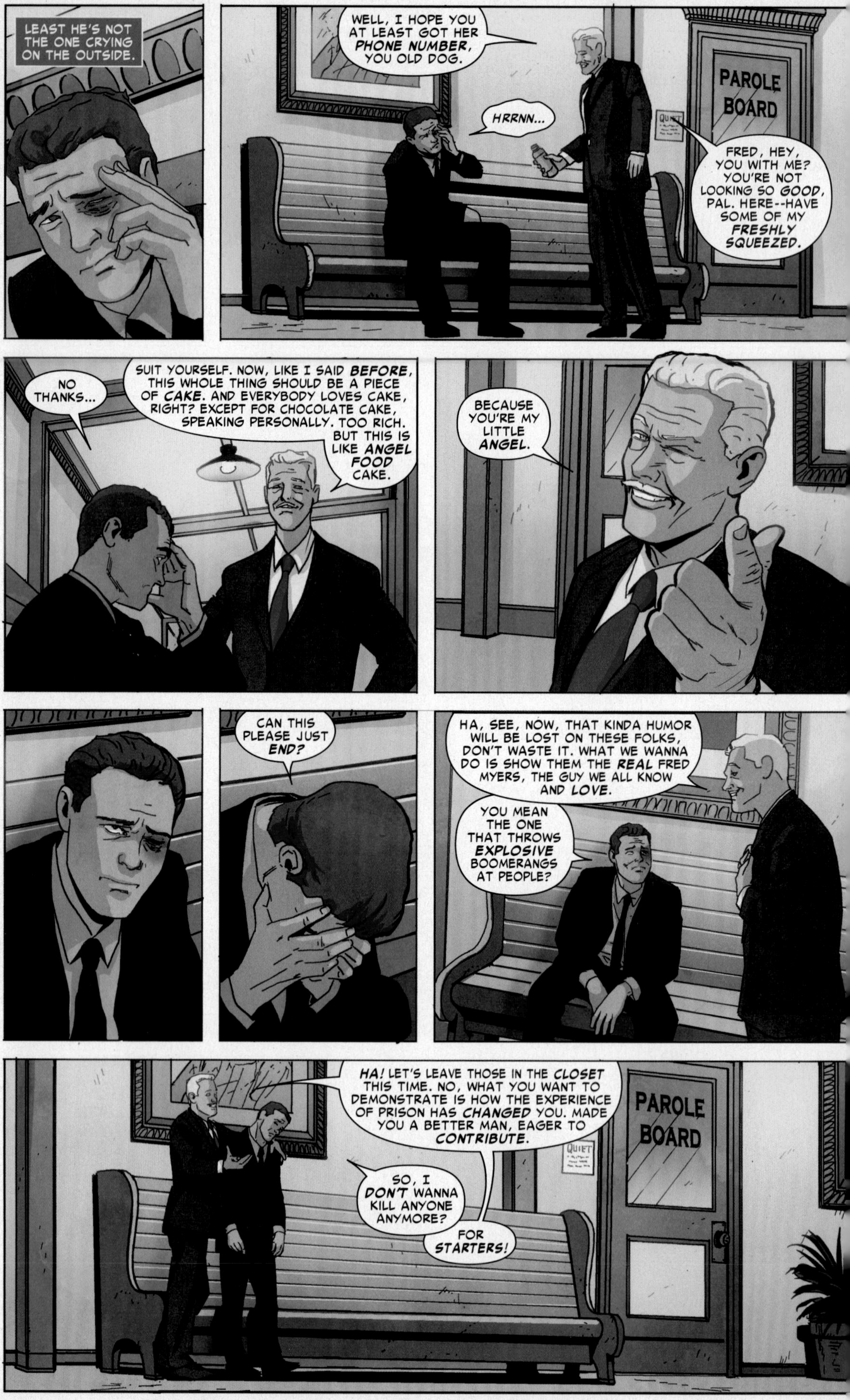
LEAST HE'S NOT THE ONE CRYING ON THE OUTSIDE.
WELL, I HOPE YOU AT LEAST GOT HER PHONE NUMBER, YOU OLD DOG.
HRRNN...
PAROLE BOARD
QUIET
FRED, HEY, YOU WITH ME? YOU'RE NOT LOOKING SO GOOD, PAL. HERE--HAVE SOME OF MY FRESHLY SQUEEZED.
NO THANKS...
SUIT YOURSELF. NOW, LIKE I SAID BEFORE, THIS WHOLE THING SHOULD BE A PIECE OF CAKE. AND EVERYBODY LOVES CAKE, RIGHT? EXCEPT FOR CHOCOLATE CAKE, SPEAKING PERSONALLY. TOO RICH. BUT THIS IS LIKE ANGEL FOOD CAKE.
BECAUSE YOU'RE MY LITTLE ANGEL.
CAN THIS PLEASE JUST END?
HA, SEE, NOW, THAT KINDA HUMOR WILL BE LOST ON THESE FOLKS, DON'T WASTE IT. WHAT WE WANNA DO IS SHOW THEM THE REAL FRED MYERS, THE GUY WE ALL KNOW AND LOVE.
YOU MEAN THE ONE THAT THROWS EXPLOSIVE BOOMERANGS AT PEOPLE?
HA! LET'S LEAVE THOSE IN THE CLOSET THIS TIME. NO, WHAT YOU WANT TO DEMONSTRATE IS HOW THE EXPERIENCE OF PRISON HAS CHANGED YOU. MADE YOU A BETTER MAN, EAGER TO CONTRIBUTE.
PAROLE BOARD
QUIET
SO, I DON'T WANNA KILL ANYONE ANYMORE?
FOR STARTERS!

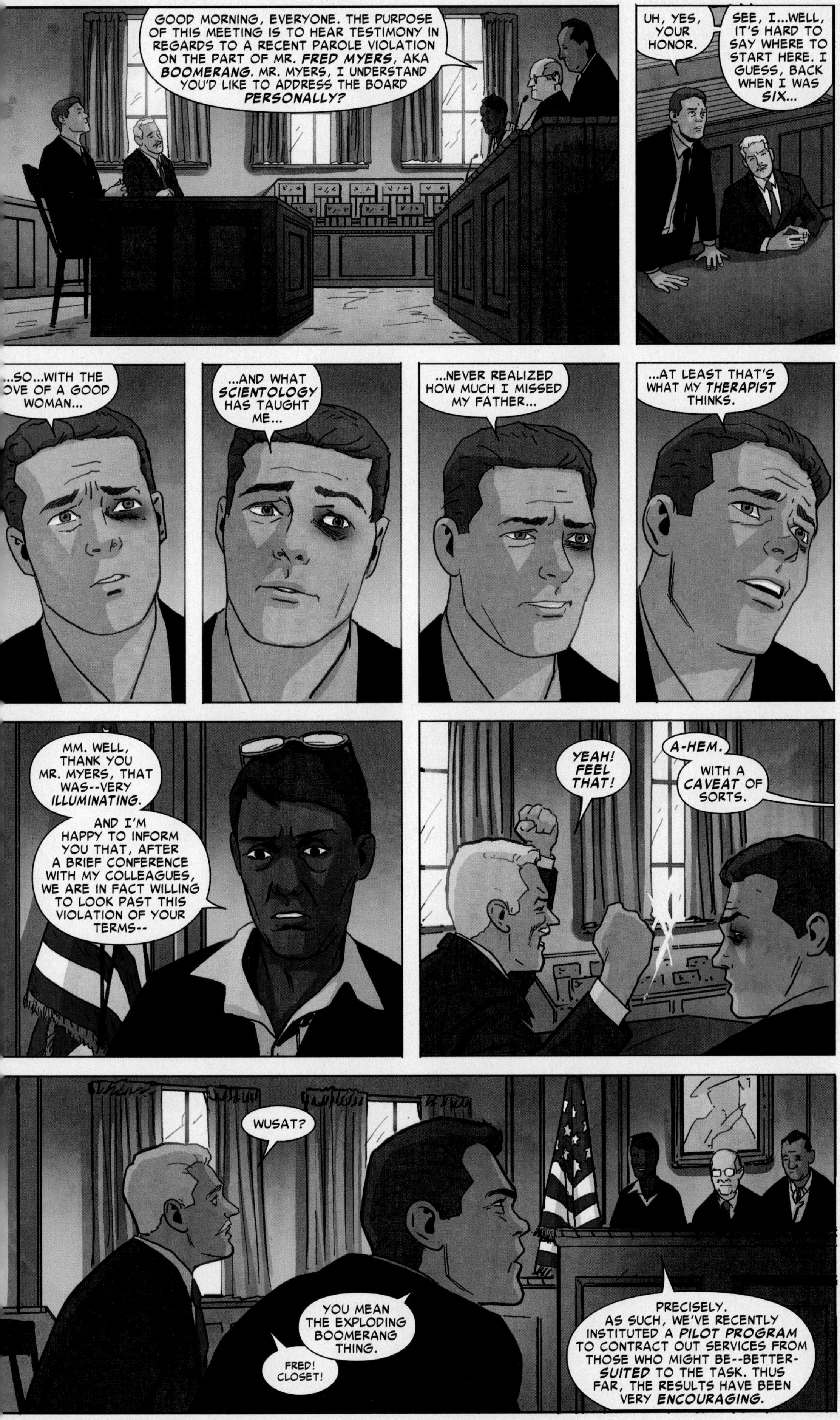
GOOD MORNING, EVERYONE. THE PURPOSE OF THIS MEETING IS TO HEAR TESTIMONY IN REGARDS TO A RECENT PAROLE VIOLATION ON THE PART OF MR. FRED MYERS, AKA BOOMERANG. MR. MYERS, I UNDERSTAND YOU'D LIKE TO ADDRESS THE BOARD PERSONALLY?
UH, YES, YOUR HONOR.
SEE, I...WELL, IT'S HARD TO SAY WHERE TO START HERE. I GUESS, BACK WHEN I WAS SIX...
...SO...WITH THE OVE OF A GOOD WOMAN...
...AND WHAT SCIENTOLOGY HAS TAUGHT ME...
...NEVER REALIZED HOW MUCH I MISSED MY FATHER...
...AT LEAST THAT'S WHAT MY THERAPIST THINKS.
MM. WELL, THANK YOU MR. MYERS, THAT WAS--VERY ILLUMINATING.
AND I'M HAPPY TO INFORM YOU THAT, AFTER A BRIEF CONFERENCE WITH MY COLLEAGUES, WE ARE IN FACT WILLING TO LOOK PAST THIS VIOLATION OF YOUR TERMS--
YEAH! FEEL THAT!
A-HEM.
WITH A CAVEAT OF SORTS.
WUSAT?
YOU MEAN THE EXPLODING BOOMERANG THING.
FRED! CLOSET!
PRECISELY. AS SUCH, WE'VE RECENTLY INSTITUTED A PILOT PROGRAM TO CONTRACT OUT SERVICES FROM THOSE WHO MIGHT BE--BETTER-SUITED TO THE TASK. THUS FAR, THE RESULTS HAVE BEEN VERY ENCOURAGING.

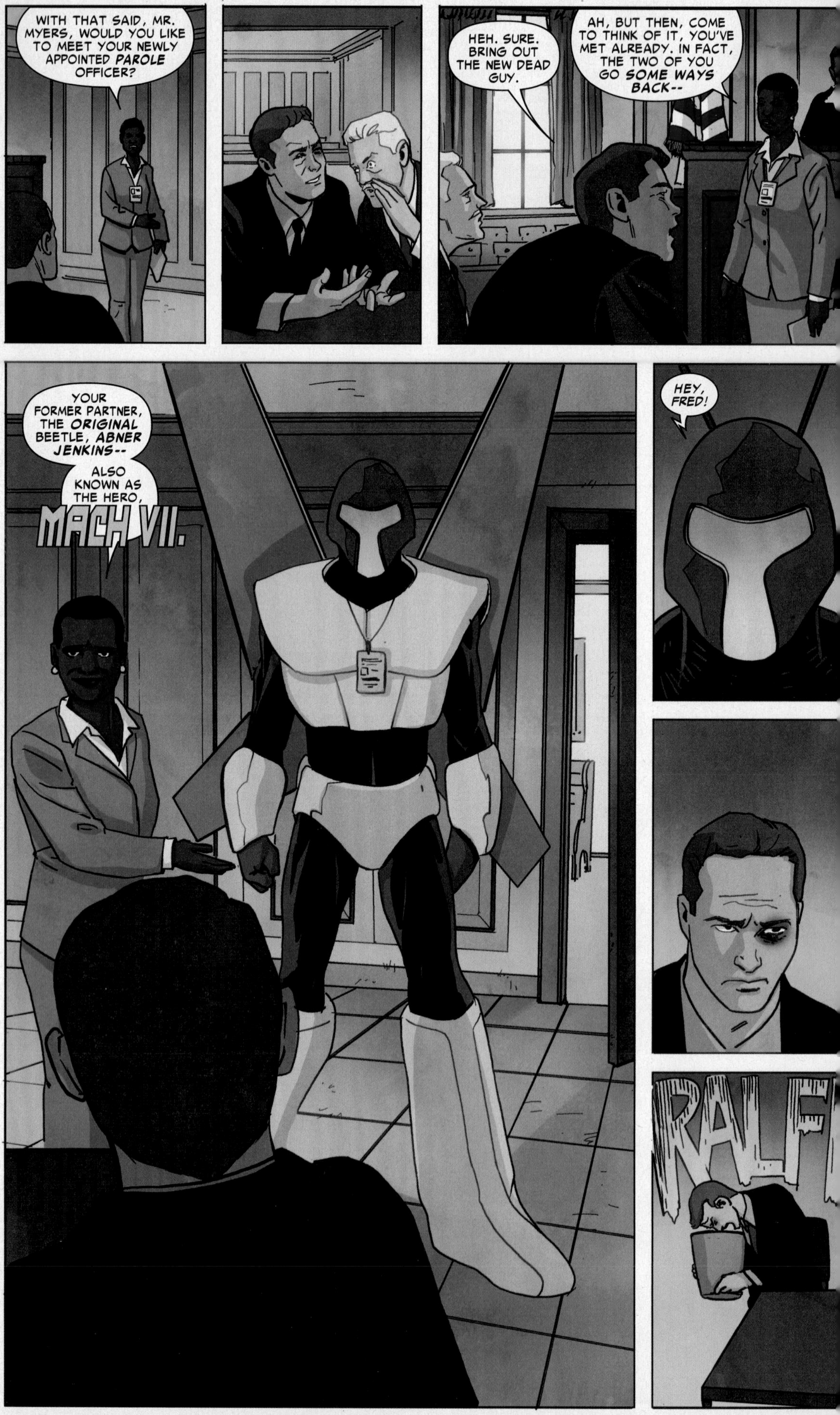
WITH THAT SAID, MR. MYERS, WOULD YOU LIKE TO MEET YOUR NEWLY APPOINTED PAROLE OFFICER?
HEH. SURE. BRING OUT THE NEW DEAD GUY.
AH, BUT THEN, COME TO THINK OF IT, YOU'VE MET ALREADY. IN FACT, THE TWO OF YOU GO SOME WAYS BACK--
YOUR FORMER PARTNER, THE ORIGINAL BEETLE, ABNER JENKINS--
ALSO KNOWN AS THE HERO,
MACH VII.
HEY, FRED!
RALF

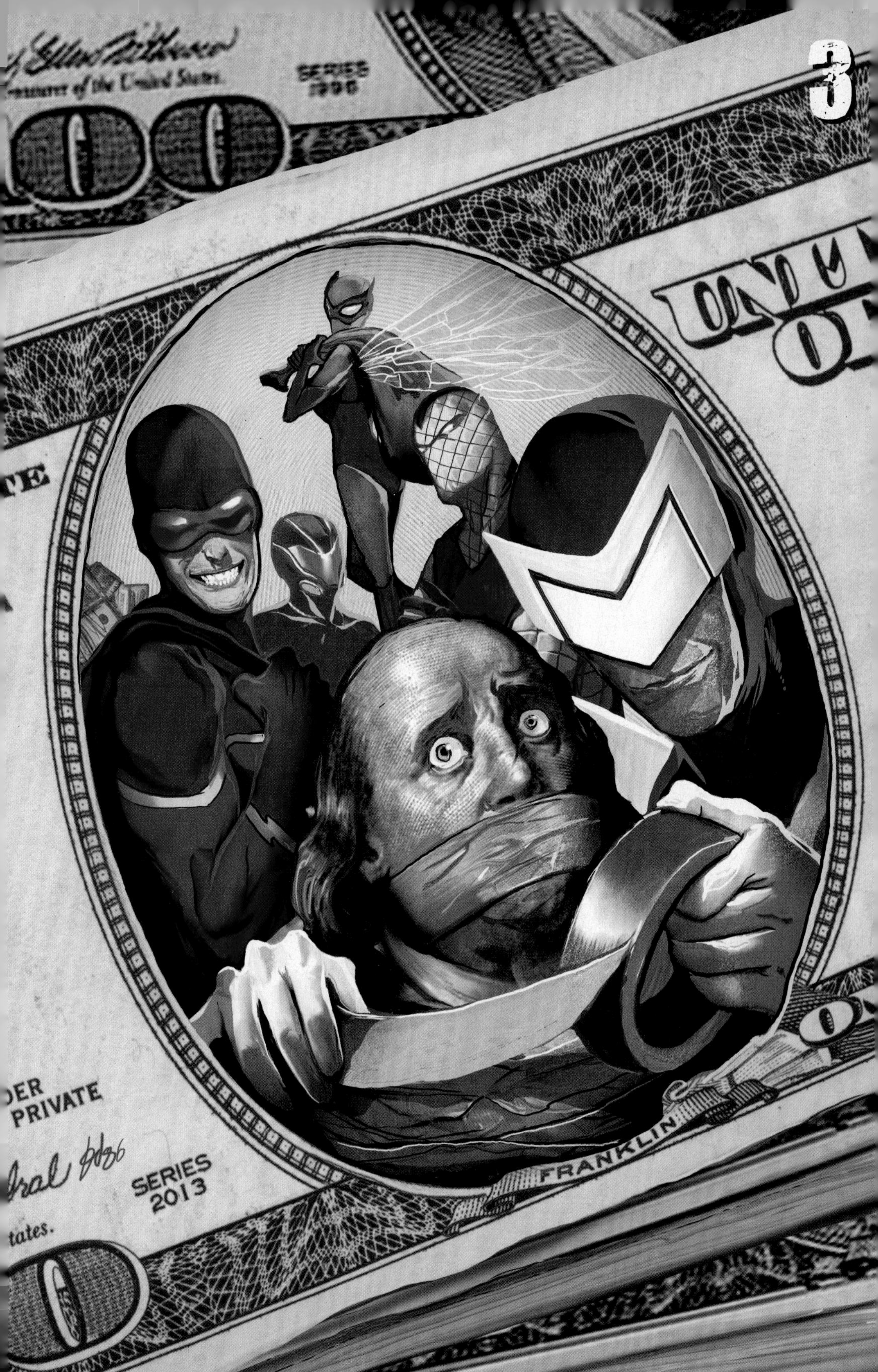
3
PRIVATE
SERIES
2013
FRANKLIN

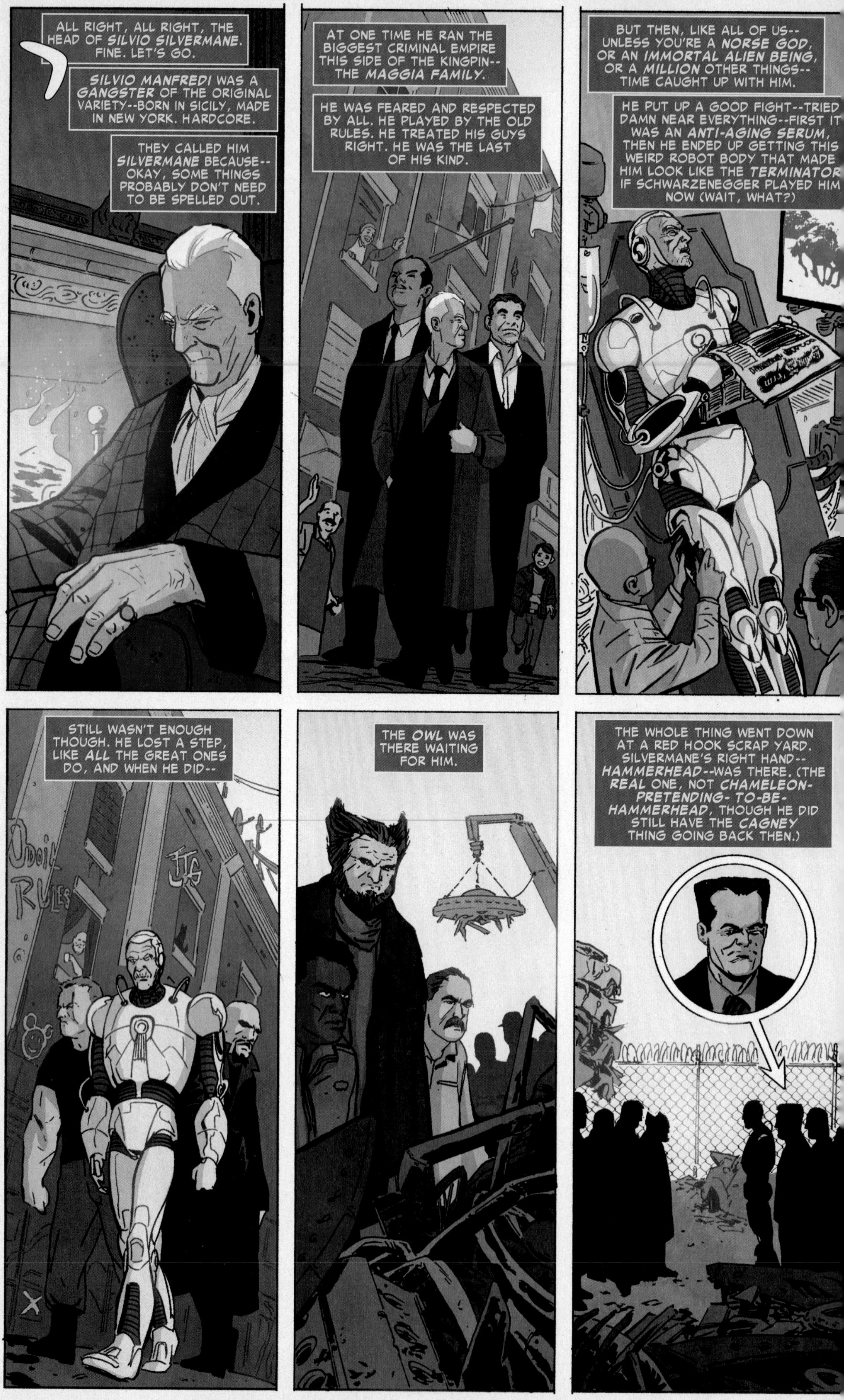
ALL RIGHT, ALL RIGHT, THE HEAD OF SILVIO SILVERMANE. FINE. LET'S GO.
SILVIO MANFREDI WAS A GANGSTER OF THE ORIGINAL VARIETY--BORN IN SICILY, MADE IN NEW YORK. HARDCORE.
THEY CALLED HIM SILVERMANE BECAUSE--OKAY, SOME THINGS PROBABLY DON'T NEED TO BE SPELLED OUT.
AT ONE TIME HE RAN THE BIGGEST CRIMINAL EMPIRE THIS SIDE OF THE KINGPIN--THE MAGGIA FAMILY.
HE WAS FEARED AND RESPECTED BY ALL. HE PLAYED BY THE OLD RULES. HE TREATED HIS GUYS RIGHT. HE WAS THE LAST OF HIS KIND.
BUT THEN, LIKE ALL OF US--UNLESS YOU'RE A NORSE GOD, OR AN IMMORTAL ALIEN BEING, OR A MILLION OTHER THINGS--TIME CAUGHT UP WITH HIM.
HE PUT UP A GOOD FIGHT--TRIED DAMN NEAR EVERYTHING--FIRST IT WAS AN ANTI-AGING SERUM, THEN HE ENDED UP GETTING THIS WEIRD ROBOT BODY THAT MADE HIM LOOK LIKE THE TERMINATOR IF SCHWARZENEGGER PLAYED HIM NOW (WAIT, WHAT?)
STILL WASN'T ENOUGH THOUGH. HE LOST A STEP, LIKE ALL THE GREAT ONES DO, AND WHEN HE DID--
RULES
THE OWL WAS THERE WAITING FOR HIM.
THE WHOLE THING WENT DOWN AT A RED HOOK SCRAP YARD. SILVERMANE'S RIGHT HAND--HAMMERHEAD--WAS THERE. (THE REAL ONE, NOT CHAMELEON-PRETENDING-TO-BE-HAMMERHEAD, THOUGH HE DID STILL HAVE THE CAGNEY THING GOING BACK THEN.)

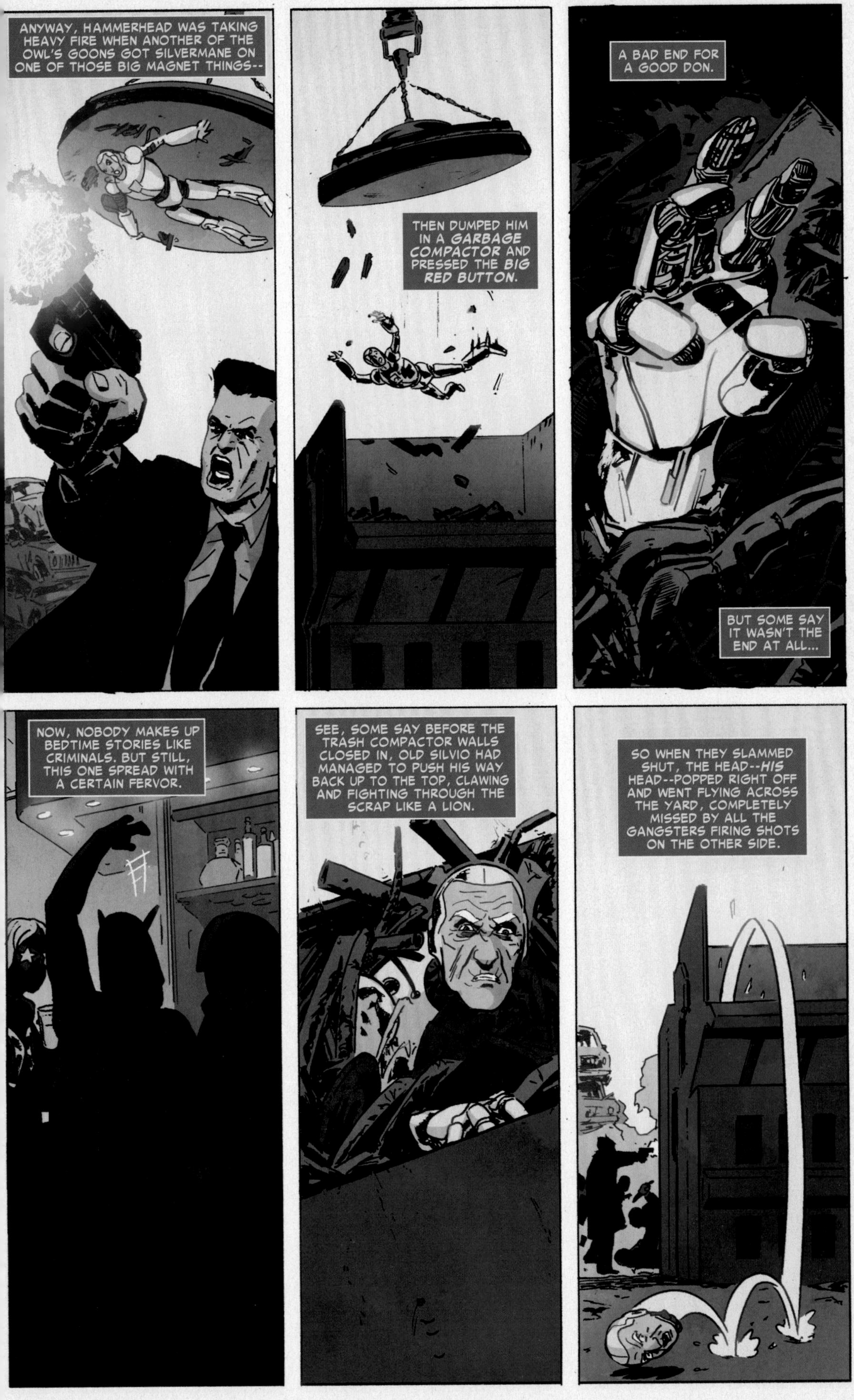
ANYWAY, HAMMERHEAD WAS TAKING HEAVY FIRE WHEN ANOTHER OF THE OWL'S GOONS GOT SILVERMANE ON ONE OF THOSE BIG MAGNET THINGS--
THEN DUMPED HIM IN A GARBAGE COMPACTOR AND PRESSED THE BIG RED BUTTON.
A BAD END FOR A GOOD DON.
BUT SOME SAY IT WASN'T THE END AT ALL...
NOW, NOBODY MAKES UP BEDTIME STORIES LIKE CRIMINALS. BUT STILL, THIS ONE SPREAD WITH A CERTAIN FERVOR.
SEE, SOME SAY BEFORE THE TRASH COMPACTOR WALLS CLOSED IN, OLD SILVIO HAD MANAGED TO PUSH HIS WAY BACK UP TO THE TOP, CLAWING AND FIGHTING THROUGH THE SCRAP LIKE A LION.
SO WHEN THEY SLAMMED SHUT, THE HEAD--HIS HEAD--POPPED RIGHT OFF AND WENT FLYING ACROSS THE YARD, COMPLETELY MISSED BY ALL THE GANGSTERS FIRING SHOTS ON THE OTHER SIDE.

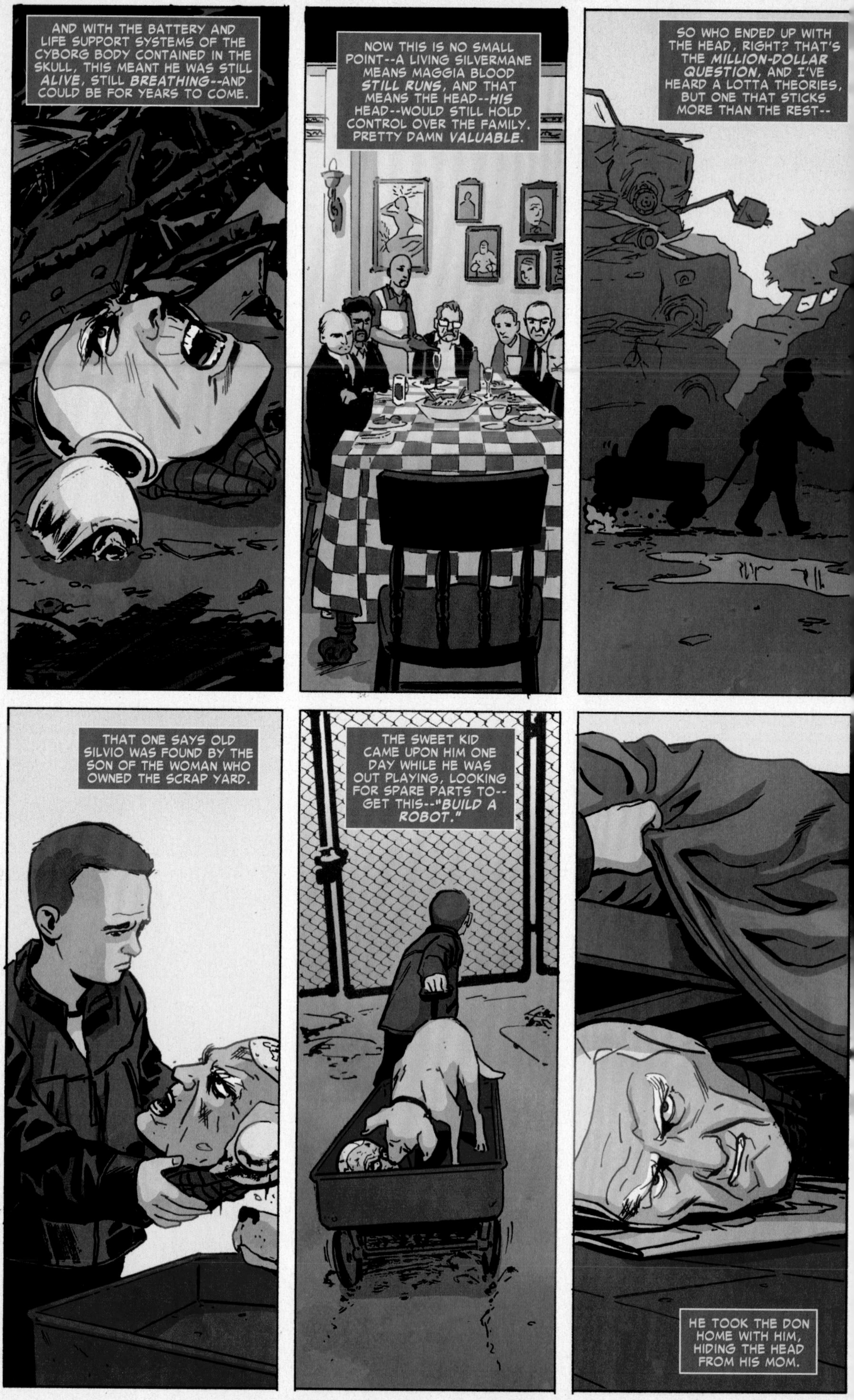
AND WITH THE BATTERY AND LIFE SUPPORT SYSTEMS OF THE CYBORG BODY CONTAINED IN THE SKULL, THIS MEANT HE WAS STILL *ALIVE*, STILL *BREATHING*--AND COULD BE FOR YEARS TO COME.
NOW THIS IS NO SMALL POINT--A LIVING SILVERMANE MEANS MAGGIA BLOOD *STILL RUNS*, AND THAT MEANS THE HEAD--*HIS* HEAD--WOULD STILL HOLD CONTROL OVER THE FAMILY. PRETTY DAMN *VALUABLE*.
SO WHO ENDED UP WITH THE HEAD, RIGHT? THAT'S THE *MILLION-DOLLAR QUESTION*, AND I'VE HEARD A LOTTA THEORIES, BUT ONE THAT STICKS MORE THAN THE REST--
THAT ONE SAYS OLD SILVIO WAS FOUND BY THE SON OF THE WOMAN WHO OWNED THE SCRAP YARD.
THE SWEET KID CAME UPON HIM ONE DAY WHILE HE WAS OUT PLAYING, LOOKING FOR SPARE PARTS TO-- GET THIS--"*BUILD A ROBOT*."
HE TOOK THE DON HOME WITH HIM, HIDING THE HEAD FROM HIS MOM.

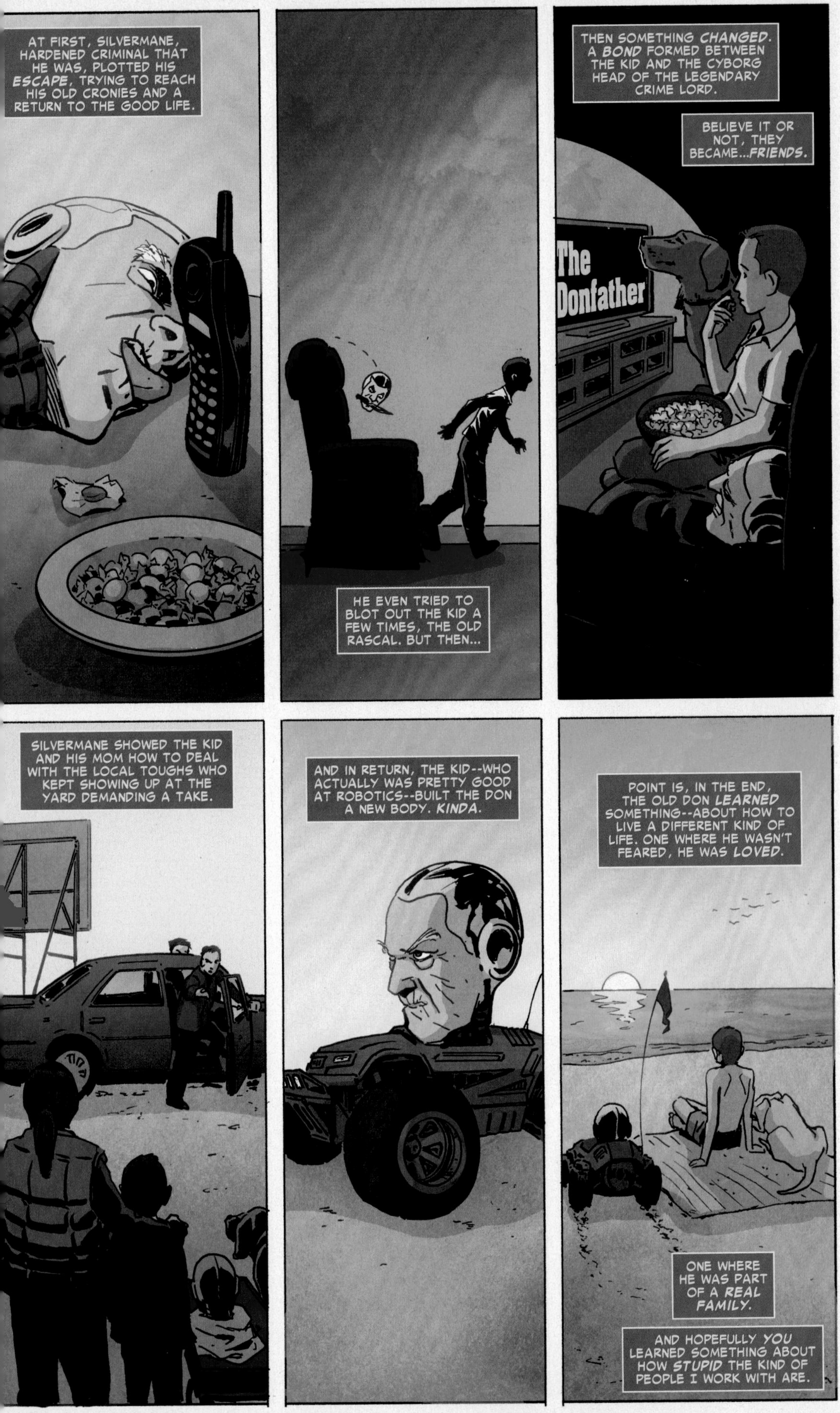
AT FIRST, SILVERMANE, HARDENED CRIMINAL THAT HE WAS, PLOTTED HIS *ESCAPE*, TRYING TO REACH HIS OLD CRONIES AND A RETURN TO THE GOOD LIFE.
HE EVEN TRIED TO BLOT OUT THE KID A FEW TIMES, THE OLD RASCAL. BUT THEN...
THEN SOMETHING *CHANGED*. A *BOND* FORMED BETWEEN THE KID AND THE CYBORG HEAD OF THE LEGENDARY CRIME LORD.
BELIEVE IT OR NOT, THEY BECAME...*FRIENDS*.
The Donfather
SILVERMANE SHOWED THE KID AND HIS MOM HOW TO DEAL WITH THE LOCAL TOUGHS WHO KEPT SHOWING UP AT THE YARD DEMANDING A TAKE.
AND IN RETURN, THE KID--WHO ACTUALLY WAS PRETTY GOOD AT ROBOTICS--BUILT THE DON A NEW BODY. *KINDA*.
POINT IS, IN THE END, THE OLD DON *LEARNED* SOMETHING--ABOUT HOW TO LIVE A DIFFERENT KIND OF LIFE. ONE WHERE HE WASN'T FEARED, HE WAS *LOVED*.
ONE WHERE HE WAS PART OF A *REAL FAMILY*.
AND HOPEFULLY *YOU* LEARNED SOMETHING ABOUT HOW *STUPID* THE KIND OF PEOPLE I WORK WITH ARE.

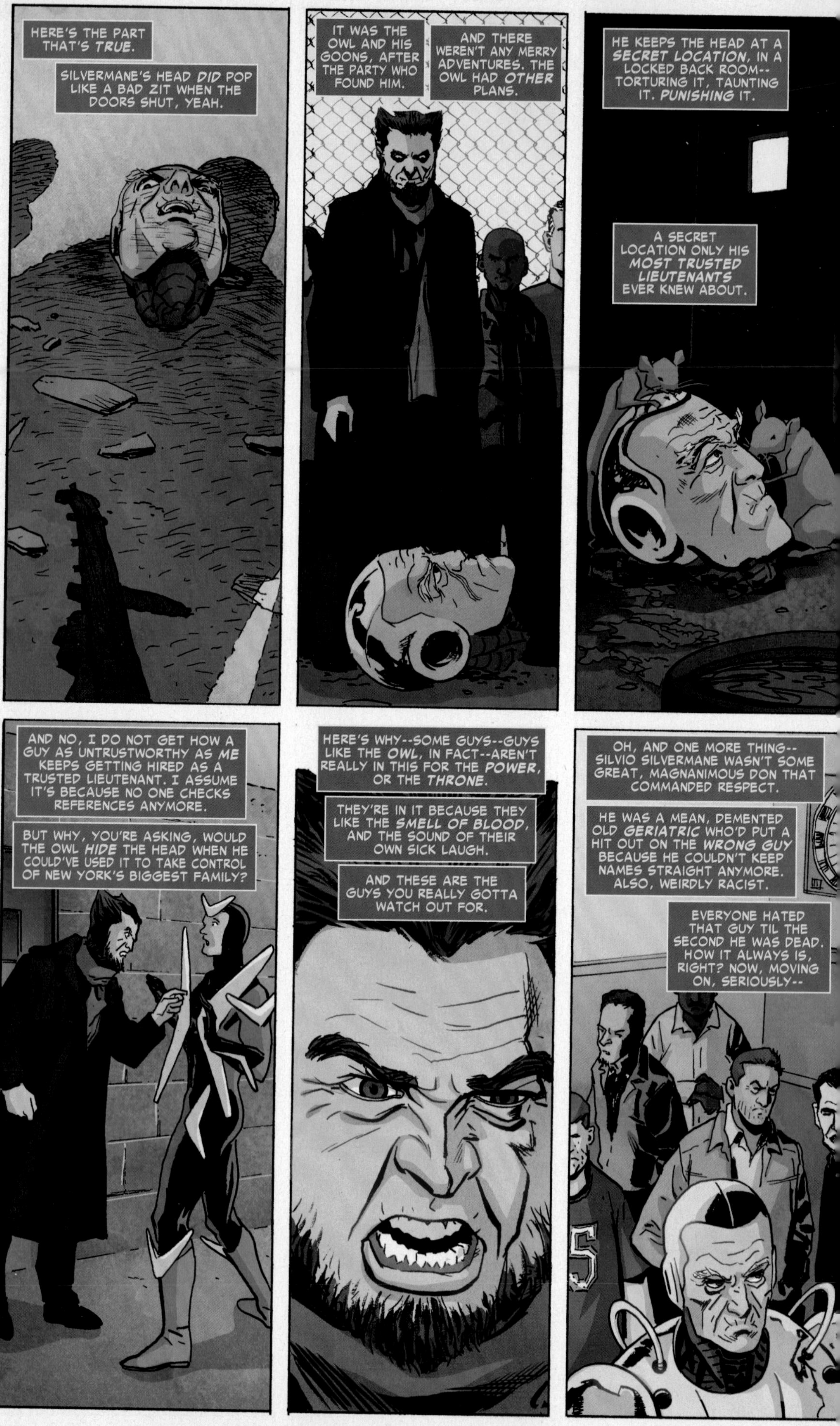
HERE'S THE PART THAT'S *TRUE*.
SILVERMANE'S HEAD *DID* POP LIKE A BAD ZIT WHEN THE DOORS SHUT, YEAH.
IT WAS THE OWL AND HIS GOONS, AFTER THE PARTY WHO FOUND HIM.
AND THERE WEREN'T ANY MERRY ADVENTURES. THE OWL HAD *OTHER* PLANS.
HE KEEPS THE HEAD AT A *SECRET LOCATION*, IN A LOCKED BACK ROOM-- TORTURING IT, TAUNTING IT. *PUNISHING* IT.
A SECRET LOCATION ONLY HIS *MOST TRUSTED LIEUTENANTS* EVER KNEW ABOUT.
AND NO, I DO NOT GET HOW A GUY AS UNTRUSTWORTHY AS *ME* KEEPS GETTING HIRED AS A TRUSTED LIEUTENANT. I ASSUME IT'S BECAUSE NO ONE CHECKS REFERENCES ANYMORE.
BUT WHY, YOU'RE ASKING, WOULD THE OWL *HIDE* THE HEAD WHEN HE COULD'VE USED IT TO TAKE CONTROL OF NEW YORK'S BIGGEST FAMILY?
HERE'S WHY--SOME GUYS--GUYS LIKE THE *OWL*, IN FACT--AREN'T REALLY IN THIS FOR THE *POWER*, OR THE *THRONE*.
THEY'RE IN IT BECAUSE THEY LIKE THE *SMELL OF BLOOD*, AND THE SOUND OF THEIR OWN SICK LAUGH.
AND THESE ARE THE GUYS YOU REALLY GOTTA WATCH OUT FOR.
OH, AND ONE MORE THING-- SILVIO SILVERMANE WASN'T SOME GREAT, MAGNANIMOUS DON THAT COMMANDED RESPECT.
HE WAS A MEAN, DEMENTED OLD *GERIATRIC* WHO'D PUT A HIT OUT ON THE *WRONG GUY* BECAUSE HE COULDN'T KEEP NAMES STRAIGHT ANYMORE. ALSO, WEIRDLY RACIST.
EVERYONE HATED THAT GUY TIL THE SECOND HE WAS DEAD. HOW IT ALWAYS IS, RIGHT? NOW, MOVING ON, SERIOUSLY--

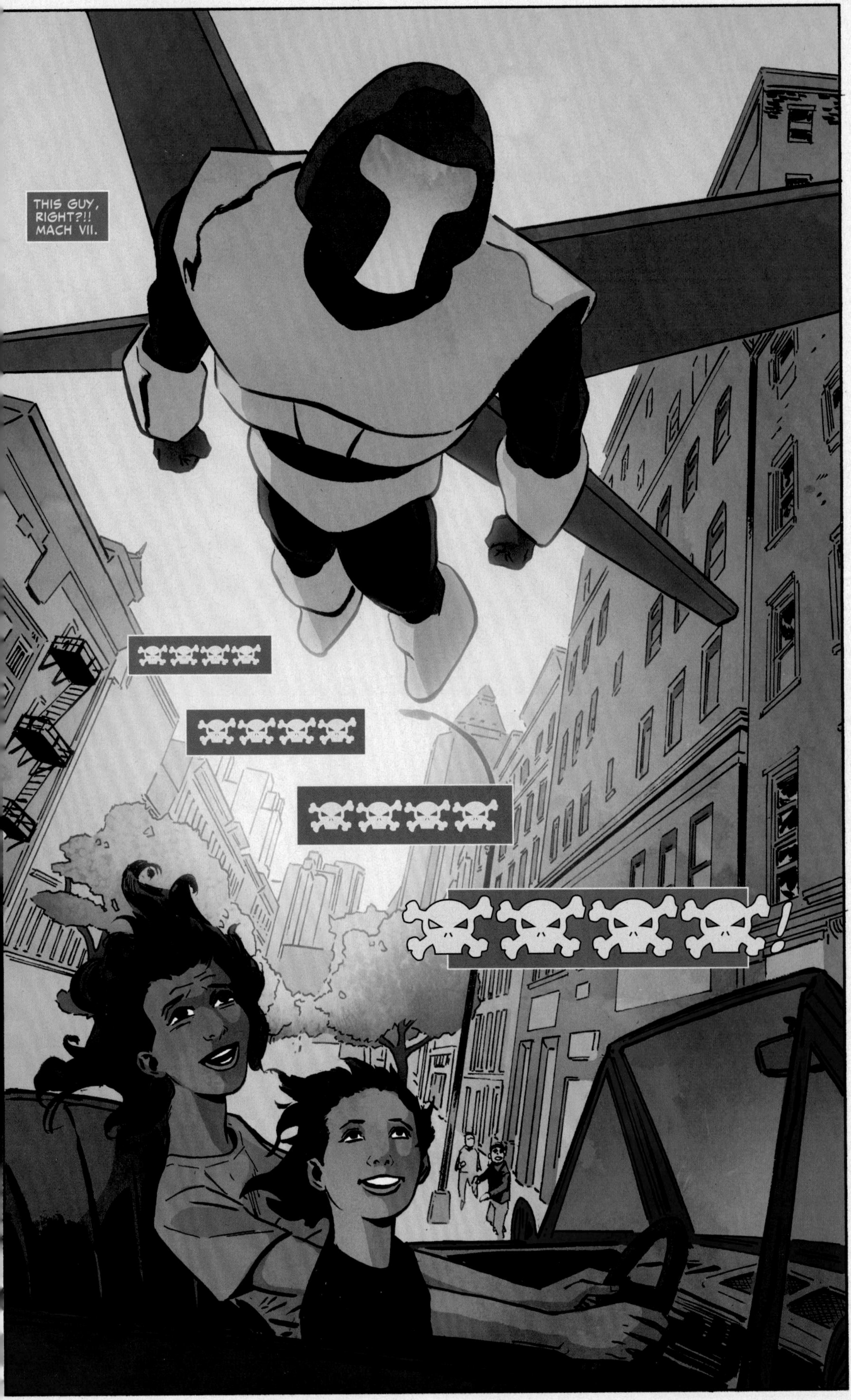
THIS GUY, RIGHT?!! MACH VII.

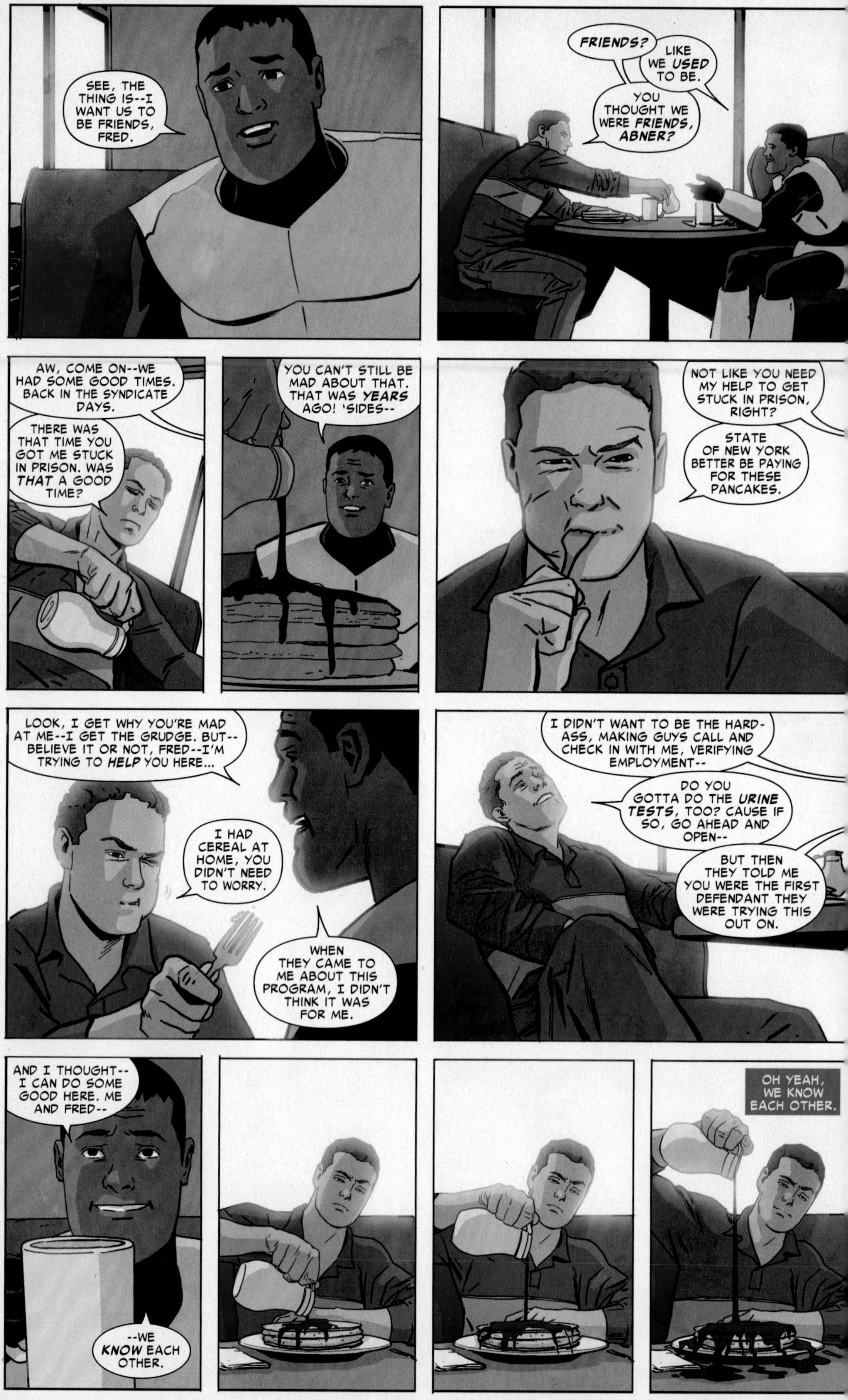
SEE, THE THING IS--I WANT US TO BE FRIENDS, FRED.
FRIENDS?
LIKE WE USED TO BE.
YOU THOUGHT WE WERE FRIENDS, ABNER?
AW, COME ON--WE HAD SOME GOOD TIMES. BACK IN THE SYNDICATE DAYS.
THERE WAS THAT TIME YOU GOT ME STUCK IN PRISON. WAS THAT A GOOD TIME?
YOU CAN'T STILL BE MAD ABOUT THAT. THAT WAS YEARS AGO! 'SIDES--
NOT LIKE YOU NEED MY HELP TO GET STUCK IN PRISON, RIGHT?
STATE OF NEW YORK BETTER BE PAYING FOR THESE PANCAKES.
LOOK, I GET WHY YOU'RE MAD AT ME--I GET THE GRUDGE. BUT--BELIEVE IT OR NOT, FRED--I'M TRYING TO HELP YOU HERE...
I HAD CEREAL AT HOME, YOU DIDN'T NEED TO WORRY.
WHEN THEY CAME TO ME ABOUT THIS PROGRAM, I DIDN'T THINK IT WAS FOR ME.
I DIDN'T WANT TO BE THE HARD-ASS, MAKING GUYS CALL AND CHECK IN WITH ME, VERIFYING EMPLOYMENT--
DO YOU GOTTA DO THE URINE TESTS, TOO? CAUSE IF SO, GO AHEAD AND OPEN--
BUT THEN THEY TOLD ME YOU WERE THE FIRST DEFENDANT THEY WERE TRYING THIS OUT ON.
AND I THOUGHT--I CAN DO SOME GOOD HERE. ME AND FRED--
--WE KNOW EACH OTHER.
OH YEAH, WE KNOW EACH OTHER.

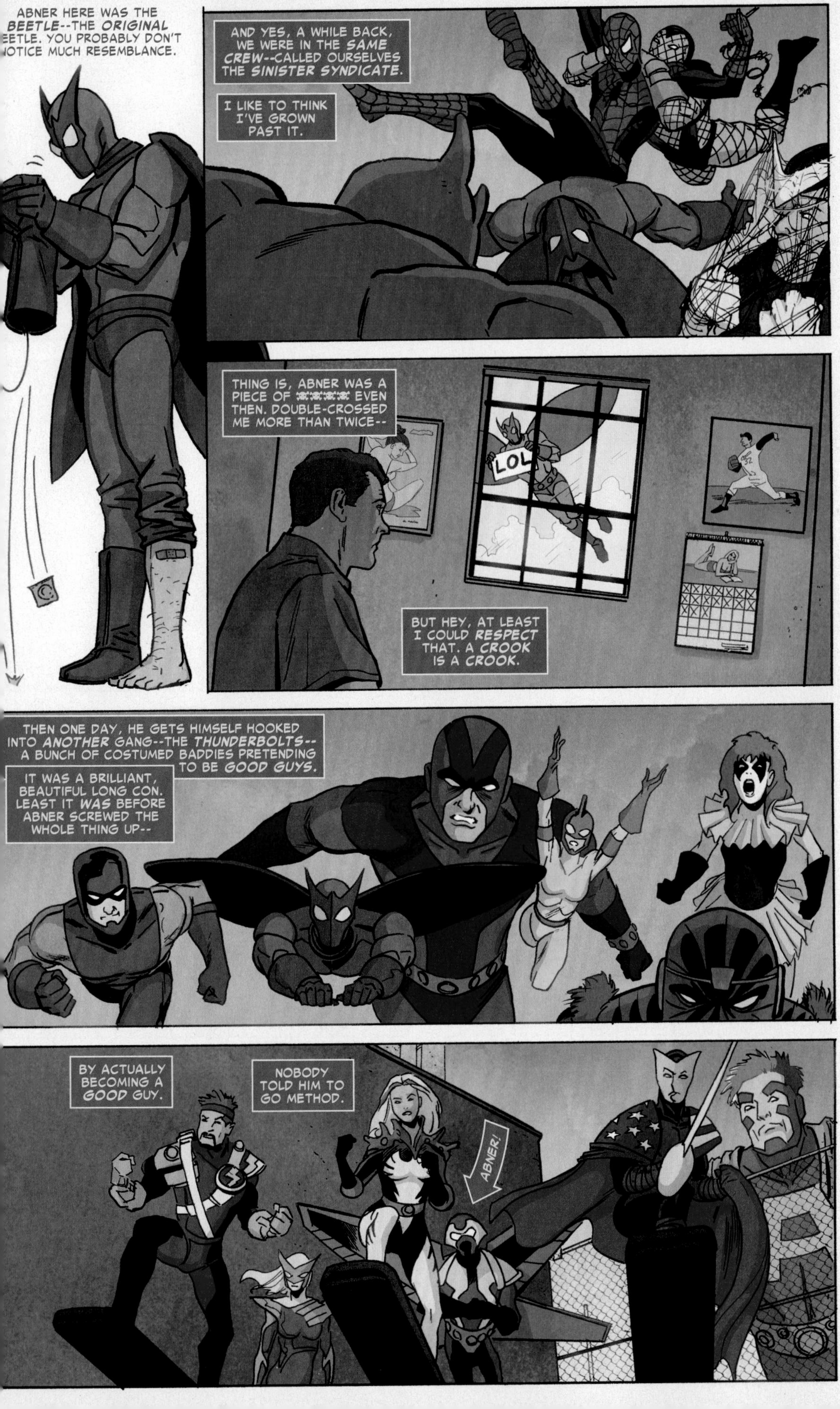

ABNER HERE WAS THE BEETLE--THE ORIGINAL EETLE. YOU PROBABLY DON'T IOTICE MUCH RESEMBLANCE.
AND YES, A WHILE BACK, WE WERE IN THE SAME CREW--CALLED OURSELVES THE SINISTER SYNDICATE.
I LIKE TO THINK I'VE GROWN PAST IT.
THING IS, ABNER WAS A PIECE OF ☠☠☠☠ EVEN THEN. DOUBLE-CROSSED ME MORE THAN TWICE--
LOL
BUT HEY, AT LEAST I COULD RESPECT THAT. A CROOK IS A CROOK.
THEN ONE DAY, HE GETS HIMSELF HOOKED INTO ANOTHER GANG--THE THUNDERBOLTS--A BUNCH OF COSTUMED BADDIES PRETENDING TO BE GOOD GUYS.
IT WAS A BRILLIANT, BEAUTIFUL LONG CON. LEAST IT WAS BEFORE ABNER SCREWED THE WHOLE THING UP--
BY ACTUALLY BECOMING A GOOD GUY.
NOBODY TOLD HIM TO GO METHOD.
ABNER!

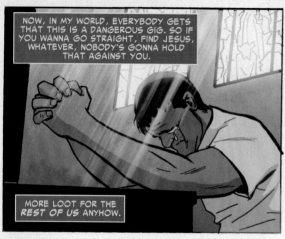

NOW, IN MY WORLD, EVERYBODY GETS THAT THIS IS A DANGEROUS GIG. SO IF YOU WANNA GO STRAIGHT, FIND JESUS, WHATEVER, NOBODY'S GONNA HOLD THAT AGAINST YOU.

MORE LOOT FOR THE *REST OF US* ANYHOW.

AND IF YOU GET PINCHED, AND DECIDE TO TURN STATE'S, GO RAT, WELL-- IF *YOU* DO THAT, WE'LL PROBABLY *KILL* YOU. SURE.

BUT WE MIGHT FEEL *BAD* ABOUT IT. A TWINGE OF SYMPATHY. MAYBE MAKE IT QUICK.

YOU DECIDE TO TAKE YOUR *JETPACK* OR *PET DRAGON* OR WHATEVER, THOUGH, AND USE IT AGAINST YOUR OWN--

YOU DECIDE TO BECOME ONE OF THE GUYS WE SPEND OUR WHOLE LIVES GETTING *CHASED DOWN* BY, *KNOCKED AROUND* BY--

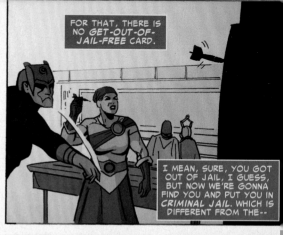

FOR THAT, THERE IS NO *GET-OUT-OF- JAIL-FREE* CARD.

I MEAN, SURE, YOU GOT OUT OF JAIL, I GUESS, BUT NOW WE'RE GONNA FIND YOU AND PUT YOU IN *CRIMINAL JAIL*. WHICH IS DIFFERENT FROM THE--

MY POINT IS ABNER JENKINS IS A *TRAITOROUS, BACK-STABBING, TURNCOAT* ✕✕✕✕✕✕✕✕ ALL RIGHT?!

ALSO THAT NEW COSTUME MAKES HIM LOOK LIKE SOMETHING YOUR WIFE SAYS SHE DOESN'T OWN.

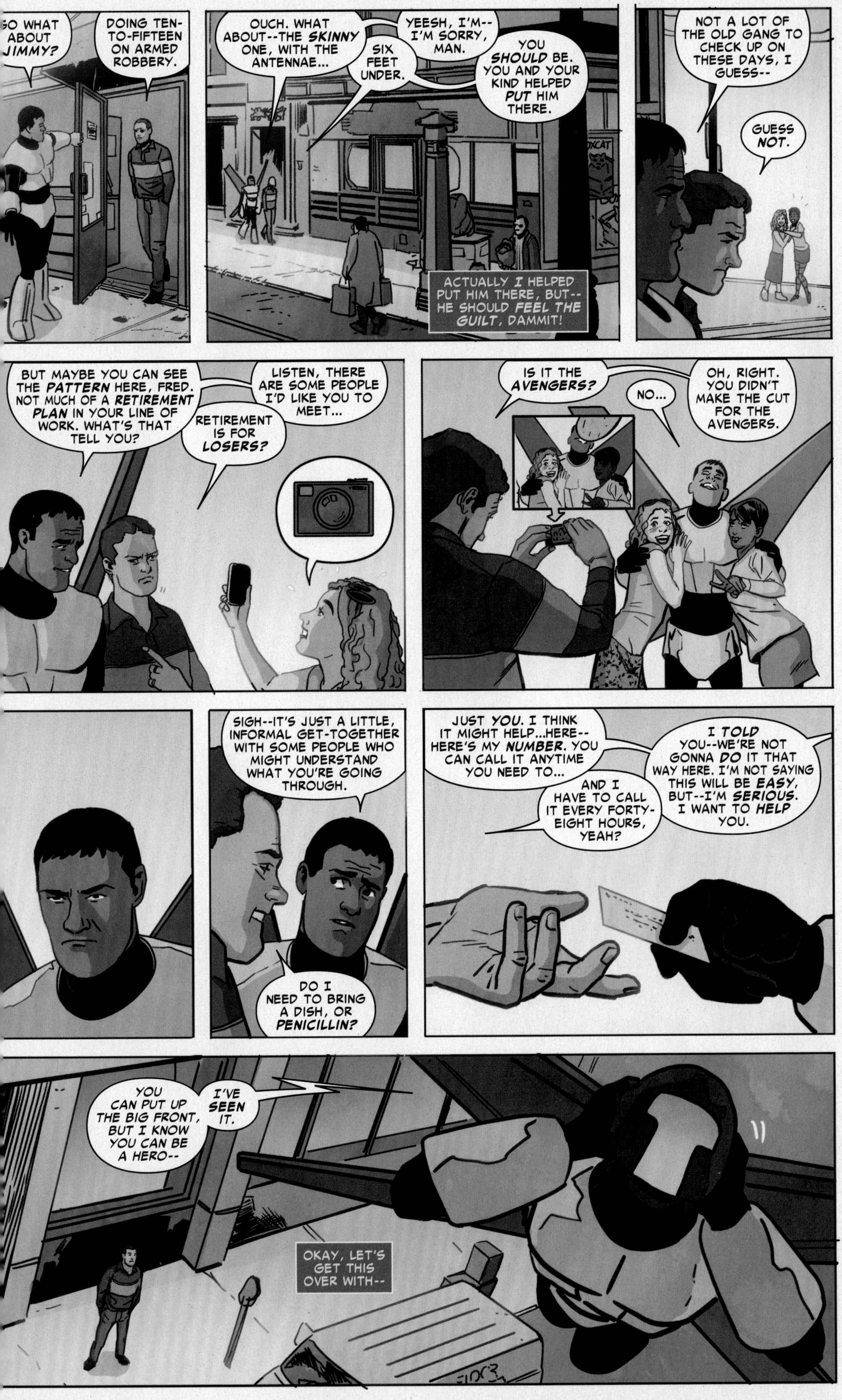
SO WHAT ABOUT JIMMY?
DOING TEN-TO-FIFTEEN ON ARMED ROBBERY.
OUCH. WHAT ABOUT--THE SKINNY ONE, WITH THE ANTENNAE...
SIX FEET UNDER.
YEESH, I'M--I'M SORRY, MAN.
YOU SHOULD BE. YOU AND YOUR KIND HELPED PUT HIM THERE.
ACTUALLY I HELPED PUT HIM THERE, BUT--HE SHOULD FEEL THE GUILT, DAMMIT!
NOT A LOT OF THE OLD GANG TO CHECK UP ON THESE DAYS, I GUESS--
GUESS NOT.
BUT MAYBE YOU CAN SEE THE PATTERN HERE, FRED. NOT MUCH OF A RETIREMENT PLAN IN YOUR LINE OF WORK. WHAT'S THAT TELL YOU?
RETIREMENT IS FOR LOSERS?
LISTEN, THERE ARE SOME PEOPLE I'D LIKE YOU TO MEET...
IS IT THE AVENGERS?
NO...
OH, RIGHT. YOU DIDN'T MAKE THE CUT FOR THE AVENGERS.
SIGH--IT'S JUST A LITTLE, INFORMAL GET-TOGETHER WITH SOME PEOPLE WHO MIGHT UNDERSTAND WHAT YOU'RE GOING THROUGH.
DO I NEED TO BRING A DISH, OR PENICILLIN?
JUST YOU. I THINK IT MIGHT HELP...HERE--HERE'S MY NUMBER. YOU CAN CALL IT ANYTIME YOU NEED TO...
AND I HAVE TO CALL IT EVERY FORTY-EIGHT HOURS, YEAH?
I TOLD YOU--WE'RE NOT GONNA DO IT THAT WAY HERE. I'M NOT SAYING THIS WILL BE EASY, BUT--I'M SERIOUS. I WANT TO HELP YOU.
YOU CAN PUT UP THE BIG FRONT, BUT I KNOW YOU CAN BE A HERO--
I'VE SEEN IT.
OKAY, LET'S GET THIS OVER WITH--

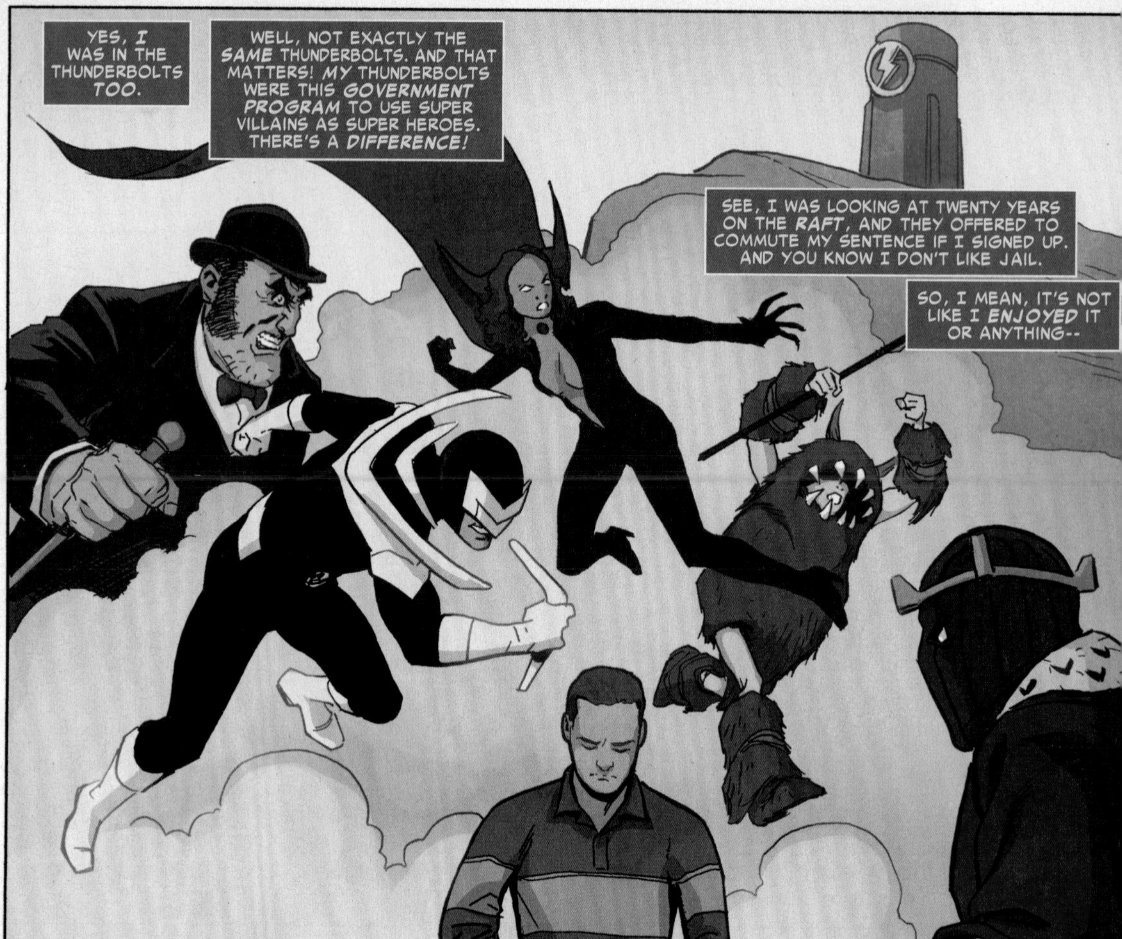
YES, I WAS IN THE THUNDERBOLTS TOO.
WELL, NOT EXACTLY THE SAME THUNDERBOLTS. AND THAT MATTERS! MY THUNDERBOLTS WERE THIS GOVERNMENT PROGRAM TO USE SUPER VILLAINS AS SUPER HEROES. THERE'S A DIFFERENCE!
SEE, I WAS LOOKING AT TWENTY YEARS ON THE RAFT, AND THEY OFFERED TO COMMUTE MY SENTENCE IF I SIGNED UP. AND YOU KNOW I DON'T LIKE JAIL.
SO, I MEAN, IT'S NOT LIKE I ENJOYED IT OR ANYTHING--
IT'S NOT LIKE I'D HAD SOME BIG CHANGE OF HEART AND WANTED TO DO RIGHT SUDDENLY--
I WAS JUST LOOKING TO SAVE MY OWN ASS!
THAT MAKES IT TOTALLY OKAY! ANYBODY WOULD GET THAT, RIGHT?

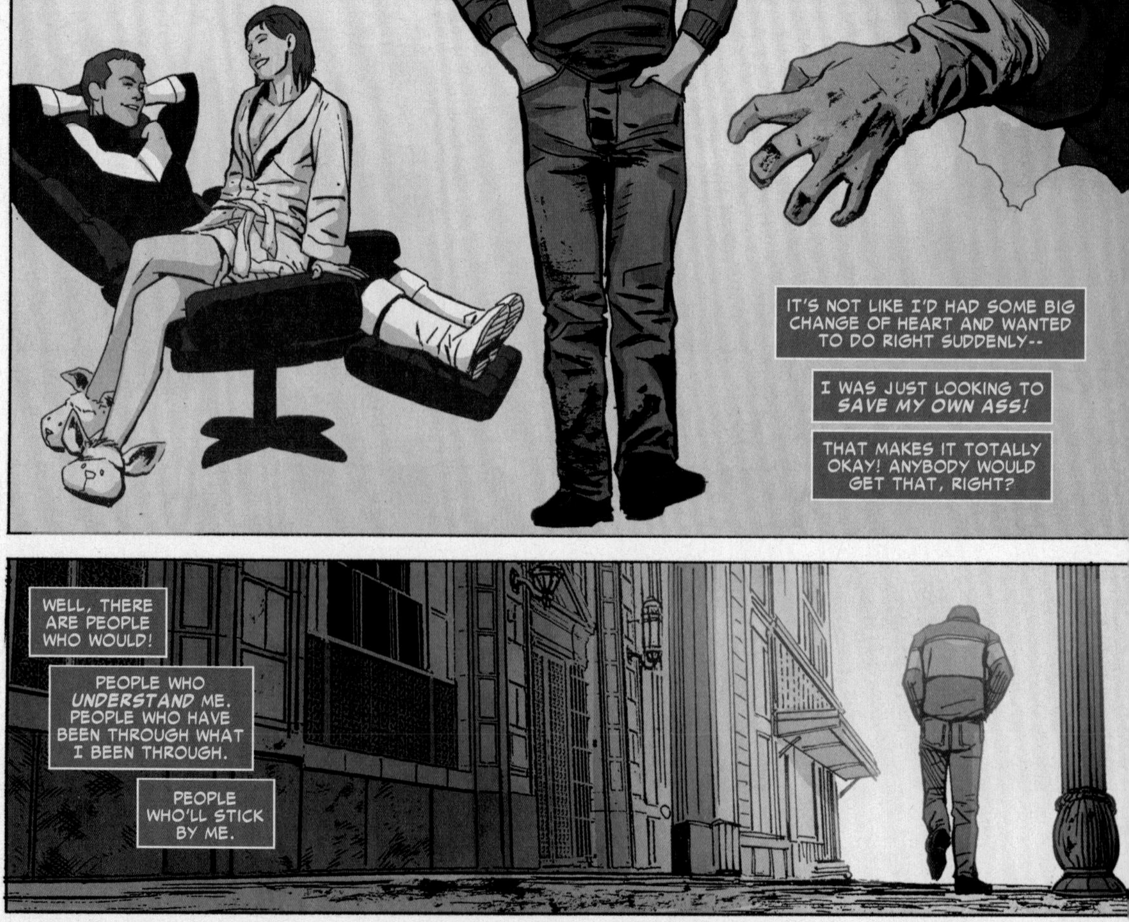
WELL, THERE ARE PEOPLE WHO WOULD!
PEOPLE WHO UNDERSTAND ME. PEOPLE WHO HAVE BEEN THROUGH WHAT I BEEN THROUGH.
PEOPLE WHO'LL STICK BY ME.

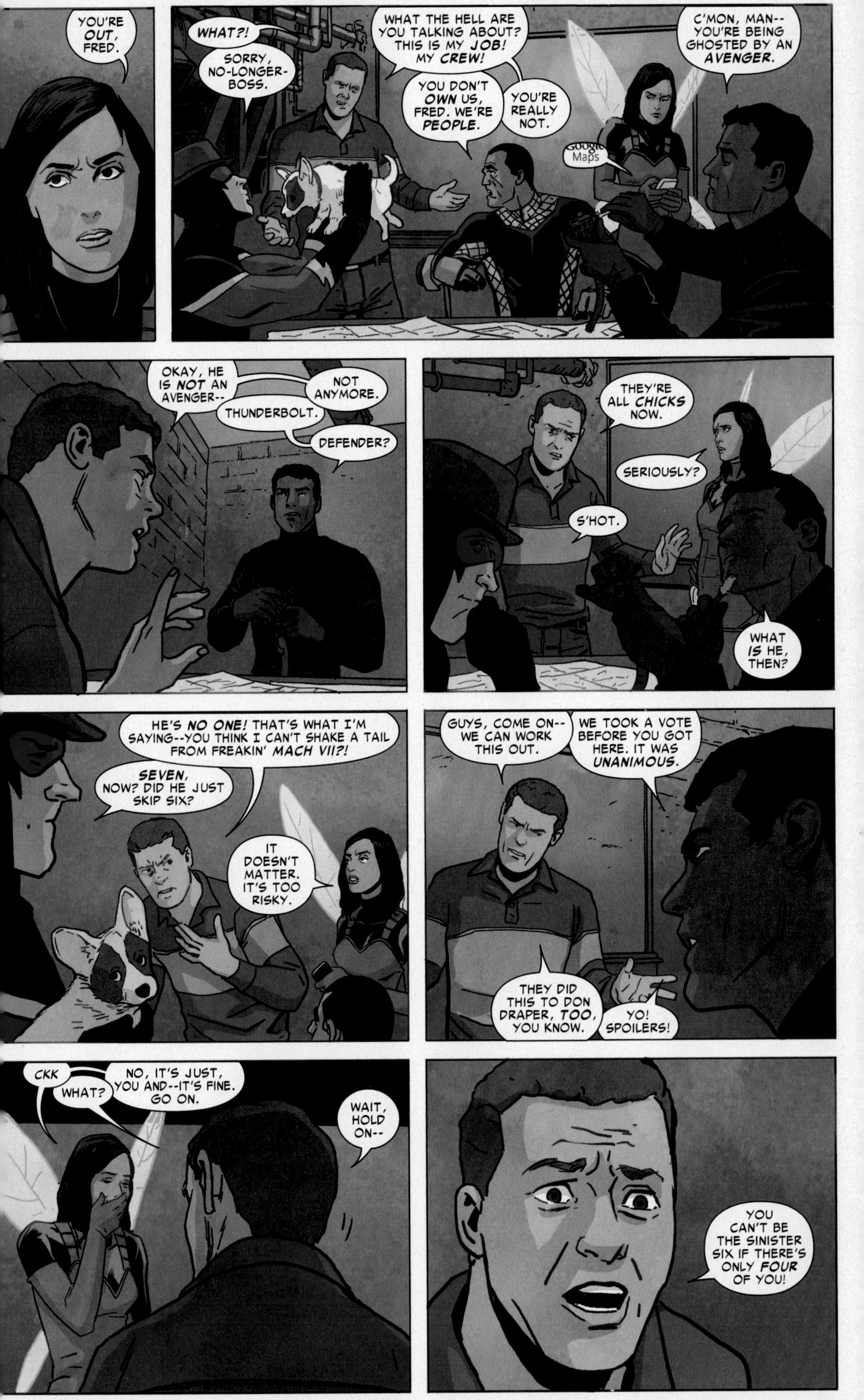
YOU'RE OUT, FRED.
WHAT?!
SORRY, NO-LONGER-BOSS.
WHAT THE HELL ARE YOU TALKING ABOUT? THIS IS MY JOB! MY CREW!
YOU DON'T OWN US, FRED. WE'RE PEOPLE.
YOU'RE REALLY NOT.
Google Maps
C'MON, MAN--YOU'RE BEING GHOSTED BY AN AVENGER.
OKAY, HE IS NOT AN AVENGER--
NOT ANYMORE.
THUNDERBOLT.
DEFENDER?
THEY'RE ALL CHICKS NOW.
SERIOUSLY?
S'HOT.
WHAT IS HE, THEN?
HE'S NO ONE! THAT'S WHAT I'M SAYING--YOU THINK I CAN'T SHAKE A TAIL FROM FREAKIN' MACH VII?!
SEVEN, NOW? DID HE JUST SKIP SIX?
IT DOESN'T MATTER. IT'S TOO RISKY.
GUYS, COME ON--WE CAN WORK THIS OUT.
WE TOOK A VOTE BEFORE YOU GOT HERE. IT WAS UNANIMOUS.
THEY DID THIS TO DON DRAPER, TOO, YOU KNOW.
YO! SPOILERS!
CKK
WHAT?
NO, IT'S JUST, YOU AND--IT'S FINE. GO ON.
WAIT, HOLD ON--
YOU CAN'T BE THE SINISTER SIX IF THERE'S ONLY FOUR OF YOU!

DUDE, I KNOW YOU'RE UPSET, BUT LOOK ON THE BRIGHT SIDE--YOU COULD GO BE A HENCHMAN AGAIN! YOU *LIKED* THAT, RIGHT?

BEIN' A *HENCHMAN?*

YOU ALL THINK YOU'RE SO SMART... ESPECIALLY *YOU!*

I FIND IT INTERESTING IT'S *ME* YOU CHOOSE TO HAVE A PROBLEM WITH.

YOU AND OVERDRIVE, YEAH-- WHO THE HELL DO YOU THINK YOU ARE, ANYWAY? I BEEN PULLING OFF HEISTS LONGER THAN YOU--

SORRY, EXCUSE ME--WHICH ONES DID YOU *ACTUALLY* PULL OFF?

OH, SEE, THERE YOU GO--YOU THINK IT'S SO *EASY*, YEAH? WAIT 'TIL THE FIRST TIME YOU'RE OUT IN THE FIELD AND *THE PUNISHER* WALKS IN ON YOU--

DIDN'T THAT HAPPEN *LAST WEEK?*

UH... RIGHT. YEAH.

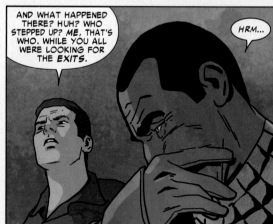

AND WHAT HAPPENED THERE? HUH? WHO STEPPED UP? *ME*, THAT'S WHO. WHILE YOU ALL WERE LOOKING FOR THE *EXITS.*

HRM...

YOU GOT SOMETHING TO SAY, SHOCKER?

...FORGET IT.

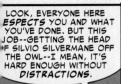

LOOK, EVERYONE HERE RESPECTS YOU AND WHAT YOU'VE DONE. BUT THIS JOB--GETTING THE HEAD OF SILVIO SILVERMANE OFF THE OWL--I MEAN, IT'S HARD ENOUGH WITHOUT DISTRACTIONS.

DISTRACTIONS?! THIS IS MY JOB! I'M THE ONE THAT SAW --, I'M THE ONE WHO HAD THE IDEA, I'M THE ONE WHO PLANNED IT, AND-- HEY WAITASECOND...

YOU DON'T EVEN KNOW WHERE THE HEAD IS!

squeeze

YOU TOLD US WHERE HIS HIDEOUT IS ALREADY.

YEAH, BUT THAT PLACE IS HUGE, IT'S LIKE A MAZE.

YOU DON'T KNOW WHERE HE KEEPS IT!

IS IT WHERE YOU MARKED THIS BIG RED X ON THE FLOOR PLAN?

...

NO?

THOSE GUYS DIDN'T STICK BY ME AT ALL!

UNBELIEVABLE-- WHAT HAPPENED TO LOYALTY, RIGHT? JUST A LITTLE HEAT, AND WHAT DO THEY DO?

WELL, THAT'S FINE. NOT LIKE I DON'T HAVE FRIENDS OF MY OWN--

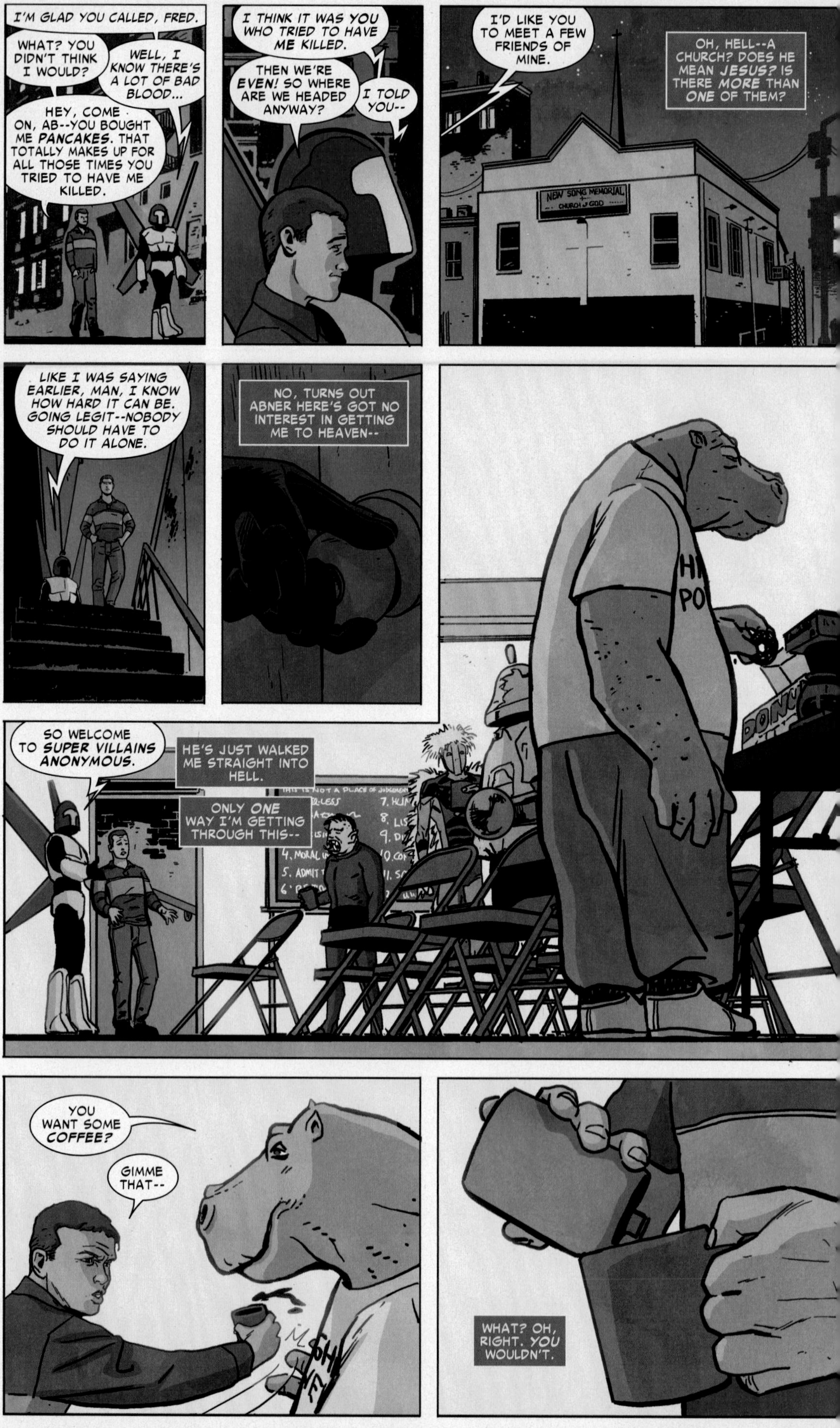
I'M GLAD YOU CALLED, FRED.
WHAT? YOU DIDN'T THINK I WOULD?
WELL, I KNOW THERE'S A LOT OF BAD BLOOD...
HEY, COME ON, AB--YOU BOUGHT ME PANCAKES. THAT TOTALLY MAKES UP FOR ALL THOSE TIMES YOU TRIED TO HAVE ME KILLED.
I THINK IT WAS YOU WHO TRIED TO HAVE ME KILLED.
THEN WE'RE EVEN! SO WHERE ARE WE HEADED ANYWAY?
I TOLD YOU--
I'D LIKE YOU TO MEET A FEW FRIENDS OF MINE.
OH, HELL--A CHURCH? DOES HE MEAN JESUS? IS THERE MORE THAN ONE OF THEM?
NEW SONG MEMORIAL CHURCH OF GOD
LIKE I WAS SAYING EARLIER, MAN, I KNOW HOW HARD IT CAN BE. GOING LEGIT--NOBODY SHOULD HAVE TO DO IT ALONE.
NO, TURNS OUT ABNER HERE'S GOT NO INTEREST IN GETTING ME TO HEAVEN--
SO WELCOME TO SUPER VILLAINS ANONYMOUS.
HE'S JUST WALKED ME STRAIGHT INTO HELL.
ONLY ONE WAY I'M GETTING THROUGH THIS--
YOU WANT SOME COFFEE?
GIMME THAT--
WHAT? OH, RIGHT. YOU WOULDN'T.

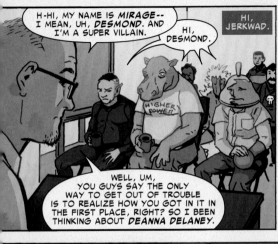

H-HI, MY NAME IS MIRAGE-- I MEAN, UH, DESMOND. AND I'M A SUPER VILLAIN.

HI, DESMOND.

HI, JERKWAD.

WELL, UM, YOU GUYS SAY THE ONLY WAY TO GET OUT OF TROUBLE IS TO REALIZE HOW YOU GOT IN IT IN THE FIRST PLACE, RIGHT? SO I BEEN THINKING ABOUT DEANNA DELANEY.

"AMY AND I WERE IN LOVE, SEE. WE HAD A REAL GOOD THING GOING. OR AT LEAST, WE DID--

"'TIL HE SHOWED UP."

"NO, NOT HIM."

"BIG-ASS MONSTER INVADES NEW YORK, FINE. THAT'S WHAT WE GET FOR BEING IN MIDTOWN ON SAINT PATRICK'S DAY, RIGHT? BUT THEN IRON MAN SWOOPS IN AND--AND--"

IT'S OKAY--I'VE GOT YOU, MISS.

KEEP AN EYE ON HER FOR ME NEXT TIME, YEAH, PAL?

"AS FAR AS AMY WAS CONCERNED, THAT WAS IT FOR ME. MIGHT AS WELL HAVE BEEN GIANT DRAGON DUDE HIMSELF.

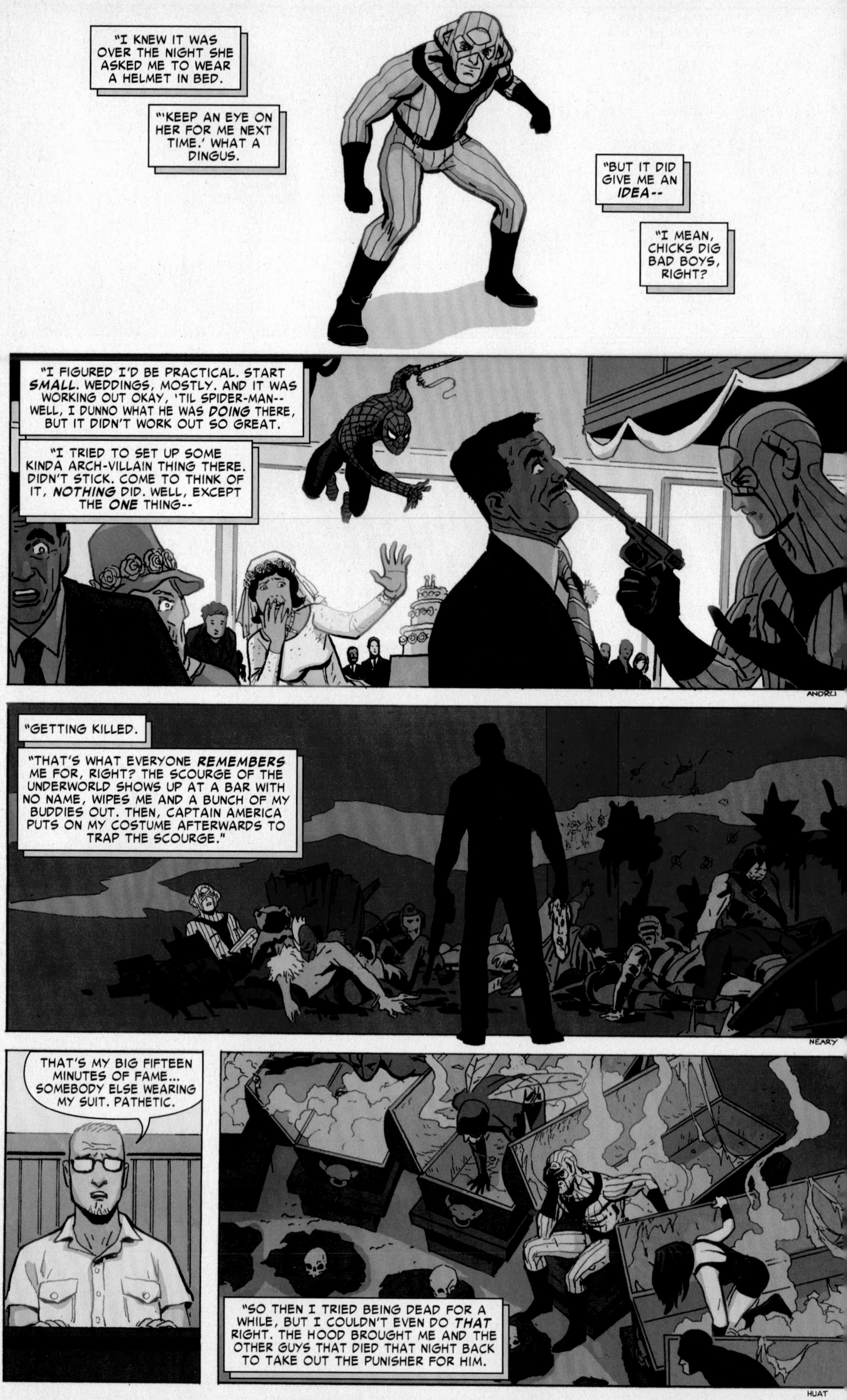
"I KNEW IT WAS OVER THE NIGHT SHE ASKED ME TO WEAR A HELMET IN BED.
"'KEEP AN EYE ON HER FOR ME NEXT TIME.' WHAT A DINGUS.
"BUT IT DID GIVE ME AN IDEA--
"I MEAN, CHICKS DIG BAD BOYS, RIGHT?
"I FIGURED I'D BE PRACTICAL. START SMALL. WEDDINGS, MOSTLY. AND IT WAS WORKING OUT OKAY, 'TIL SPIDER-MAN-- WELL, I DUNNO WHAT HE WAS DOING THERE, BUT IT DIDN'T WORK OUT SO GREAT.
"I TRIED TO SET UP SOME KINDA ARCH-VILLAIN THING THERE. DIDN'T STICK. COME TO THINK OF IT, NOTHING DID. WELL, EXCEPT THE ONE THING--
ANDRU
"GETTING KILLED.
"THAT'S WHAT EVERYONE REMEMBERS ME FOR, RIGHT? THE SCOURGE OF THE UNDERWORLD SHOWS UP AT A BAR WITH NO NAME, WIPES ME AND A BUNCH OF MY BUDDIES OUT. THEN, CAPTAIN AMERICA PUTS ON MY COSTUME AFTERWARDS TO TRAP THE SCOURGE."
NEARY
THAT'S MY BIG FIFTEEN MINUTES OF FAME... SOMEBODY ELSE WEARING MY SUIT. PATHETIC.
"SO THEN I TRIED BEING DEAD FOR A WHILE, BUT I COULDN'T EVEN DO THAT RIGHT. THE HOOD BROUGHT ME AND THE OTHER GUYS THAT DIED THAT NIGHT BACK TO TAKE OUT THE PUNISHER FOR HIM.
HUAT

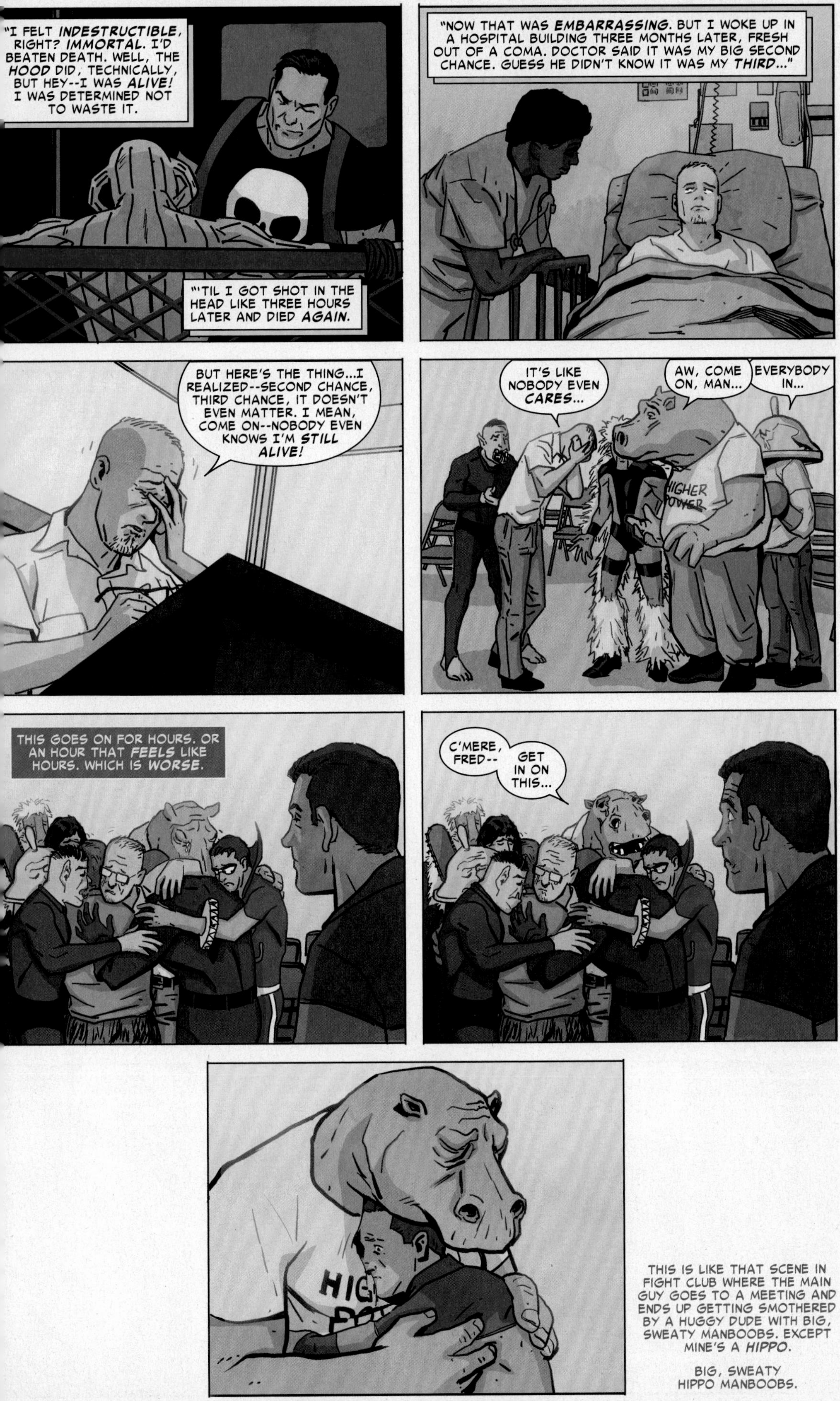
"I FELT INDESTRUCTIBLE, RIGHT? IMMORTAL. I'D BEATEN DEATH. WELL, THE HOOD DID, TECHNICALLY, BUT HEY--I WAS ALIVE! I WAS DETERMINED NOT TO WASTE IT.
"'TIL I GOT SHOT IN THE HEAD LIKE THREE HOURS LATER AND DIED AGAIN.
"NOW THAT WAS EMBARRASSING. BUT I WOKE UP IN A HOSPITAL BUILDING THREE MONTHS LATER, FRESH OUT OF A COMA. DOCTOR SAID IT WAS MY BIG SECOND CHANCE. GUESS HE DIDN'T KNOW IT WAS MY THIRD..."
BUT HERE'S THE THING...I REALIZED--SECOND CHANCE, THIRD CHANCE, IT DOESN'T EVEN MATTER. I MEAN, COME ON--NOBODY EVEN KNOWS I'M STILL ALIVE!
IT'S LIKE NOBODY EVEN CARES...
AW, COME ON, MAN...
EVERYBODY IN...
HIGHER POWER
THIS GOES ON FOR HOURS. OR AN HOUR THAT FEELS LIKE HOURS. WHICH IS WORSE.
C'MERE, FRED--
GET IN ON THIS...
THIS IS LIKE THAT SCENE IN FIGHT CLUB WHERE THE MAIN GUY GOES TO A MEETING AND ENDS UP GETTING SMOTHERED BY A HUGGY DUDE WITH BIG, SWEATY MANBOOBS. EXCEPT MINE'S A HIPPO.
BIG, SWEATY HIPPO MANBOOBS.

BEFORE YOU ASK, YES, HE *DID* CARRY ME UP HERE. IT WAS HUMILIATING.

DON'T FEEL BAD ABOUT NOT SPEAKING TONIGHT, FRED.

OH BELIEVE ME, I *DON'T*.

I MEAN...*YEAH*. SORRY. I'M SHY?

I'M JUST SAYING, I KNOW IT TAKES TIME. BUT I FEEL LIKE WE MADE REAL *PROGRESS* TODAY, RIGHT?

OH YEAH. *LOTS* OF PROGRESS. I DON'T EVEN KNOW WHERE I *AM* ANYMORE.

STICK WITH IT.

SURE. I DO GOTTA SAY THOUGH...SOME OF THAT STUFF IN THERE, IT DID HIT HOME--

YEAH?

YEAH. THAT STUFF ABOU[T] MAKING A *CLEAN BREA*[K,] CUTTING OFF BAD INFLUENCES--

THAT STUFF'S IMPORTANT.

I BET. AND IT GOT ME THINKING. I HAVEN'T-- WELL, HELL, MAN...I HAVEN'T BEEN TOTALLY HONEST WITH YOU.

WHAT DO YOU *MEAN*?

WELL, SEE, THERE'S THIS *JOB*...

JOB?

YEAH. AND WHEN THEY CAME TO ME WITH IT, I WAS LIKE "NO WAY" RIGHT? I'M TRYING TO STAY *CLEAN* HERE. BUT THEY JUST KEPT PRESSING ME, IT WAS AWFUL.

AND NOW I'M THINKING, SHOULD I KEEP *QUIET* ABOUT THIS? I MEAN, THIS IS ILLEGAL!

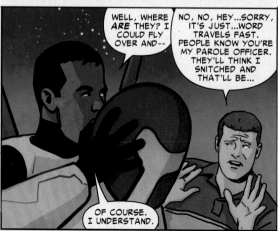

WELL, WHERE *ARE* THEY? I COULD FLY OVER AND--

NO, NO, HEY...SORRY, IT'S JUST...WORD TRAVELS FAST. PEOPLE KNOW YOU'RE MY PAROLE OFFICER. THEY'LL THINK I SNITCHED AND THAT'LL BE...

OF COURSE. I UNDERSTAND.

BUT THEN I WAS THINKING-- MAYBE YOU KNEW OF SOME- ONE YOU COULD CALL--YOU KNOW, LIKE *REAL* AVENGERS. AND THEY COULD TAKE CARE OF IT.

WELL...

I MEAN, *SOMEONE* NEEDS TO--PEOPLE COULD GET *HURT* HERE!

HMM-- IF THAT'S REALLY THE CASE...

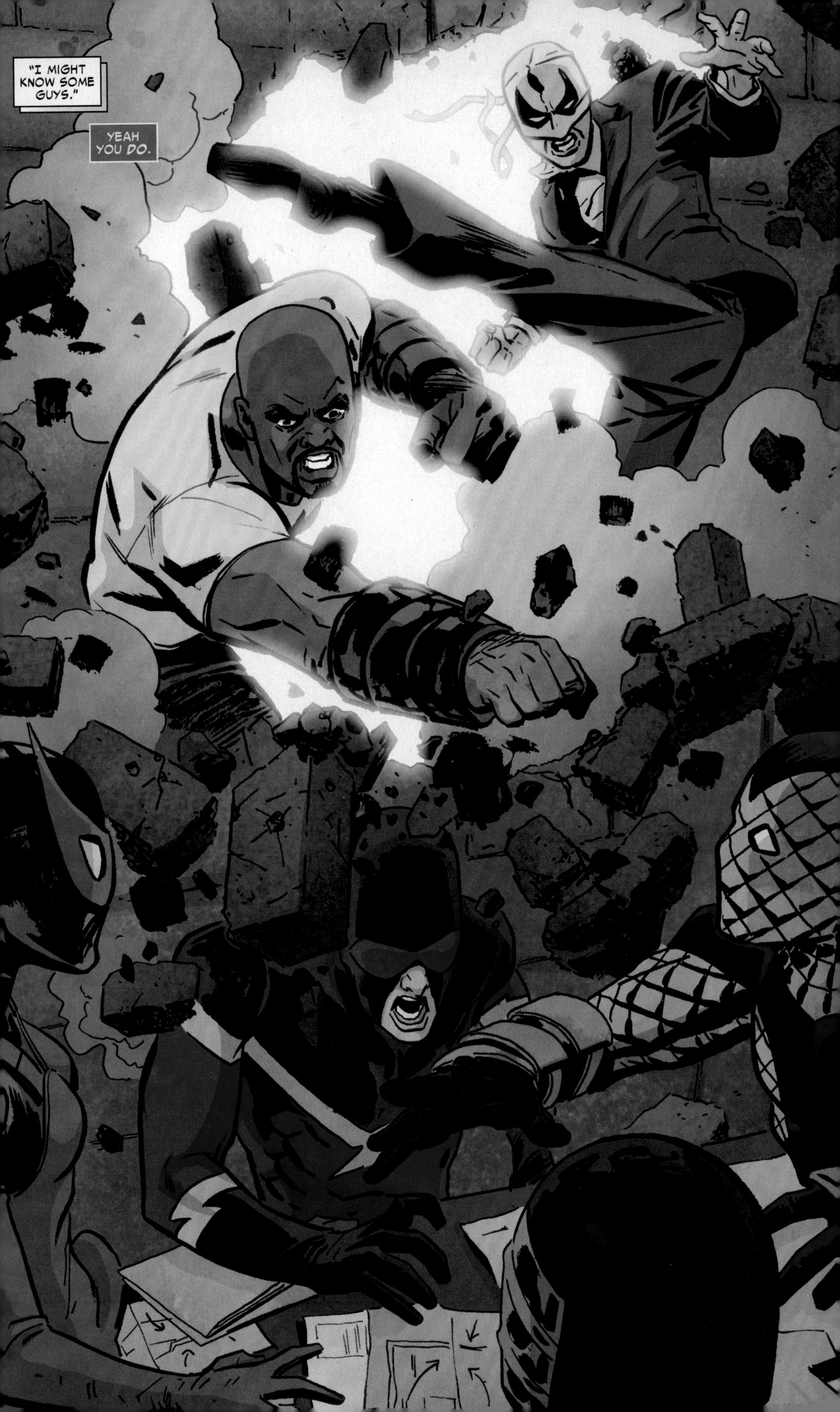
"I MIGHT KNOW SOME GUYS."
YEAH YOU DO.

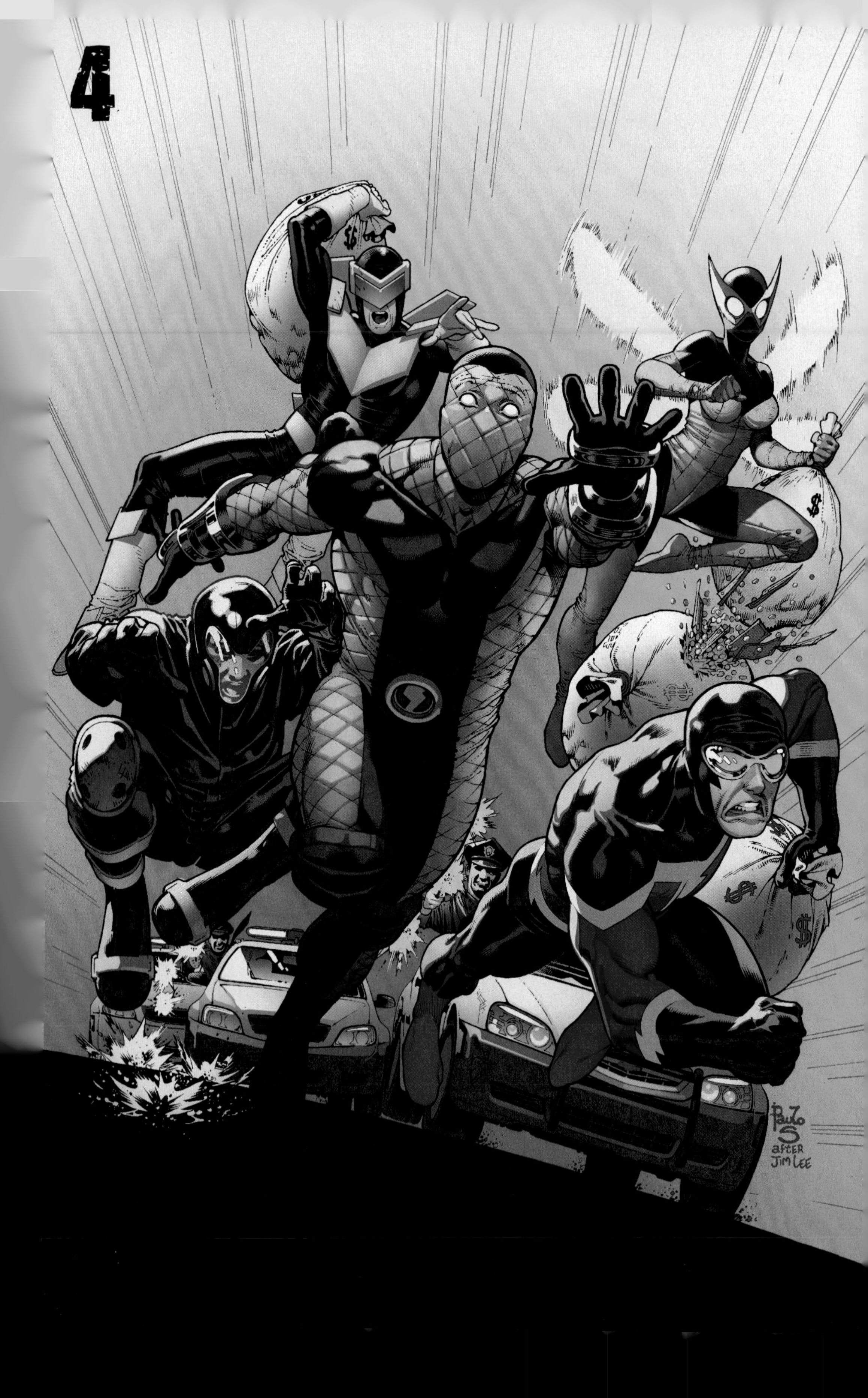
4
PAULO S AFTER JIM LEE

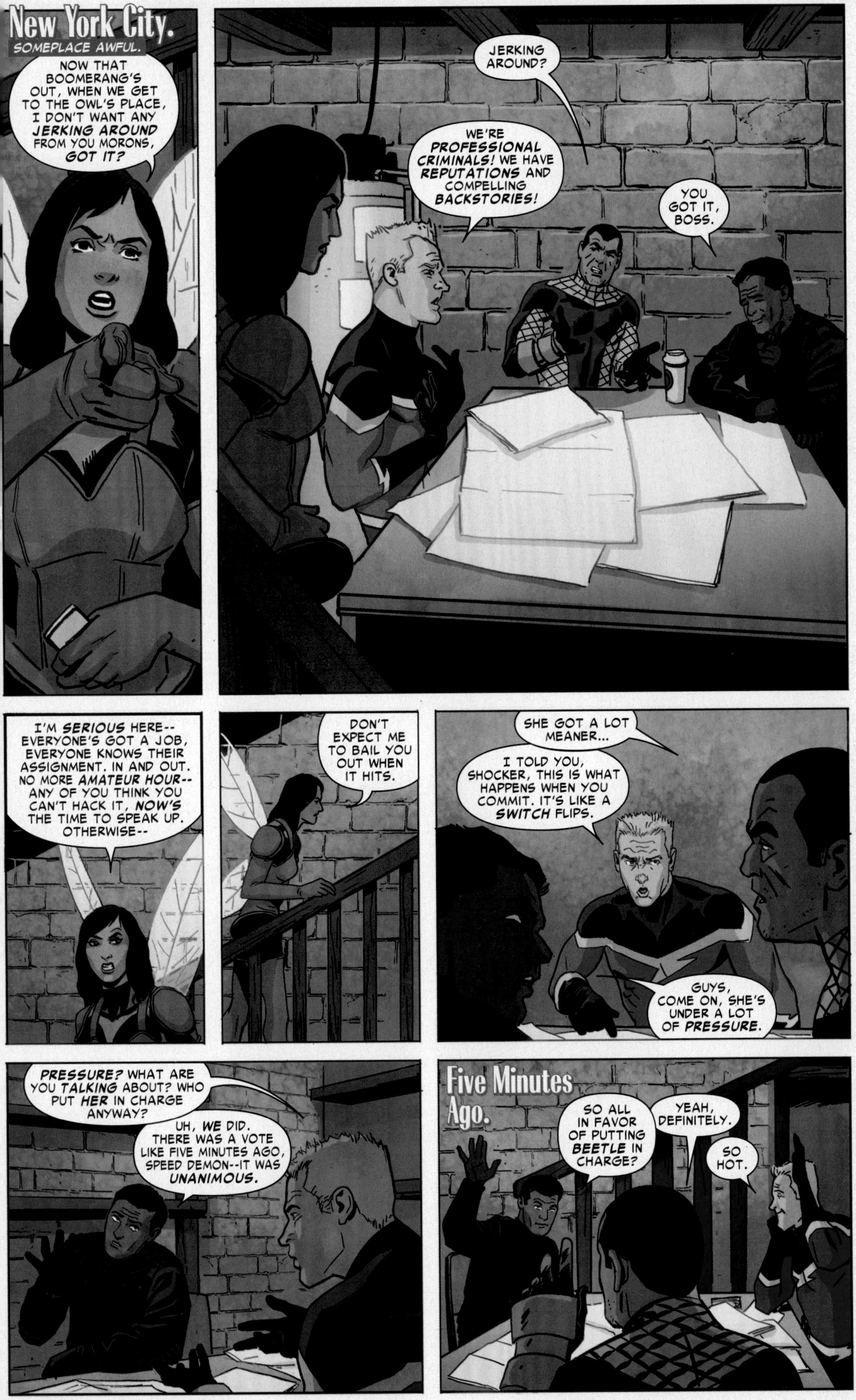

New York City.
SOMEPLACE AWFUL.
NOW THAT BOOMERANG'S OUT, WHEN WE GET TO THE OWL'S PLACE, I DON'T WANT ANY JERKING AROUND FROM YOU MORONS, GOT IT?
JERKING AROUND?
WE'RE PROFESSIONAL CRIMINALS! WE HAVE REPUTATIONS AND COMPELLING BACKSTORIES!
YOU GOT IT, BOSS.
I'M SERIOUS HERE--EVERYONE'S GOT A JOB, EVERYONE KNOWS THEIR ASSIGNMENT. IN AND OUT. NO MORE AMATEUR HOUR--ANY OF YOU THINK YOU CAN'T HACK IT, NOW'S THE TIME TO SPEAK UP. OTHERWISE--
DON'T EXPECT ME TO BAIL YOU OUT WHEN IT HITS.
SHE GOT A LOT MEANER...
I TOLD YOU, SHOCKER, THIS IS WHAT HAPPENS WHEN YOU COMMIT. IT'S LIKE A SWITCH FLIPS.
GUYS, COME ON, SHE'S UNDER A LOT OF PRESSURE.
PRESSURE? WHAT ARE YOU TALKING ABOUT? WHO PUT HER IN CHARGE ANYWAY?
UH, WE DID. THERE WAS A VOTE LIKE FIVE MINUTES AGO, SPEED DEMON--IT WAS UNANIMOUS.
Five Minutes Ago.
SO ALL IN FAVOR OF PUTTING BEETLE IN CHARGE?
YEAH, DEFINITELY.
SO HOT.

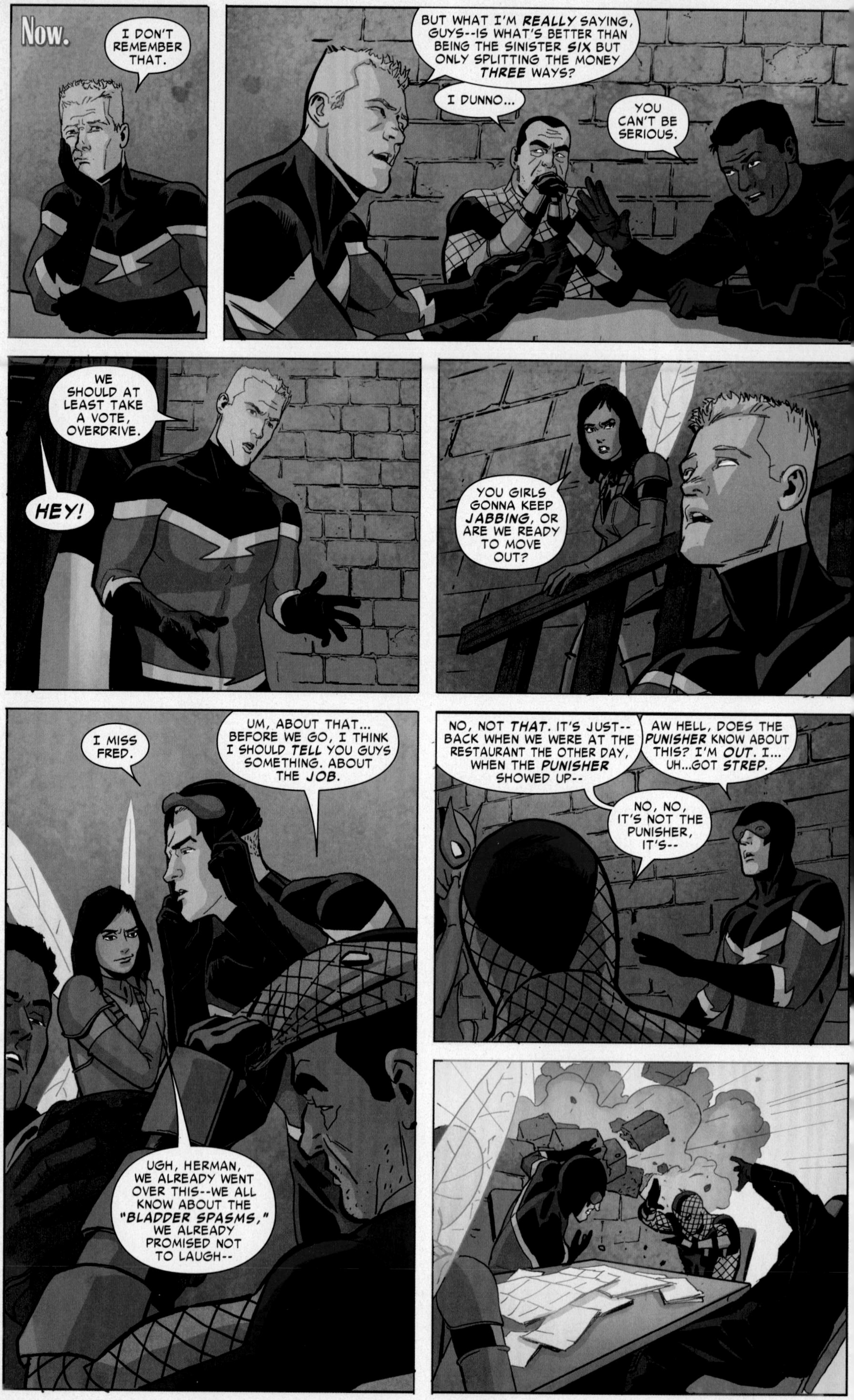

Now.
I DON'T REMEMBER THAT.
BUT WHAT I'M REALLY SAYING, GUYS--IS WHAT'S BETTER THAN BEING THE SINISTER SIX BUT ONLY SPLITTING THE MONEY THREE WAYS?
I DUNNO...
YOU CAN'T BE SERIOUS.
WE SHOULD AT LEAST TAKE A VOTE, OVERDRIVE.
HEY!
YOU GIRLS GONNA KEEP JABBING, OR ARE WE READY TO MOVE OUT?
I MISS FRED.
UM, ABOUT THAT... BEFORE WE GO, I THINK I SHOULD TELL YOU GUYS SOMETHING. ABOUT THE JOB.
UGH, HERMAN, WE ALREADY WENT OVER THIS--WE ALL KNOW ABOUT THE "BLADDER SPASMS," WE ALREADY PROMISED NOT TO LAUGH--
NO, NOT THAT. IT'S JUST--BACK WHEN WE WERE AT THE RESTAURANT THE OTHER DAY, WHEN THE PUNISHER SHOWED UP--
AW HELL, DOES THE PUNISHER KNOW ABOUT THIS? I'M OUT. I... UH...GOT STREP.
NO, NO, IT'S NOT THE PUNISHER, IT'S--

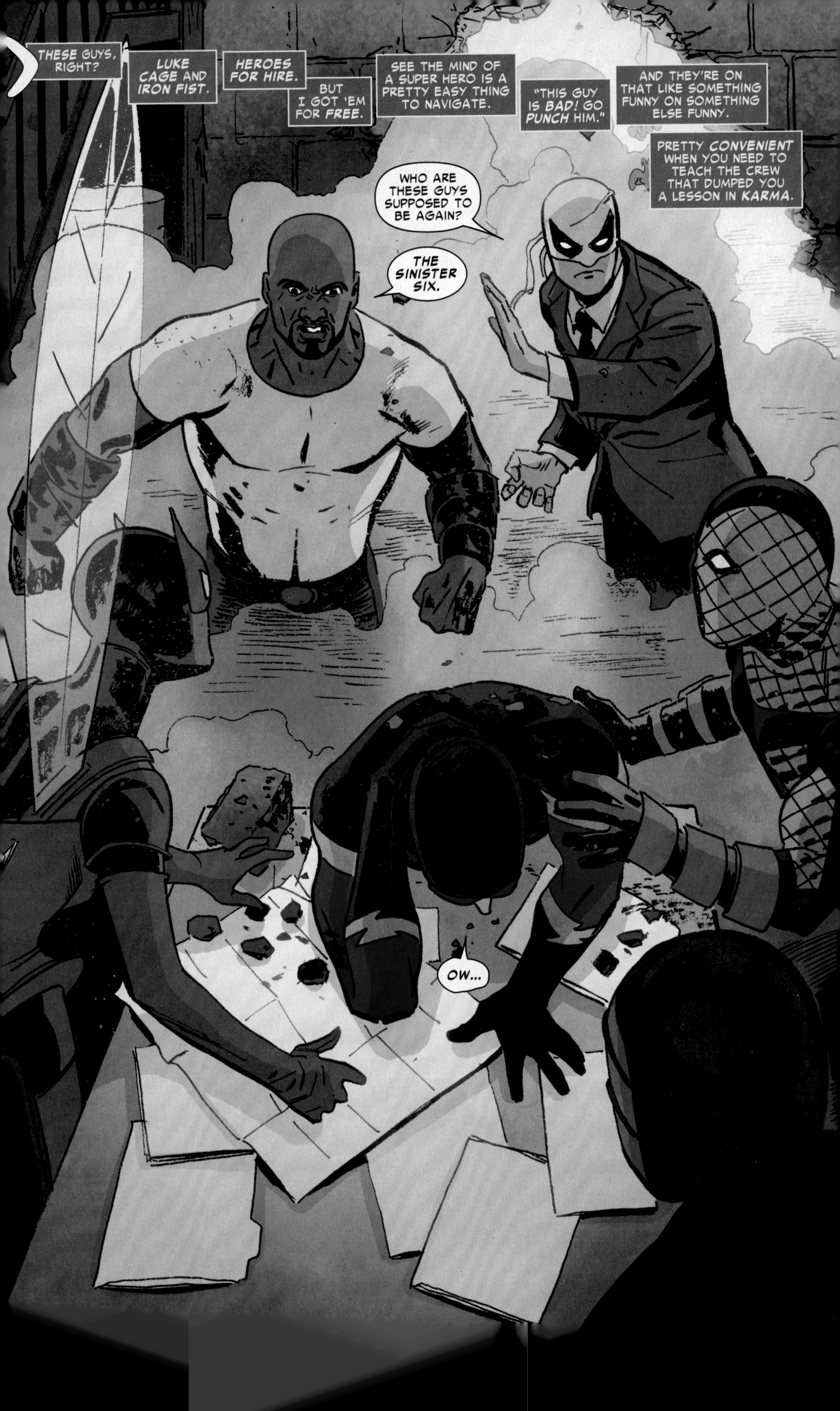
THESE GUYS, RIGHT?
LUKE CAGE AND IRON FIST.
HEROES FOR HIRE.
BUT I GOT 'EM FOR FREE.
SEE THE MIND OF A SUPER HERO IS A PRETTY EASY THING TO NAVIGATE.
"THIS GUY IS BAD! GO PUNCH HIM."
AND THEY'RE ON THAT LIKE SOMETHING FUNNY ON SOMETHING ELSE FUNNY.
PRETTY CONVENIENT WHEN YOU NEED TO TEACH THE CREW THAT DUMPED YOU A LESSON IN KARMA.
WHO ARE THESE GUYS SUPPOSED TO BE AGAIN?
THE SINISTER SIX.
OW...

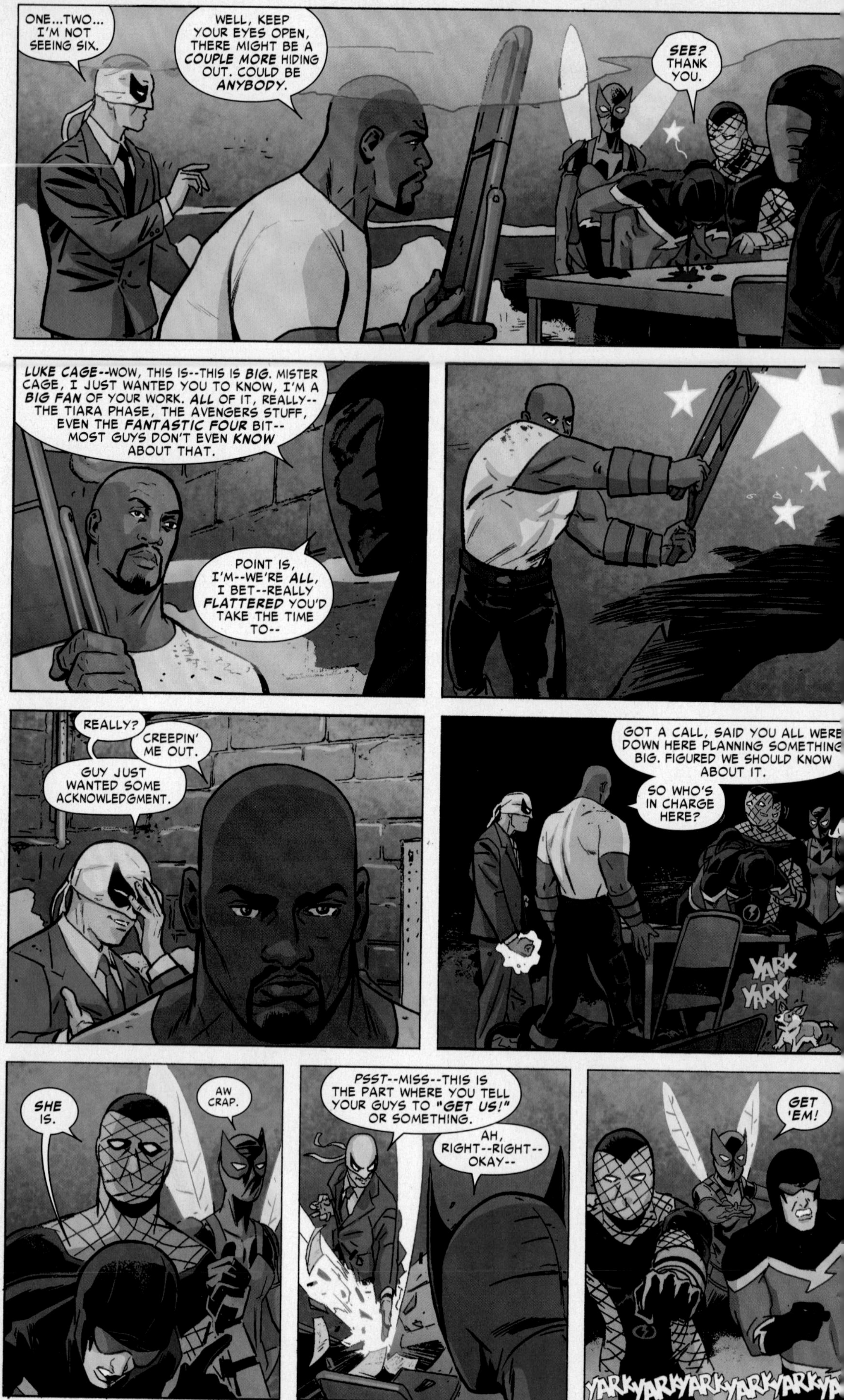
ONE...TWO... I'M NOT SEEING SIX.
WELL, KEEP YOUR EYES OPEN, THERE MIGHT BE A COUPLE MORE HIDING OUT. COULD BE ANYBODY.
SEE? THANK YOU.
LUKE CAGE--WOW, THIS IS--THIS IS BIG. MISTER CAGE, I JUST WANTED YOU TO KNOW, I'M A BIG FAN OF YOUR WORK. ALL OF IT, REALLY--THE TIARA PHASE, THE AVENGERS STUFF, EVEN THE FANTASTIC FOUR BIT--MOST GUYS DON'T EVEN KNOW ABOUT THAT.
POINT IS, I'M--WE'RE ALL, I BET--REALLY FLATTERED YOU'D TAKE THE TIME TO--
REALLY?
CREEPIN' ME OUT.
GUY JUST WANTED SOME ACKNOWLEDGMENT.
GOT A CALL, SAID YOU ALL WERE DOWN HERE PLANNING SOMETHING BIG. FIGURED WE SHOULD KNOW ABOUT IT.
SO WHO'S IN CHARGE HERE?
YARK YARK
SHE IS.
AW CRAP.
PSST--MISS--THIS IS THE PART WHERE YOU TELL YOUR GUYS TO "GET US!" OR SOMETHING.
AH, RIGHT--RIGHT--OKAY--
GET 'EM!
YARKYARKYARKYARKYARKYA

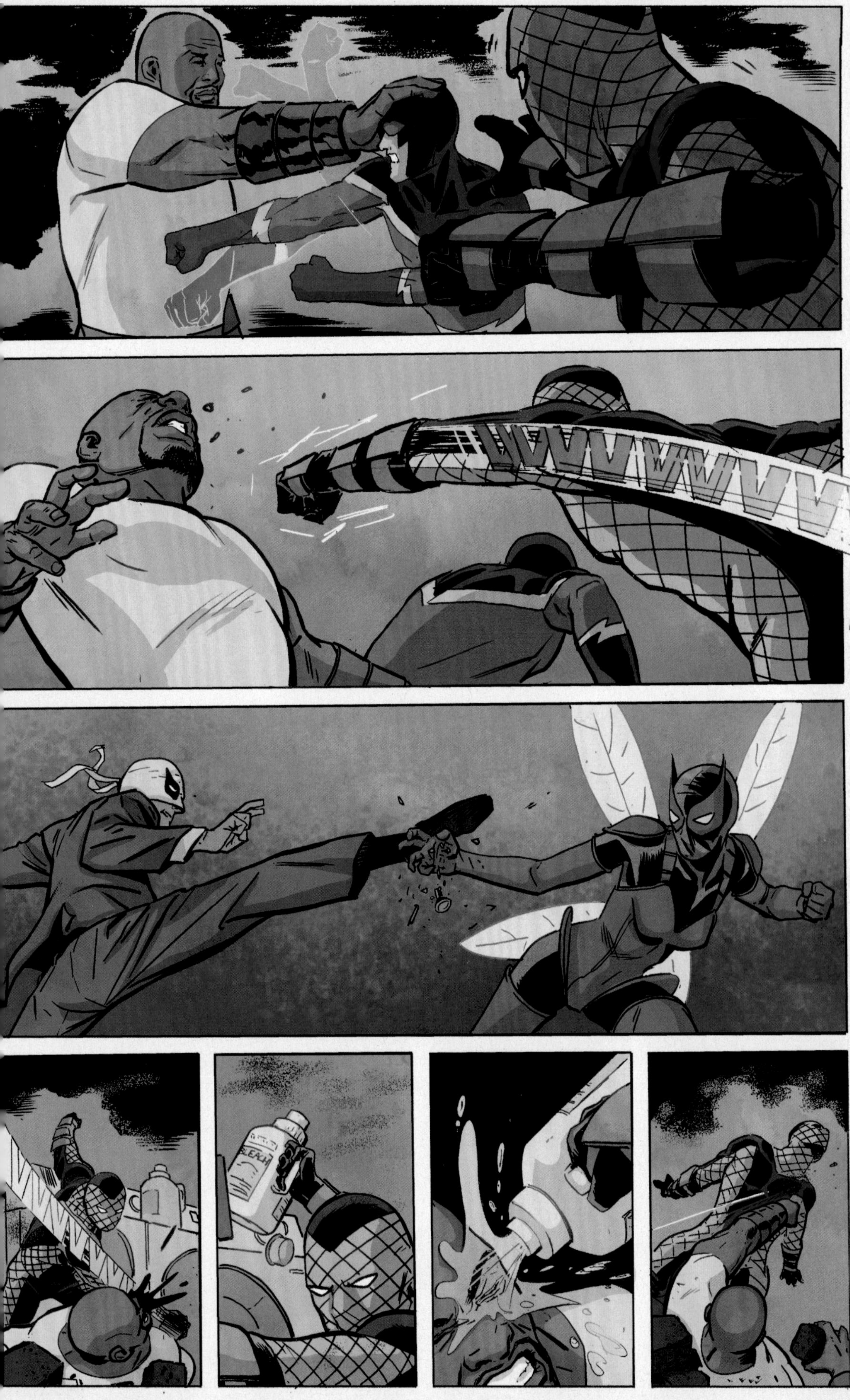
BLEACH

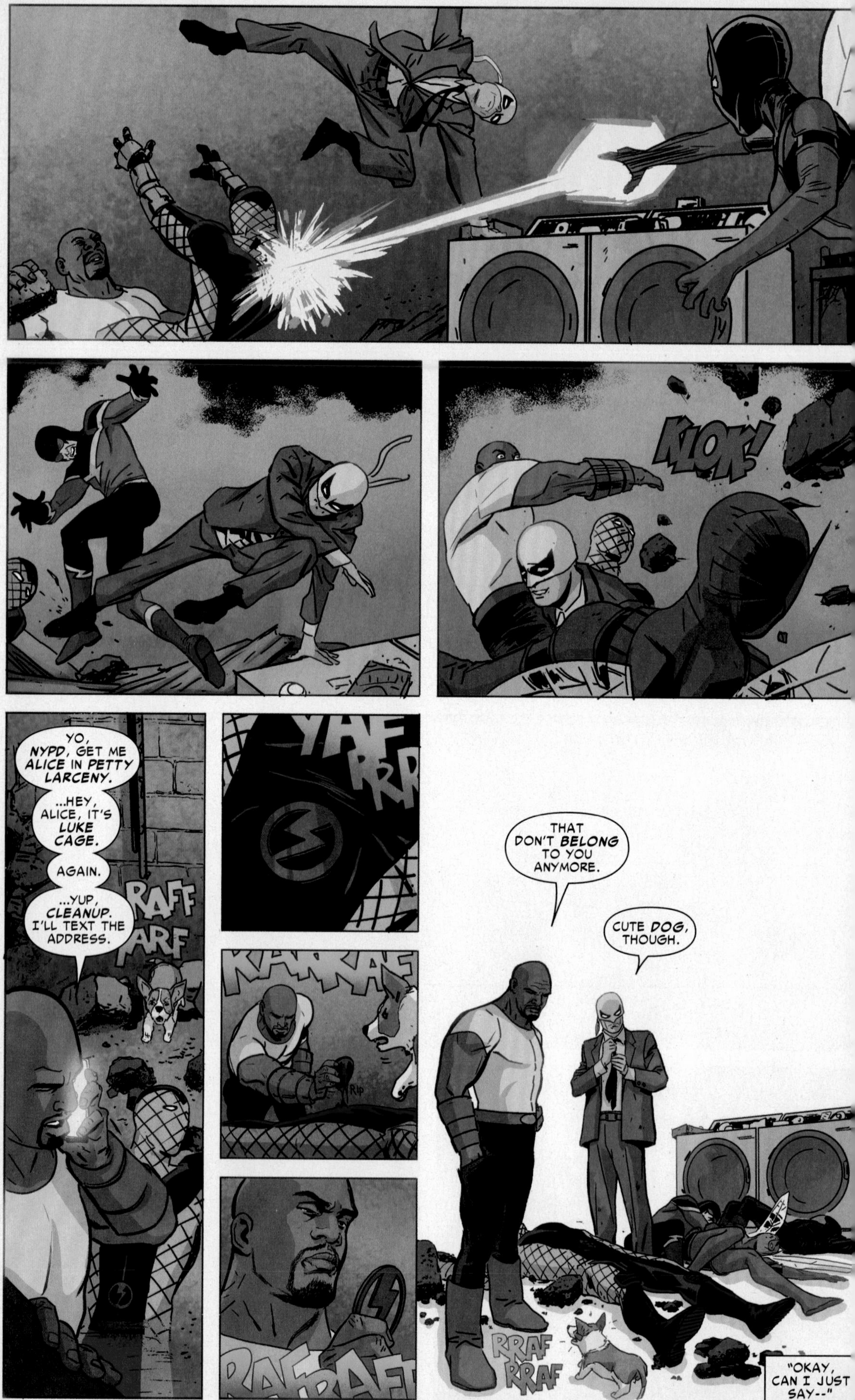
KLOK!
YO, NYPD, GET ME ALICE IN PETTY LARCENY.
...HEY, ALICE, IT'S LUKE CAGE.
AGAIN.
...YUP, CLEANUP. I'LL TEXT THE ADDRESS.
RAFF
ARF
YAF
RRR
RAFF
RIP
RAFRAFF
THAT DON'T BELONG TO YOU ANYMORE.
CUTE DOG, THOUGH.
RRAF
RRAF
"OKAY, CAN I JUST SAY--"

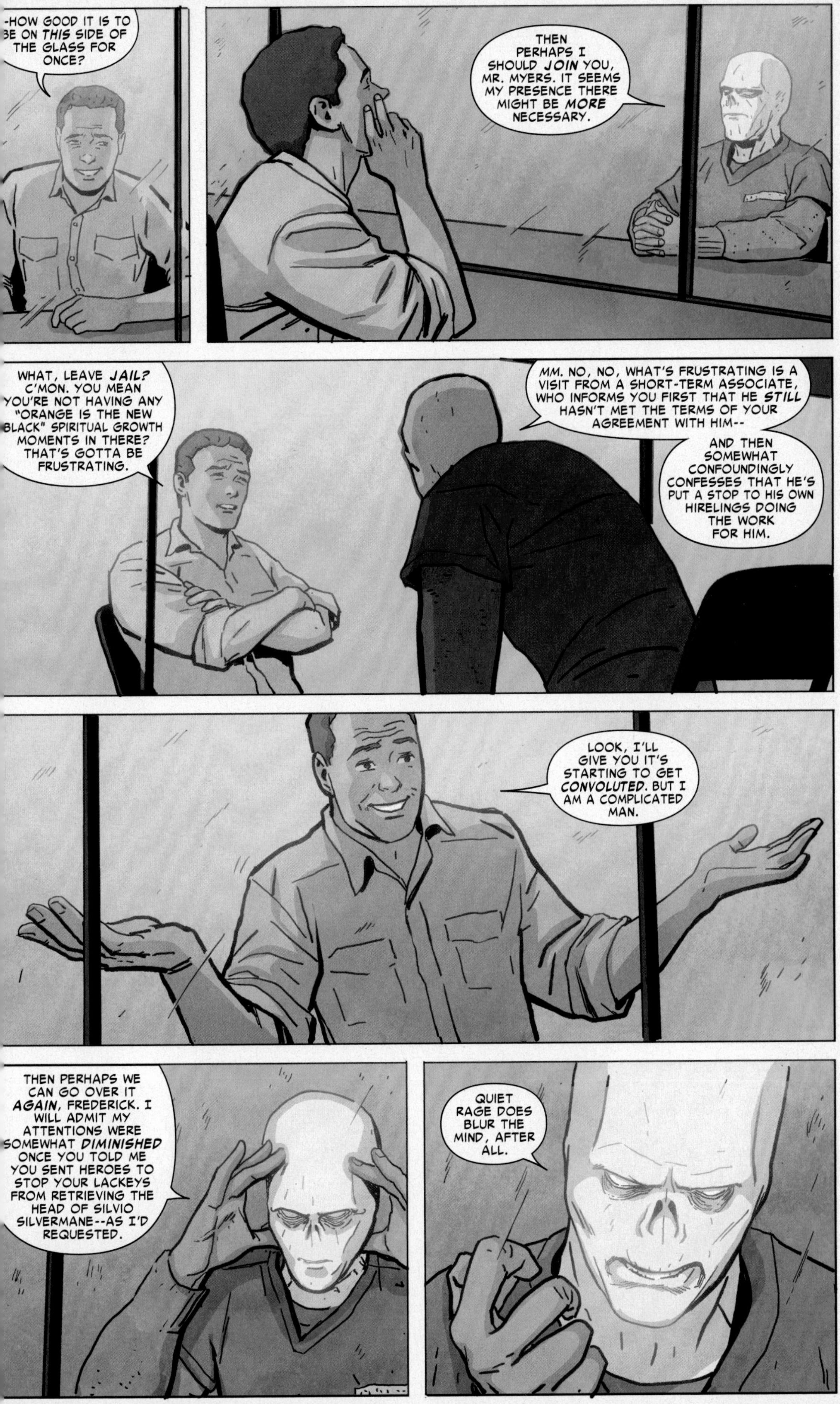
-HOW GOOD IT IS TO BE ON THIS SIDE OF THE GLASS FOR ONCE?
THEN PERHAPS I SHOULD JOIN YOU, MR. MYERS. IT SEEMS MY PRESENCE THERE MIGHT BE MORE NECESSARY.
WHAT, LEAVE JAIL? C'MON. YOU MEAN YOU'RE NOT HAVING ANY "ORANGE IS THE NEW BLACK" SPIRITUAL GROWTH MOMENTS IN THERE? THAT'S GOTTA BE FRUSTRATING.
MM. NO, NO, WHAT'S FRUSTRATING IS A VISIT FROM A SHORT-TERM ASSOCIATE, WHO INFORMS YOU FIRST THAT HE STILL HASN'T MET THE TERMS OF YOUR AGREEMENT WITH HIM--
AND THEN SOMEWHAT CONFOUNDINGLY CONFESSES THAT HE'S PUT A STOP TO HIS OWN HIRELINGS DOING THE WORK FOR HIM.
LOOK, I'LL GIVE YOU IT'S STARTING TO GET CONVOLUTED. BUT I AM A COMPLICATED MAN.
THEN PERHAPS WE CAN GO OVER IT AGAIN, FREDERICK. I WILL ADMIT MY ATTENTIONS WERE SOMEWHAT DIMINISHED ONCE YOU TOLD ME YOU SENT HEROES TO STOP YOUR LACKEYS FROM RETRIEVING THE HEAD OF SILVIO SILVERMANE--AS I'D REQUESTED.
QUIET RAGE DOES BLUR THE MIND, AFTER ALL.

PUT IT BACK IN YOUR PANTS, POWDER. I GOT THE SITUATION *ALL UNDER CONTROL.* SEE, THEY HUNG ME OUT TO DRY. *FIRED* ME! FROM *MY OWN* GANG!

I DON'T UNDERSTAND WHY THIS IS *MY* CONCERN.

YOUR--*YOUR CONCERN?!* I'M YOUR *POINT GUY!* I'M THE GUY WHO TOLD YOU ABOUT THE HEAD IN THE *FIRST PLACE!*

I SWEAR, NONE OF YOU PEOPLE GET THIS IS A BUSINESS OF *RELATIONSHIPS* ALSO ARSON, ROBBERY, AND MURDER...

BUT MOSTLY RELATIONSHIPS!

"YOU'RE NOT EVEN THINKING ABOUT WHAT WOULD HAPPEN WHEN THEY *GOT* THE HEAD. IT'S NOT LIKE THEY'D JUST *GIVE* IT TO YOU!"

"THEN I SUPPOSE I WOULD *KILL* THEM."

"WELL--YEAH, BUT-- THEN I WOULD BE OUT A GANG."

"I THOUGHT THE GANG WAS NO LONGER YOURS."

DETAILS! LISTEN, I'M TELLING YOU-- WE'RE ON THE VERGE OF A MAJOR *BREAKTHROUGH* HERE. THAT'S THE PROBLEM WITH YOU *RUSSIAN MOB* GUYS, YOU DON'T UNDERSTAND THE *AMERICAN* CRIMINAL MIND. OUR FRONTIER *SPIRIT.*

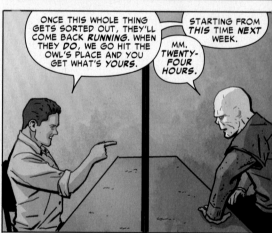

ONCE THIS WHOLE THING GETS SORTED OUT, THEY'LL COME BACK *RUNNING.* WHEN THEY *DO,* WE GO HIT THE OWL'S PLACE AND YOU GET WHAT'S *YOURS.*

STARTING FROM *THIS* TIME *NEXT* WEEK.

MM. *TWENTY- FOUR* HOURS.

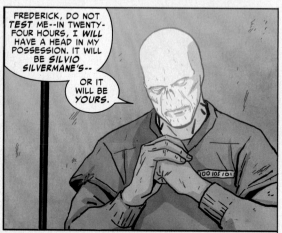

FREDERICK, DO NOT *TEST* ME--IN TWENTY- FOUR HOURS, I *WILL* HAVE A HEAD IN MY POSSESSION. IT WILL BE *SILVIO SILVERMANE'S*--

OR IT WILL BE *YOURS.*

DON'T WORRY--I'LL WAIT FOR YOU, HONEY PIE!

OKAY, YEAH--I'M PROBABLY GETTING LITTLE CARRIED AWAY WITH MYSELF HERE. SURE. BUT REALLY--

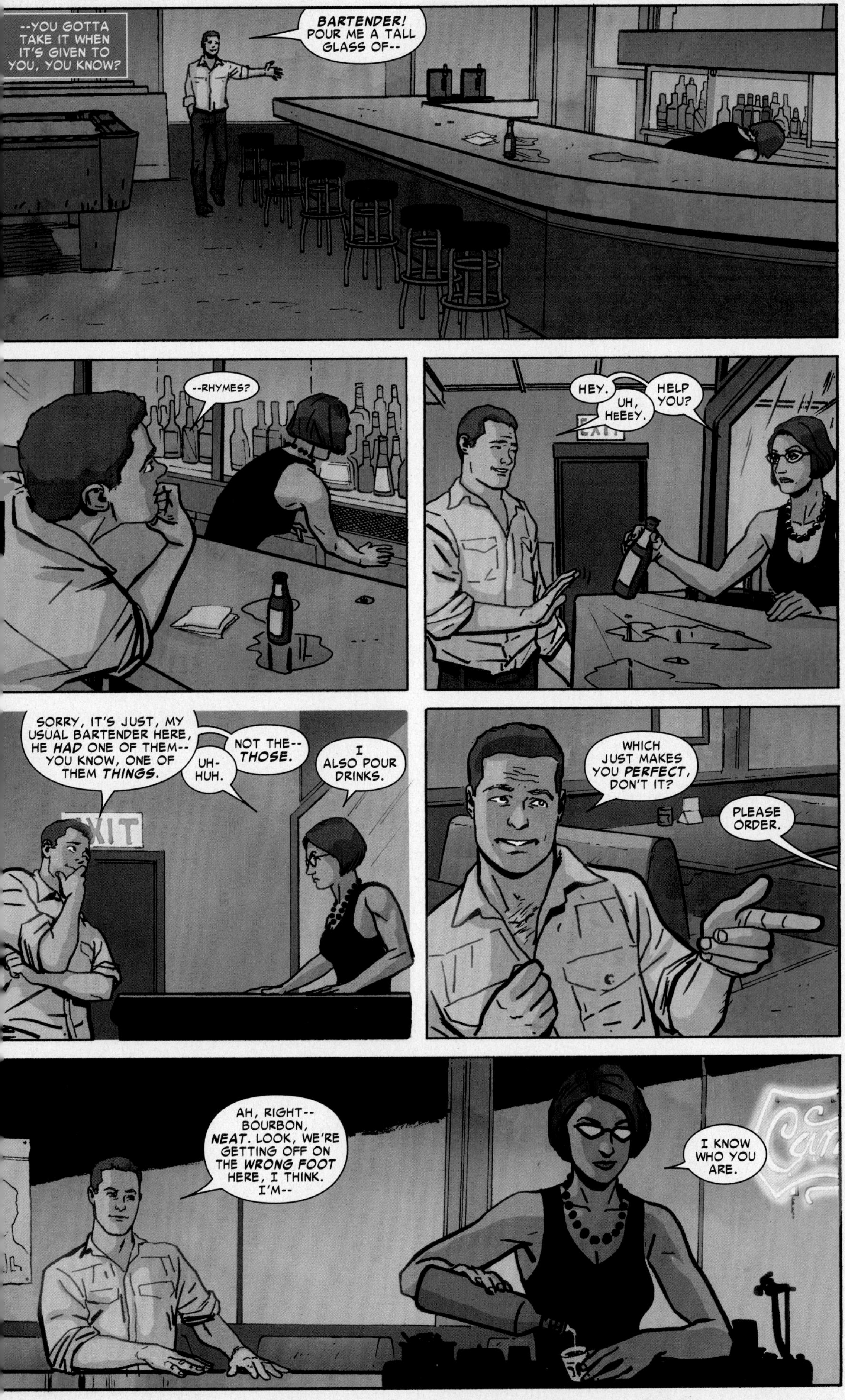
--YOU GOTTA TAKE IT WHEN IT'S GIVEN TO YOU, YOU KNOW?
BARTENDER! POUR ME A TALL GLASS OF--
--RHYMES?
HEY.
HELP YOU?
UH, HEEEY.
EXIT
SORRY, IT'S JUST, MY USUAL BARTENDER HERE, HE HAD ONE OF THEM--YOU KNOW, ONE OF THEM THINGS.
NOT THE--THOSE.
UH-HUH.
I ALSO POUR DRINKS.
EXIT
WHICH JUST MAKES YOU PERFECT, DON'T IT?
PLEASE ORDER.
AH, RIGHT--BOURBON, NEAT. LOOK, WE'RE GETTING OFF ON THE WRONG FOOT HERE, I THINK. I'M--
I KNOW WHO YOU ARE.

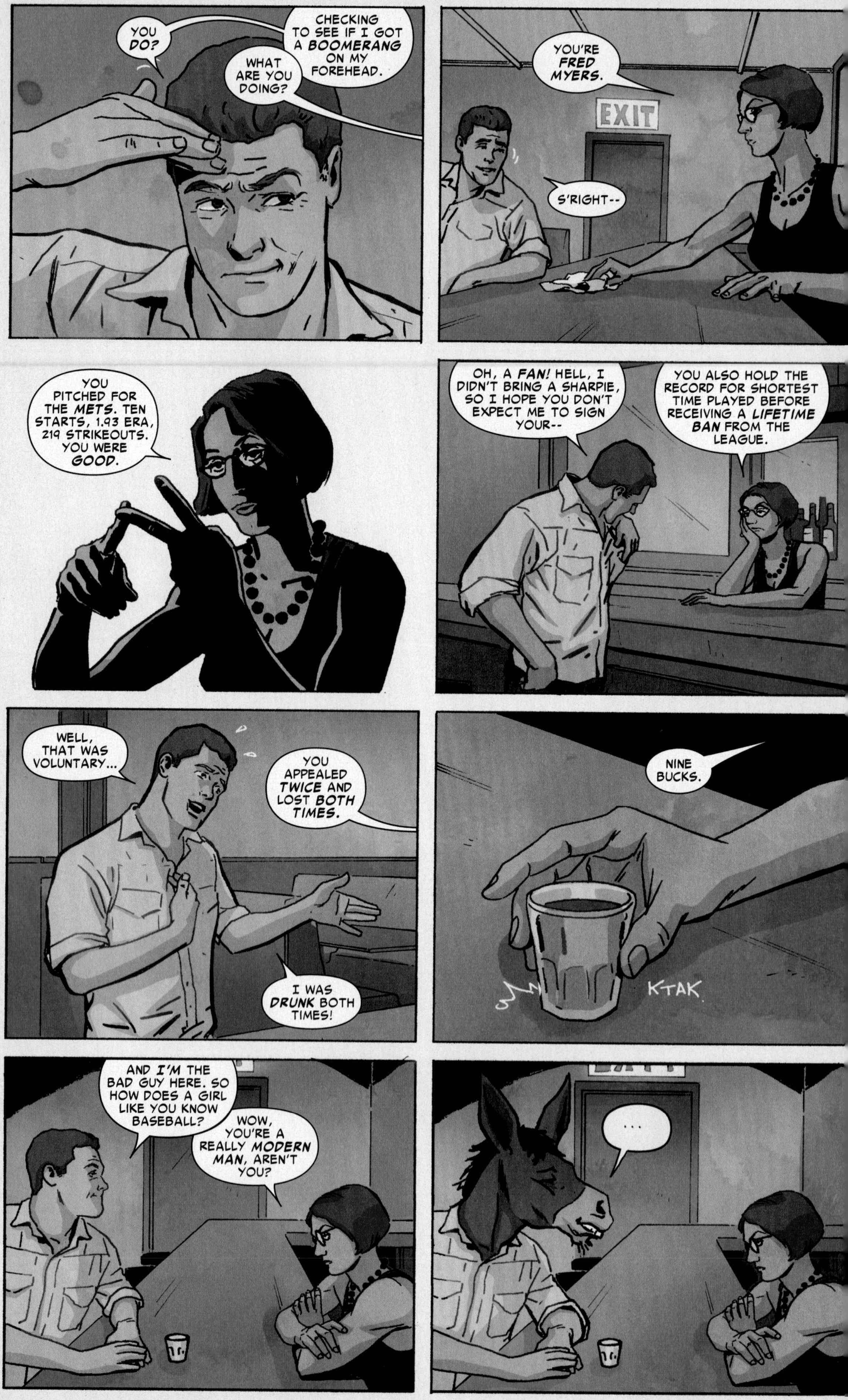

YOU DO?
CHECKING TO SEE IF I GOT A BOOMERANG ON MY FOREHEAD.
WHAT ARE YOU DOING?
YOU'RE FRED MYERS.
EXIT
S'RIGHT--
YOU PITCHED FOR THE METS. TEN STARTS, 1.93 ERA, 219 STRIKEOUTS. YOU WERE GOOD.
OH, A FAN! HELL, I DIDN'T BRING A SHARPIE, SO I HOPE YOU DON'T EXPECT ME TO SIGN YOUR--
YOU ALSO HOLD THE RECORD FOR SHORTEST TIME PLAYED BEFORE RECEIVING A LIFETIME BAN FROM THE LEAGUE.
WELL, THAT WAS VOLUNTARY...
YOU APPEALED TWICE AND LOST BOTH TIMES.
I WAS DRUNK BOTH TIMES!
NINE BUCKS.
KTAK
AND I'M THE BAD GUY HERE. SO HOW DOES A GIRL LIKE YOU KNOW BASEBALL?
WOW, YOU'RE A REALLY MODERN MAN, AREN'T YOU?
...

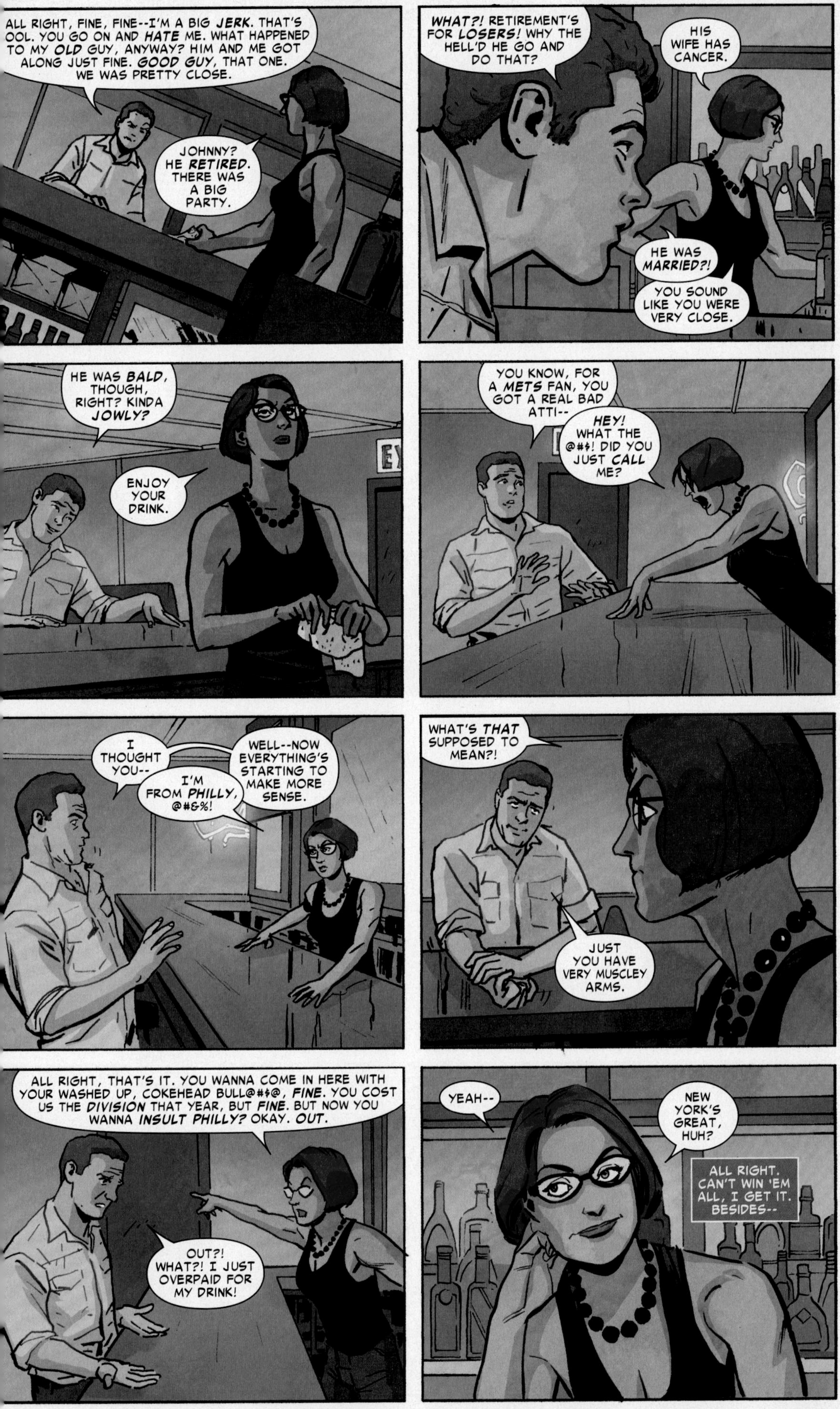

ALL RIGHT, FINE, FINE--I'M A BIG JERK. THAT'S OOL. YOU GO ON AND HATE ME. WHAT HAPPENED TO MY OLD GUY, ANYWAY? HIM AND ME GOT ALONG JUST FINE. GOOD GUY, THAT ONE. WE WAS PRETTY CLOSE.
JOHNNY? HE RETIRED. THERE WAS A BIG PARTY.
WHAT?! RETIREMENT'S FOR LOSERS! WHY THE HELL'D HE GO AND DO THAT?
HIS WIFE HAS CANCER.
HE WAS MARRIED?!
YOU SOUND LIKE YOU WERE VERY CLOSE.
HE WAS BALD, THOUGH, RIGHT? KINDA JOWLY?
ENJOY YOUR DRINK.
YOU KNOW, FOR A METS FAN, YOU GOT A REAL BAD ATTI--
HEY! WHAT THE @#$! DID YOU JUST CALL ME?
I THOUGHT YOU--
I'M FROM PHILLY, @#&%!
WELL--NOW EVERYTHING'S STARTING TO MAKE MORE SENSE.
WHAT'S THAT SUPPOSED TO MEAN?!
JUST YOU HAVE VERY MUSCLEY ARMS.
ALL RIGHT, THAT'S IT. YOU WANNA COME IN HERE WITH YOUR WASHED UP, COKEHEAD BULL@#$@, FINE. YOU COST US THE DIVISION THAT YEAR, BUT FINE. BUT NOW YOU WANNA INSULT PHILLY? OKAY. OUT.
OUT?! WHAT?! I JUST OVERPAID FOR MY DRINK!
YEAH--
NEW YORK'S GREAT, HUH?
ALL RIGHT. CAN'T WIN 'EM ALL, I GET IT. BESIDES--

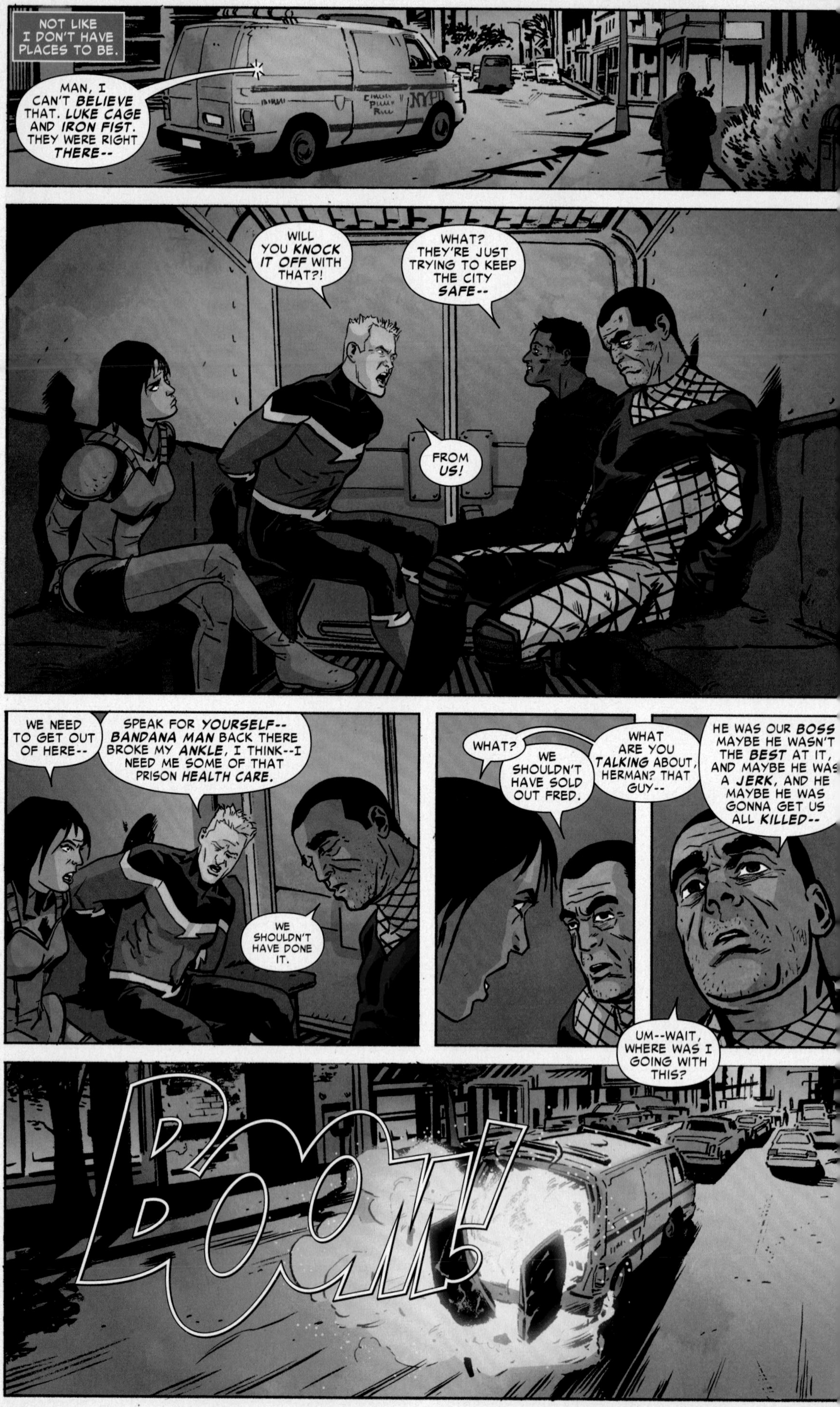
NOT LIKE I DON'T HAVE PLACES TO BE.
MAN, I CAN'T BELIEVE THAT. LUKE CAGE AND IRON FIST. THEY WERE RIGHT THERE--
WILL YOU KNOCK IT OFF WITH THAT?!
WHAT? THEY'RE JUST TRYING TO KEEP THE CITY SAFE--
FROM US!
WE NEED TO GET OUT OF HERE--
SPEAK FOR YOURSELF-- BANDANA MAN BACK THERE BROKE MY ANKLE, I THINK--I NEED ME SOME OF THAT PRISON HEALTH CARE.
WE SHOULDN'T HAVE DONE IT.
WHAT?
WE SHOULDN'T HAVE SOLD OUT FRED.
WHAT ARE YOU TALKING ABOUT, HERMAN? THAT GUY--
HE WAS OUR BOSS. MAYBE HE WASN'T THE BEST AT IT, AND MAYBE HE WAS A JERK, AND HE MAYBE HE WAS GONNA GET US ALL KILLED--
UM--WAIT, WHERE WAS I GOING WITH THIS?
BOOM!

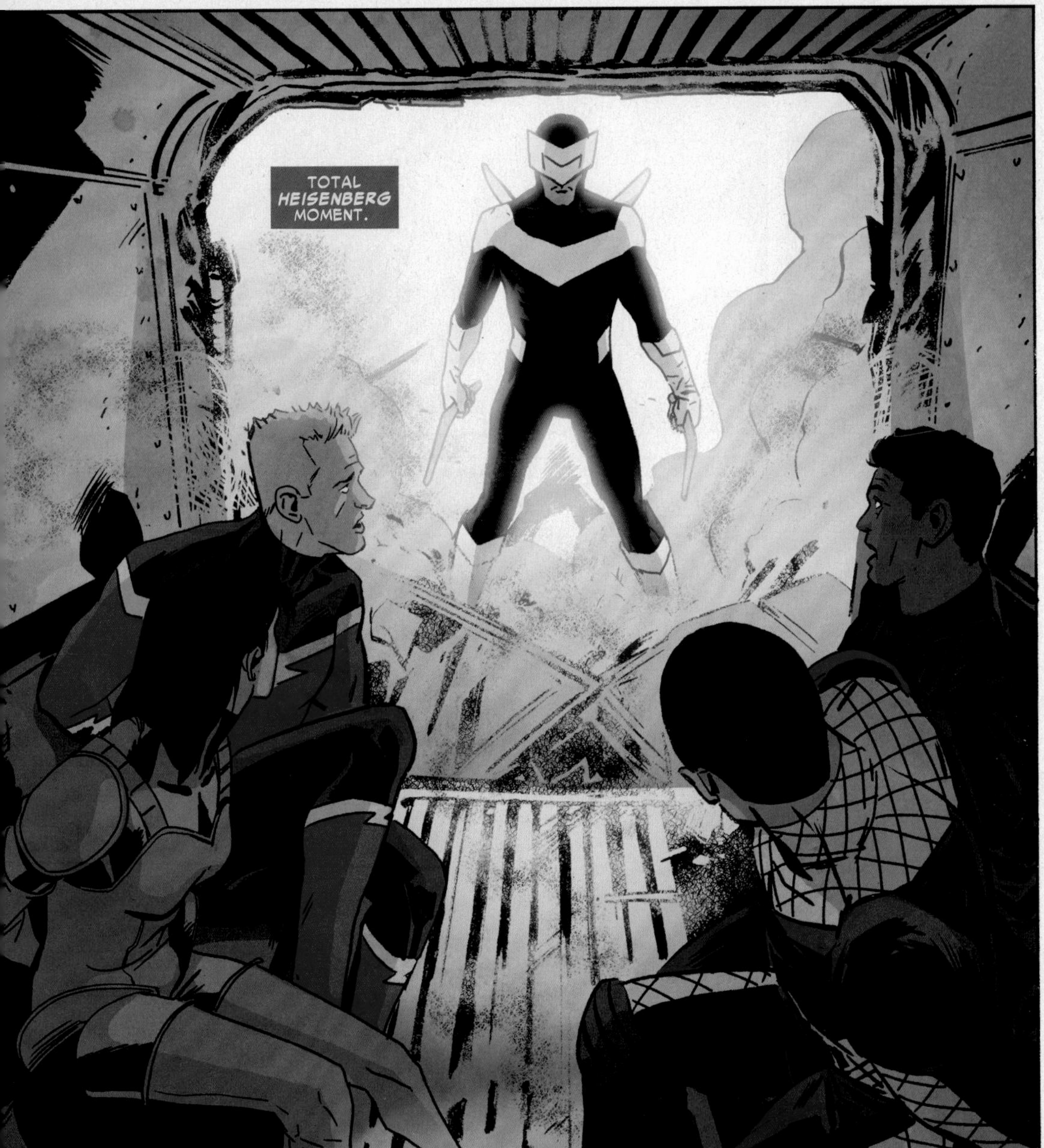
TOTAL
HEISENBERG
MOMENT.

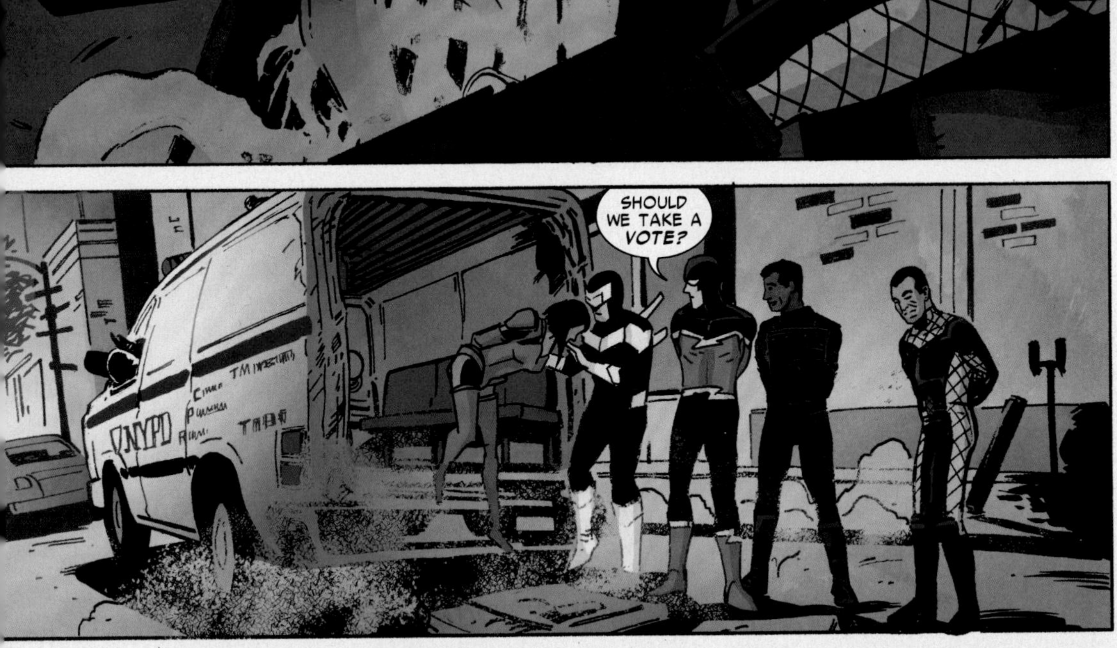
SHOULD
WE TAKE A
VOTE?
NYPD

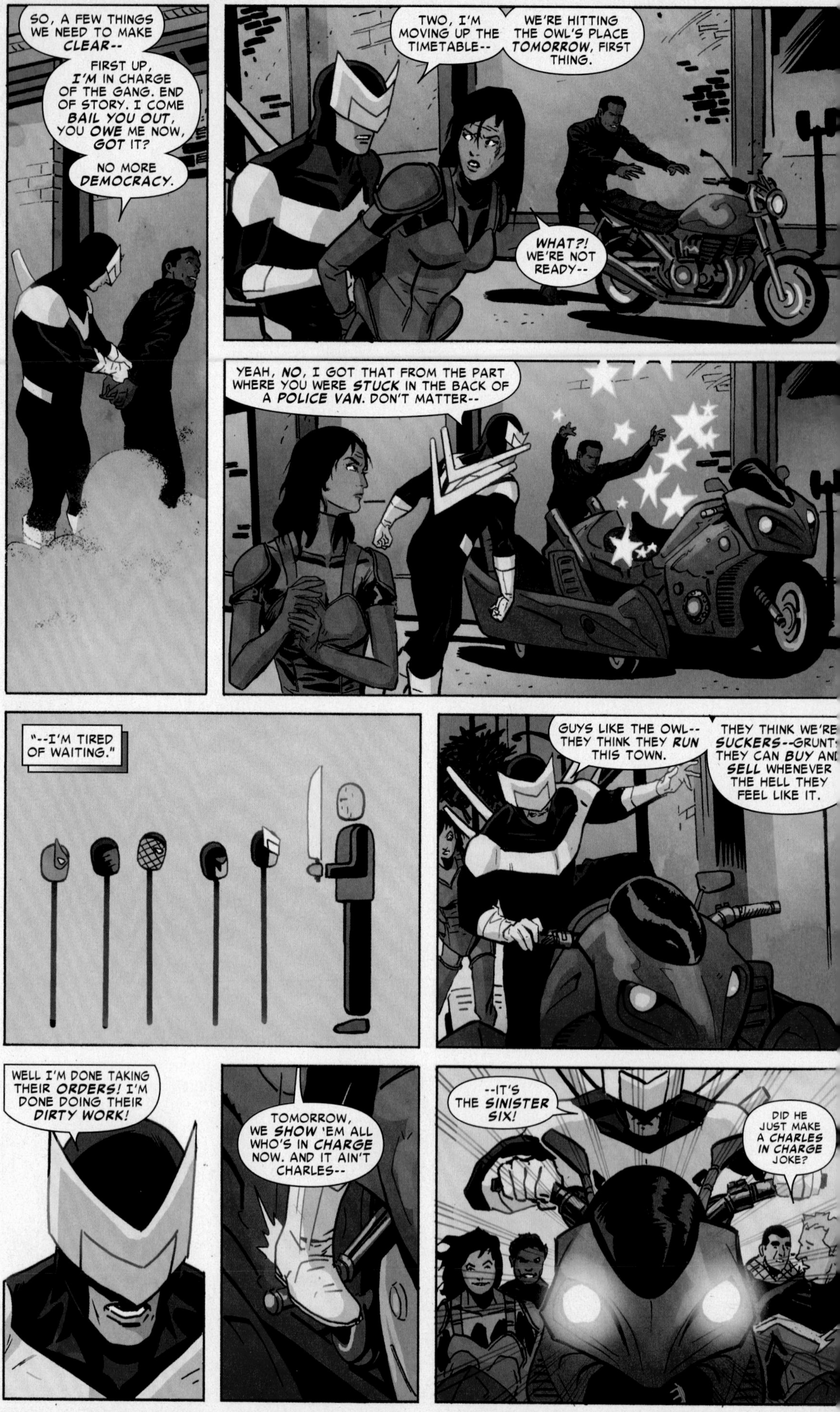

SO, A FEW THINGS WE NEED TO MAKE CLEAR--
FIRST UP, I'M IN CHARGE OF THE GANG. END OF STORY. I COME BAIL YOU OUT, YOU OWE ME NOW, GOT IT?
NO MORE DEMOCRACY.
TWO, I'M MOVING UP THE TIMETABLE--
WE'RE HITTING THE OWL'S PLACE TOMORROW, FIRST THING.
WHAT?! WE'RE NOT READY--
YEAH, NO, I GOT THAT FROM THE PART WHERE YOU WERE STUCK IN THE BACK OF A POLICE VAN. DON'T MATTER--
"--I'M TIRED OF WAITING."
GUYS LIKE THE OWL-- THEY THINK THEY RUN THIS TOWN.
THEY THINK WE'RE SUCKERS--GRUNTS THEY CAN BUY AND SELL WHENEVER THE HELL THEY FEEL LIKE IT.
WELL I'M DONE TAKING THEIR ORDERS! I'M DONE DOING THEIR DIRTY WORK!
TOMORROW, WE SHOW 'EM ALL WHO'S IN CHARGE NOW. AND IT AIN'T CHARLES--
--IT'S THE SINISTER SIX!
DID HE JUST MAKE A CHARLES IN CHARGE JOKE?

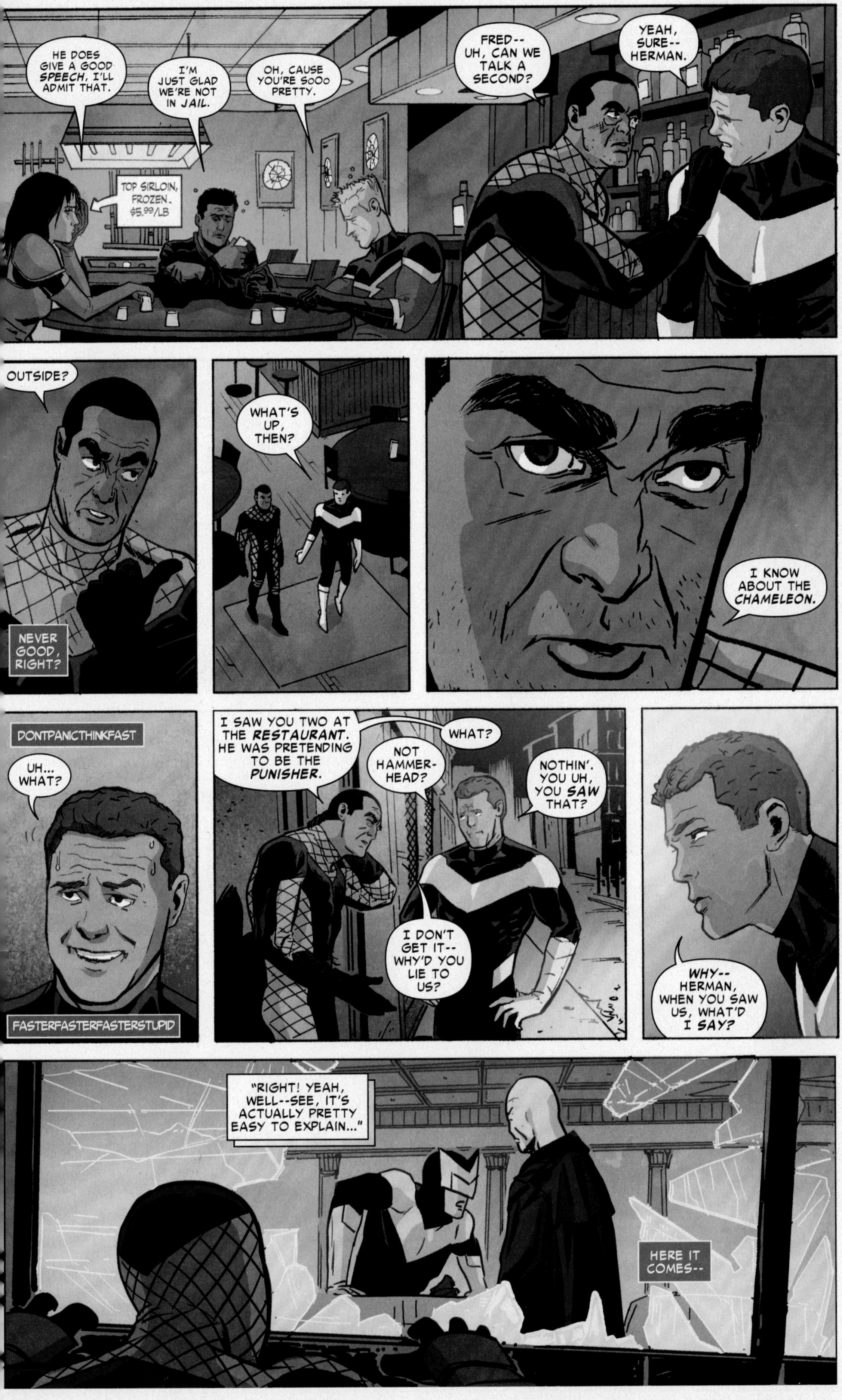

HE DOES GIVE A GOOD SPEECH, I'LL ADMIT THAT.
I'M JUST GLAD WE'RE NOT IN JAIL.
OH, CAUSE YOU'RE SOOOO PRETTY.
TOP SIRLOIN, FROZEN. $5.99/LB
FRED-- UH, CAN WE TALK A SECOND?
YEAH, SURE-- HERMAN.
OUTSIDE?
NEVER GOOD, RIGHT?
WHAT'S UP, THEN?
I KNOW ABOUT THE CHAMELEON.
DONTPANICTHINKFAST
UH... WHAT?
FASTERFASTERFASTERSTUPID
I SAW YOU TWO AT THE RESTAURANT. HE WAS PRETENDING TO BE THE PUNISHER.
WHAT?
NOT HAMMER-HEAD?
NOTHIN'. YOU UH, YOU SAW THAT?
I DON'T GET IT-- WHY'D YOU LIE TO US?
WHY-- HERMAN, WHEN YOU SAW US, WHAT'D I SAY?
"RIGHT! YEAH, WELL--SEE, IT'S ACTUALLY PRETTY EASY TO EXPLAIN..."
HERE IT COMES--

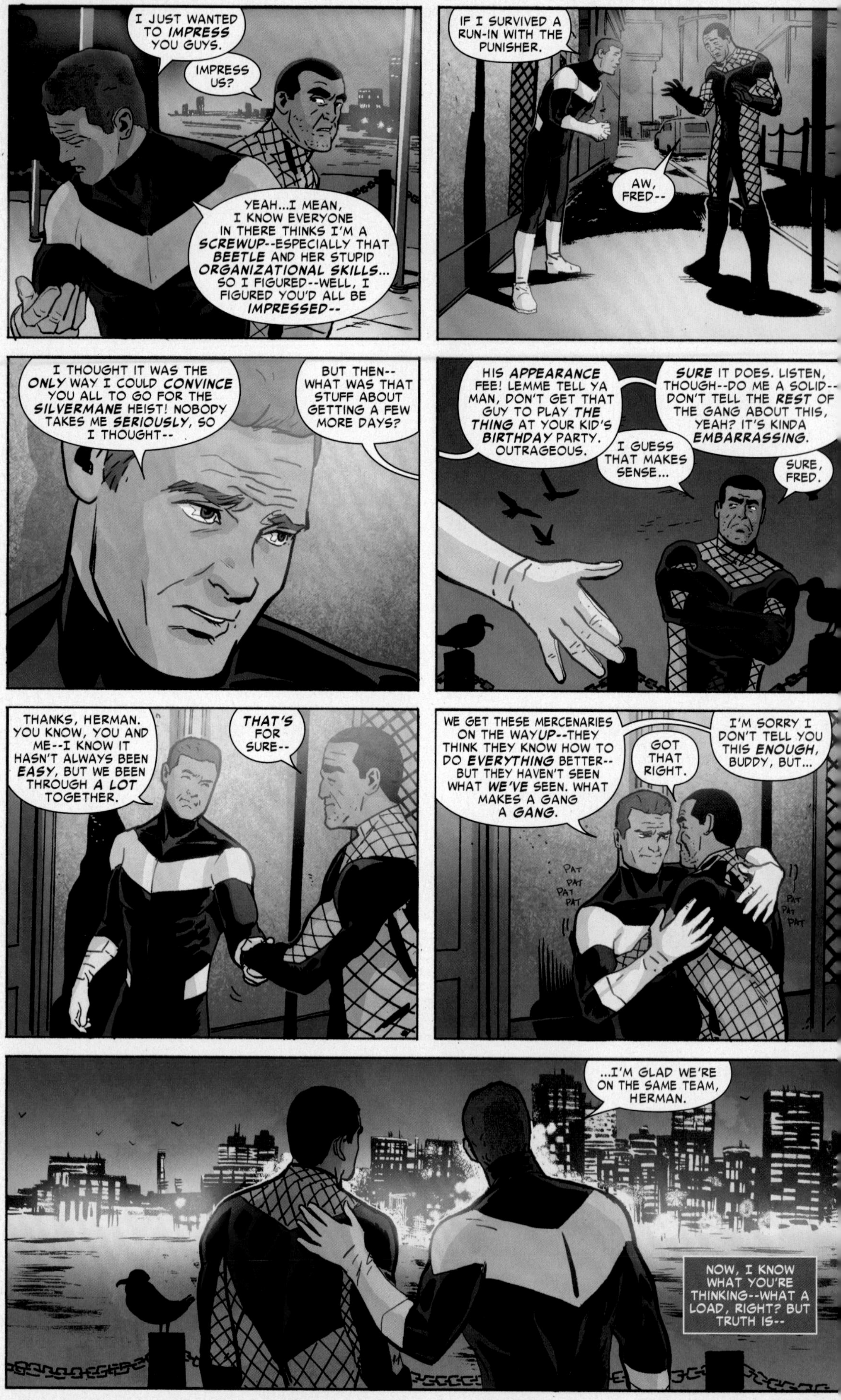
I JUST WANTED TO IMPRESS YOU GUYS.
IMPRESS US?
YEAH...I MEAN, I KNOW EVERYONE IN THERE THINKS I'M A SCREWUP--ESPECIALLY THAT BEETLE AND HER STUPID ORGANIZATIONAL SKILLS... SO I FIGURED--WELL, I FIGURED YOU'D ALL BE IMPRESSED--
IF I SURVIVED A RUN-IN WITH THE PUNISHER.
AW, FRED--
I THOUGHT IT WAS THE ONLY WAY I COULD CONVINCE YOU ALL TO GO FOR THE SILVERMANE HEIST! NOBODY TAKES ME SERIOUSLY, SO I THOUGHT--
BUT THEN-- WHAT WAS THAT STUFF ABOUT GETTING A FEW MORE DAYS?
HIS APPEARANCE FEE! LEMME TELL YA MAN, DON'T GET THAT GUY TO PLAY THE THING AT YOUR KID'S BIRTHDAY PARTY. OUTRAGEOUS.
I GUESS THAT MAKES SENSE...
SURE IT DOES. LISTEN, THOUGH--DO ME A SOLID--DON'T TELL THE REST OF THE GANG ABOUT THIS, YEAH? IT'S KINDA EMBARRASSING.
SURE, FRED.
THANKS, HERMAN. YOU KNOW, YOU AND ME--I KNOW IT HASN'T ALWAYS BEEN EASY, BUT WE BEEN THROUGH A LOT TOGETHER.
THAT'S FOR SURE--
WE GET THESE MERCENARIES ON THE WAYUP--THEY THINK THEY KNOW HOW TO DO EVERYTHING BETTER--BUT THEY HAVEN'T SEEN WHAT WE'VE SEEN. WHAT MAKES A GANG A GANG.
GOT THAT RIGHT.
I'M SORRY I DON'T TELL YOU THIS ENOUGH, BUDDY, BUT...
PAT PAT PAT PAT
PAT PAT PAT
...I'M GLAD WE'RE ON THE SAME TEAM, HERMAN.
NOW, I KNOW WHAT YOU'RE THINKING--WHAT A LOAD, RIGHT? BUT TRUTH IS--

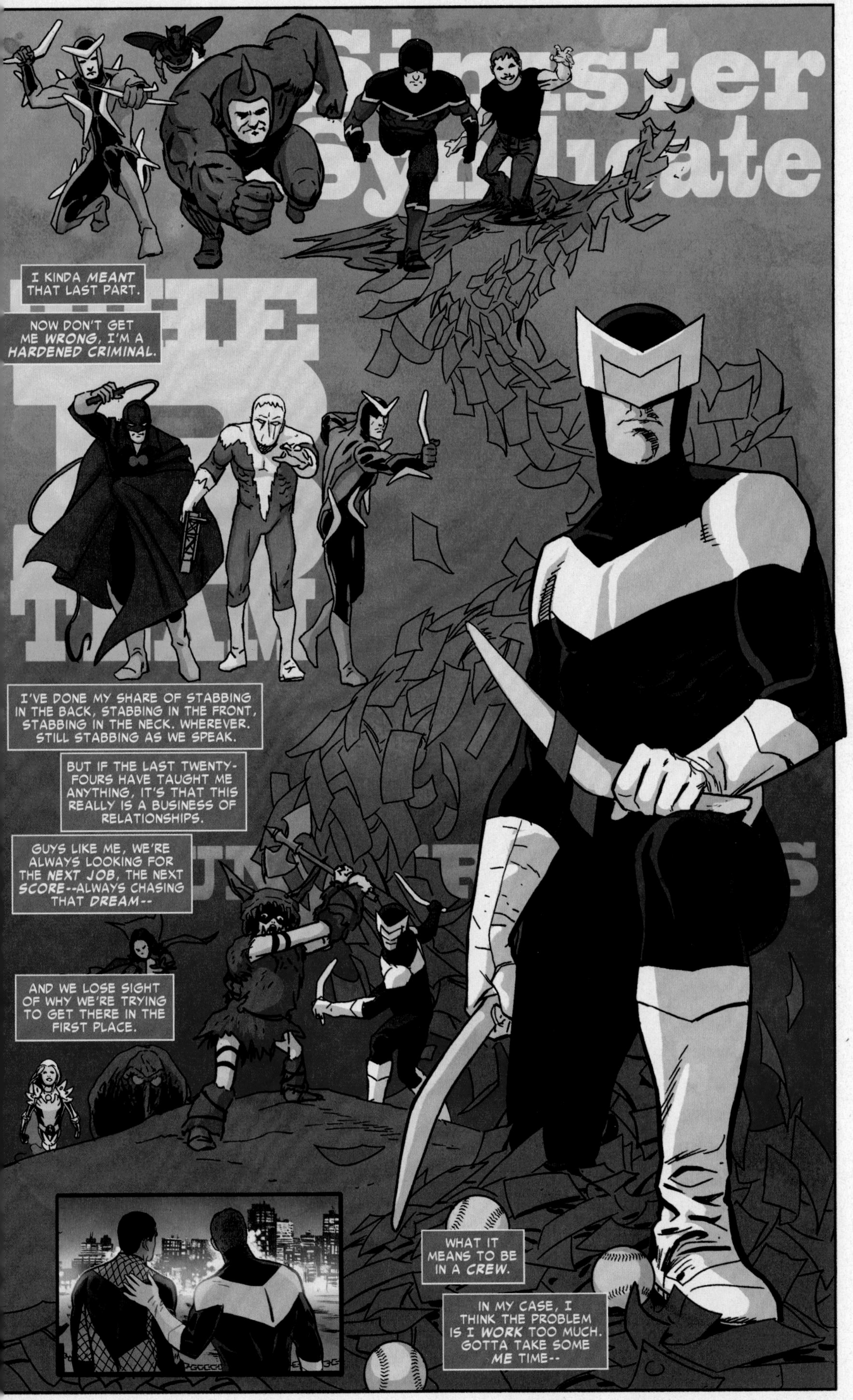

I KINDA MEANT THAT LAST PART.
NOW DON'T GET ME WRONG, I'M A HARDENED CRIMINAL.
I'VE DONE MY SHARE OF STABBING IN THE BACK, STABBING IN THE FRONT, STABBING IN THE NECK. WHEREVER. STILL STABBING AS WE SPEAK.
BUT IF THE LAST TWENTY-FOURS HAVE TAUGHT ME ANYTHING, IT'S THAT THIS REALLY IS A BUSINESS OF RELATIONSHIPS.
GUYS LIKE ME, WE'RE ALWAYS LOOKING FOR THE NEXT JOB, THE NEXT SCORE--ALWAYS CHASING THAT DREAM--
AND WE LOSE SIGHT OF WHY WE'RE TRYING TO GET THERE IN THE FIRST PLACE.
WHAT IT MEANS TO BE IN A CREW.
IN MY CASE, I THINK THE PROBLEM IS I WORK TOO MUCH. GOTTA TAKE SOME ME TIME--

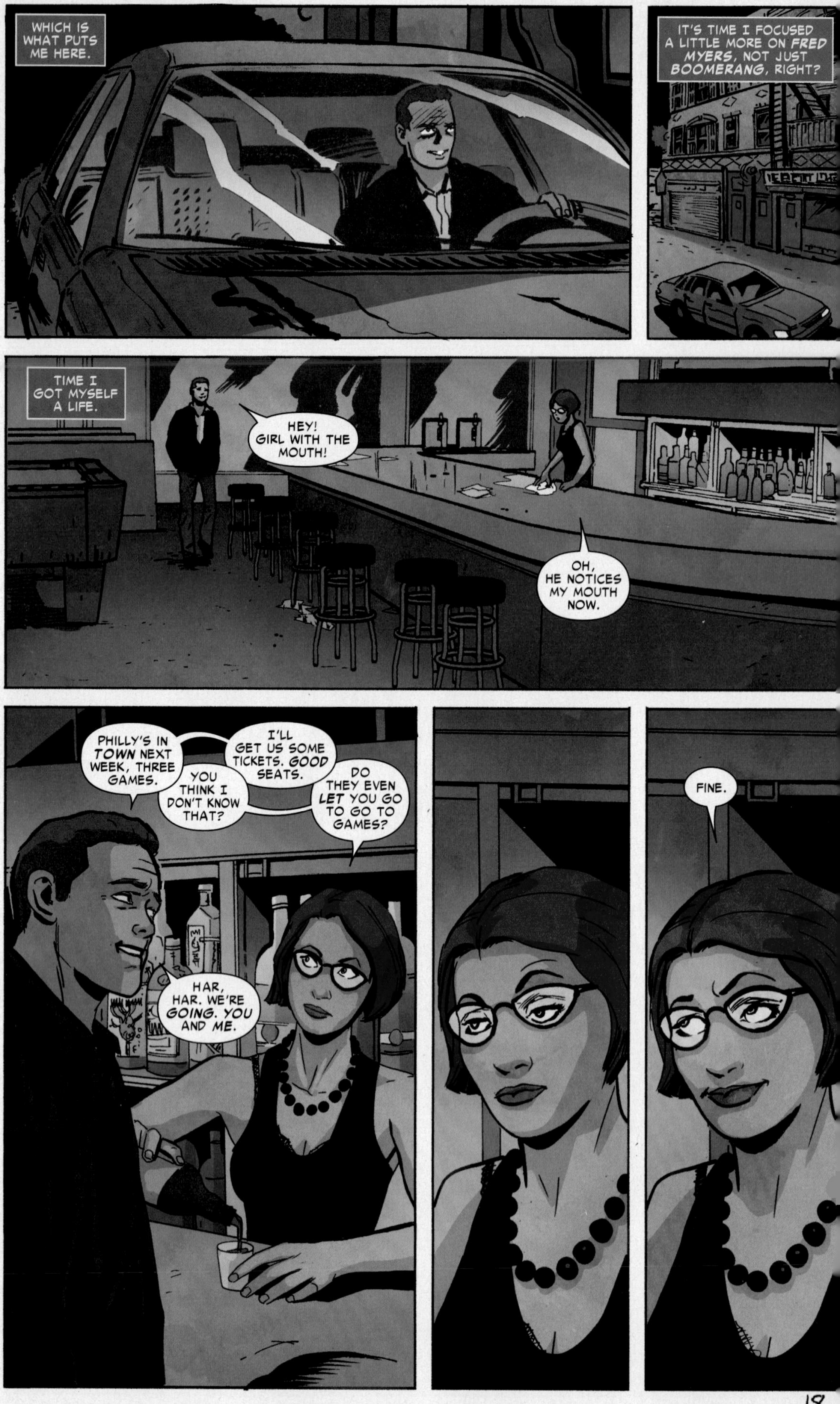
WHICH IS WHAT PUTS ME HERE.
IT'S TIME I FOCUSED A LITTLE MORE ON FRED MYERS, NOT JUST BOOMERANG, RIGHT?
TIME I GOT MYSELF A LIFE.
HEY! GIRL WITH THE MOUTH!
OH, HE NOTICES MY MOUTH NOW.
PHILLY'S IN TOWN NEXT WEEK, THREE GAMES.
YOU THINK I DON'T KNOW THAT?
I'LL GET US SOME TICKETS. GOOD SEATS.
DO THEY EVEN LET YOU GO TO GO TO GAMES?
HAR, HAR. WE'RE GOING. YOU AND ME.
FINE.

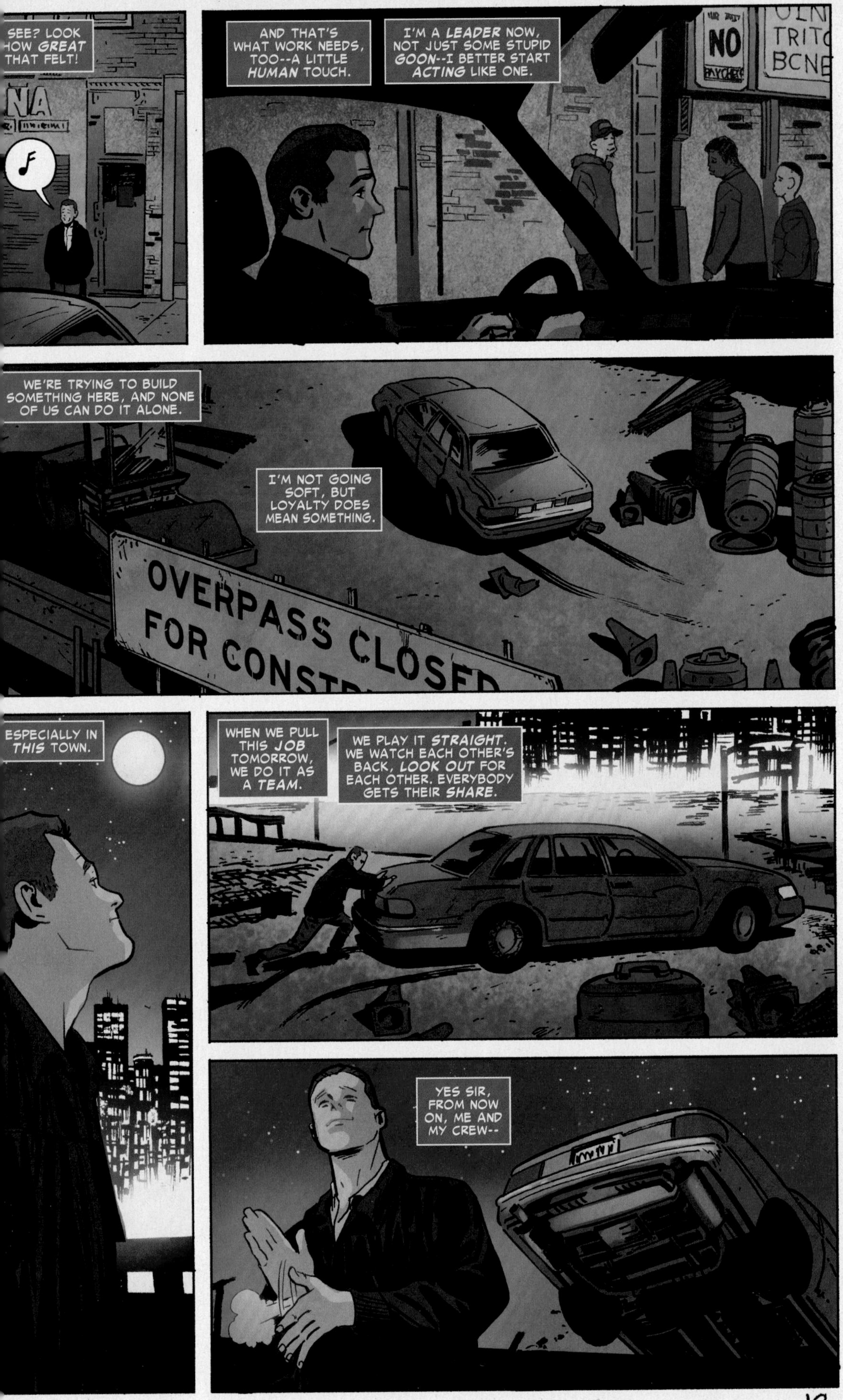

SEE? LOOK HOW GREAT THAT FELT!
AND THAT'S WHAT WORK NEEDS, TOO--A LITTLE HUMAN TOUCH.
I'M A LEADER NOW, NOT JUST SOME STUPID GOON--I BETTER START ACTING LIKE ONE.
NO
PAYCHECK
WE'RE TRYING TO BUILD SOMETHING HERE, AND NONE OF US CAN DO IT ALONE.
I'M NOT GOING SOFT, BUT LOYALTY DOES MEAN SOMETHING.
OVERPASS CLOSED FOR CONSTR
ESPECIALLY IN THIS TOWN.
WHEN WE PULL THIS JOB TOMORROW, WE DO IT AS A TEAM.
WE PLAY IT STRAIGHT. WE WATCH EACH OTHER'S BACK, LOOK OUT FOR EACH OTHER. EVERYBODY GETS THEIR SHARE.
YES SIR, FROM NOW ON, ME AND MY CREW--

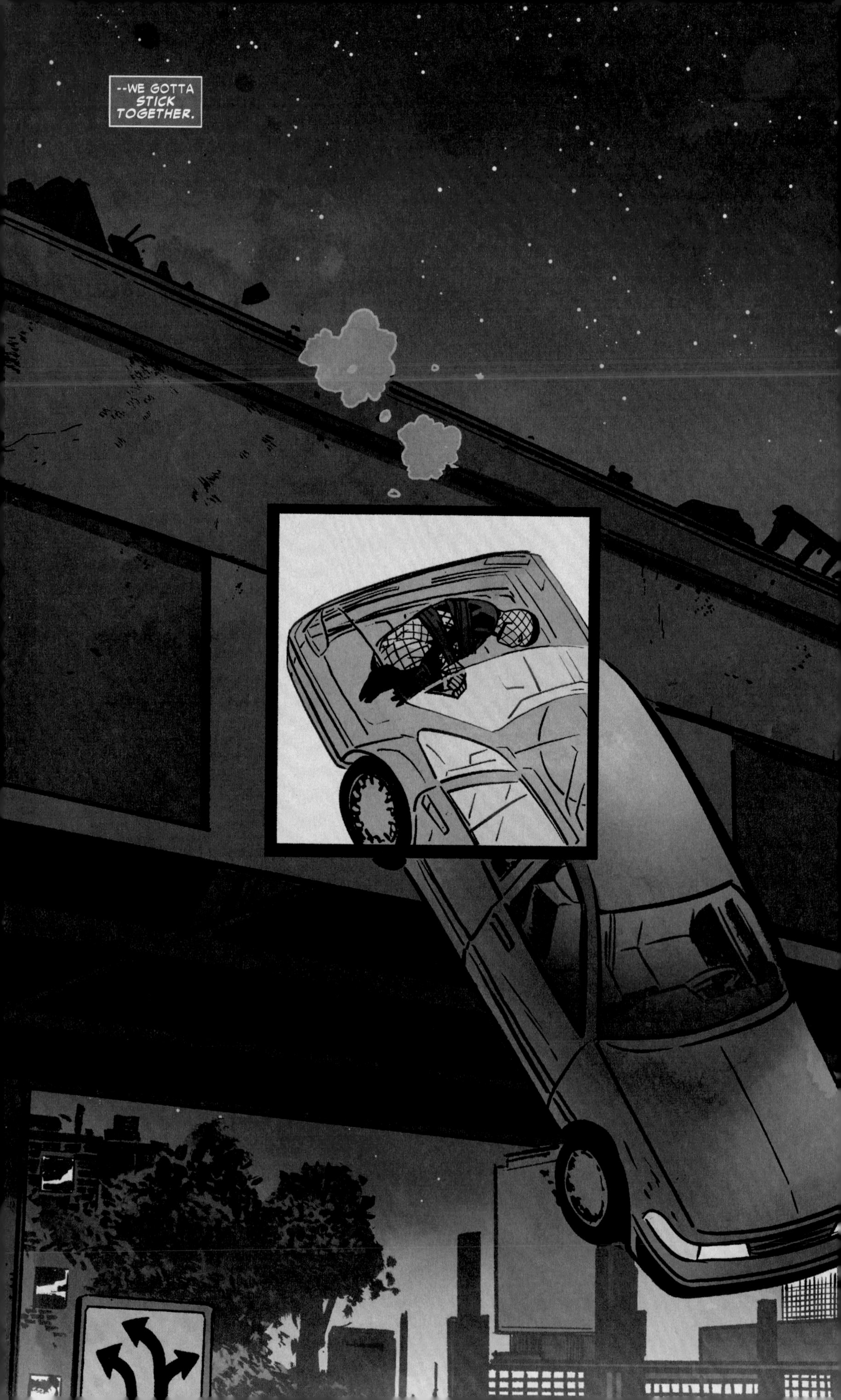
--WE GOTTA STICK TOGETHER.

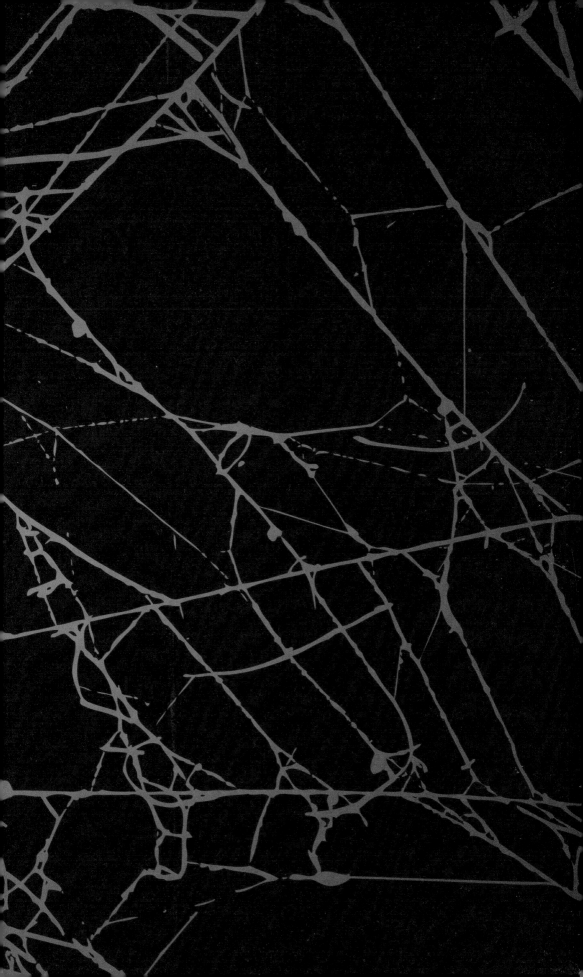

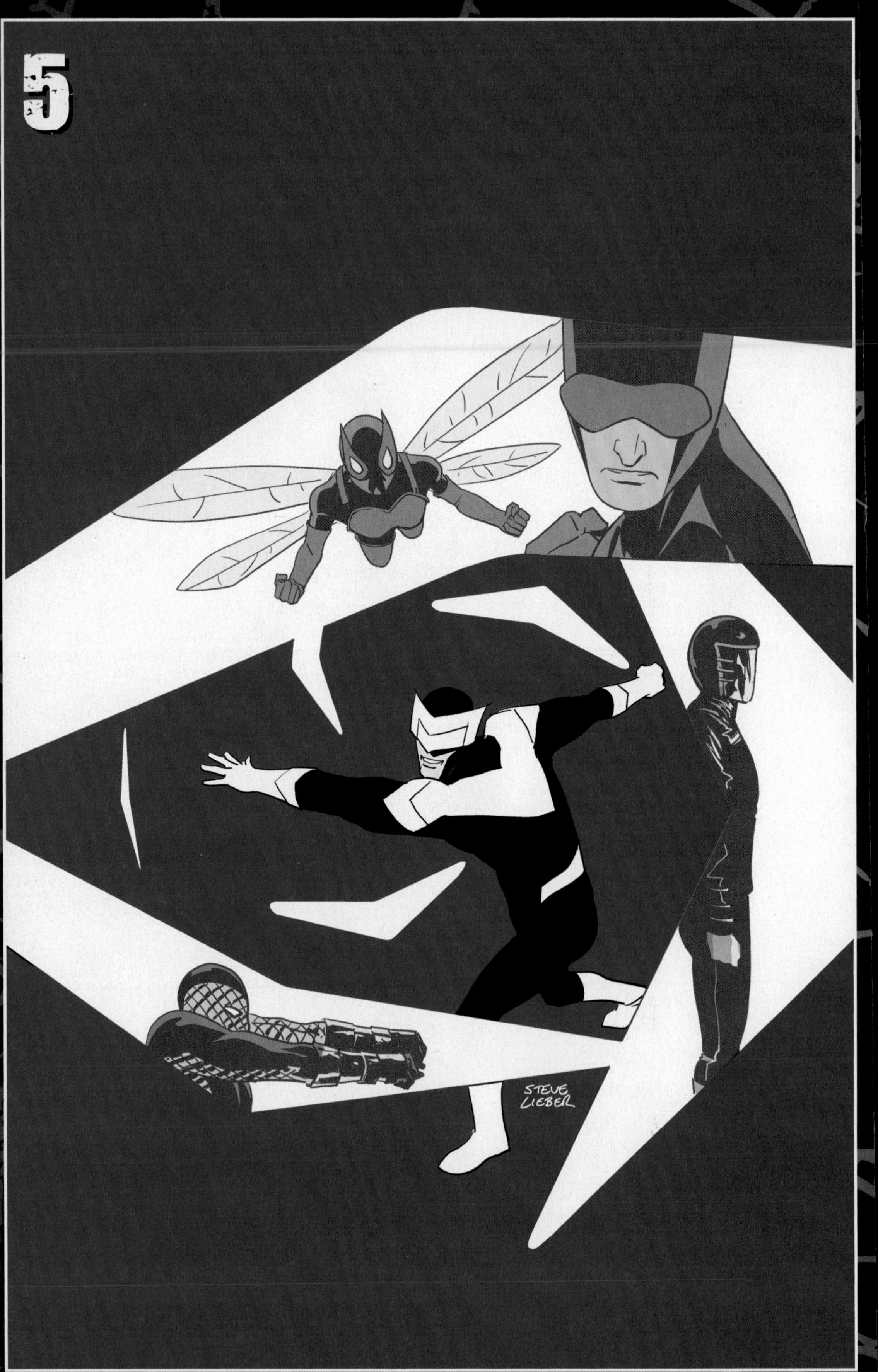
5
STEVE LIEBER

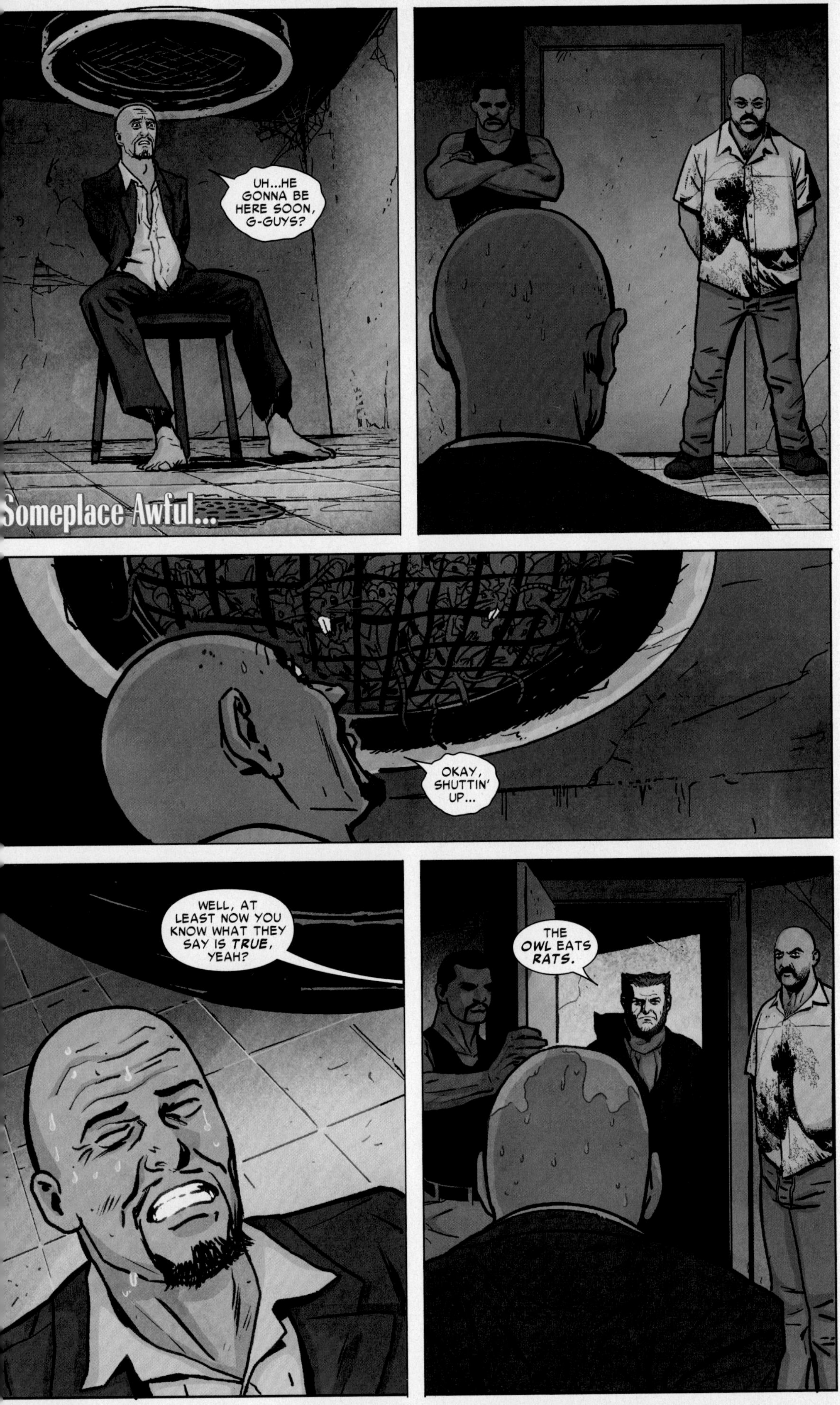
UH...HE GONNA BE HERE SOON, G-GUYS?
Someplace Awful...
OKAY, SHUTTIN' UP...
WELL, AT LEAST NOW YOU KNOW WHAT THEY SAY IS TRUE, YEAH?
THE OWL EATS RATS.

M--MISTER OWL, PLEASE--

PROBLEM I HAVE IS KEEPING THE RATS *FED*. THESE THINGS GO AT IT LIKE I'VE NEVER SEEN. THEY SAY, IF YOU PUT TWO OF THEM IN A ROOM TOGETHER, THERE'LL BE TWO *THOUSAND* OF 'EM IN A YEAR. THAT'S *SCIENCE*. AND A BURDEN ON ME.

P-PLEASE, SIR...

THE OTHER DILEMMA IS THIS--THEIR *TEETH*, THEY NEVER STOP *GROWING*. HAL A FOOT A YEAR THEY GRO DID YOU *KNOW* THAT? THE WILL CHEW YOU OUT OF HOUSE AND HOME, JUST TO KEEP GRINDING 'EM DOWN.

BUT THEY ARE *PRECIOU* LITTLE CREATURE I HAVE TO GIVE THEM THAT.

SO, TOMMY, IT SEEMS WE DON'T HAVE A LOT OF *TIME*, NOW DO WE? BEST WE GET DOWN TO THE OLD *BRASS TACKS* OF IT, YEAH?

YOU'VE BEEN CAUGHT WITH YOUR HAND IN MOMMY'S KNICKER DRAWER.

I DIDN'T KNOW IT WAS *YOU*, SIR--I SWEAR TO *GOD*, I DIDN'T KNOW!

BUT YOU DO *NOW*, DON'T YOU, TOMMY? YOU ARE *AWARE* OF THIS SORRY STATE OF AFFAIRS WE NOW FIND OURSELVES IN.

I DO, I *DO*--I JUST-- I CAN *FIX* IT-- I *SWEAR* TO YOU--

NOW THAT'S WHAT I'M HERE FOR. THAT'S WHAT I'M *HOPING* FOR. THAT YOU CAN *RETURN* THE MONEY YOU TOOK FROM ME, ALONG WITH A HEALTHY LITTLE RETURN ON *INVESTMENT*. NOTHING TOO EXTRAORDINARY.

SEE, IF YOU COULD DO *THAT*, I MIGHT EVEN CONSIDER DOING *MORE* BUSINESS WITH YOU IN THE FUTURE. I'M A VERY FORGIVING MAN THAT WAY.

CAN YOU *DO* THAT, THEN, TOMMY?

I DON'T--I DON'T *HAVE* IT RIGHT NOW...

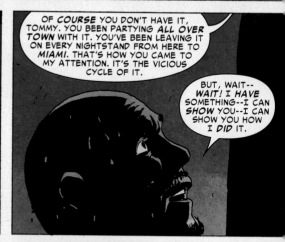

OF *COURSE* YOU DON'T HAVE IT, TOMMY. YOU BEEN PARTYING *ALL OVER TOWN* WITH IT. YOU'VE BEEN LEAVING IT ON EVERY NIGHTSTAND FROM HERE TO *MIAMI*. THAT'S HOW YOU CAME TO MY ATTENTION. IT'S THE VICIOUS CYCLE OF IT.

BUT, WAIT-- *WAIT*! I *HAVE* SOMETHING--I CAN *SHOW* YOU--I CAN SHOW YOU HOW I *DID* IT.

I CAN SHOW YOU HOW I TOOK IT WITHOUT YOU *FINDING* ME OUT FOR SO LONG. I CAN SHOW YOU THE *WEAK SPOTS* IN YOUR BOOKS. AND YOU COULD--YOU COULD APPLY IT TO YOUR *OWN* CLIENTS. YOU COULD MAKE A *LOT* MORE THAN I TOOK!

MM. YOU'LL *SHOW* ME, YEAH? HOW YOU PULLED THE *WOOL* OVER THESE *EYES*?

YES! YES!

NOW THAT IS AN INTERESTING *PROPOSITION* THERE, TOMMY. BUT IT DOES REMIND ME OF A *STORY* FROM BACK IN THE *OLD DAYS*. I CAN TELL IT TO YOU, IF YOU'D LIKE.

OH, GOD...

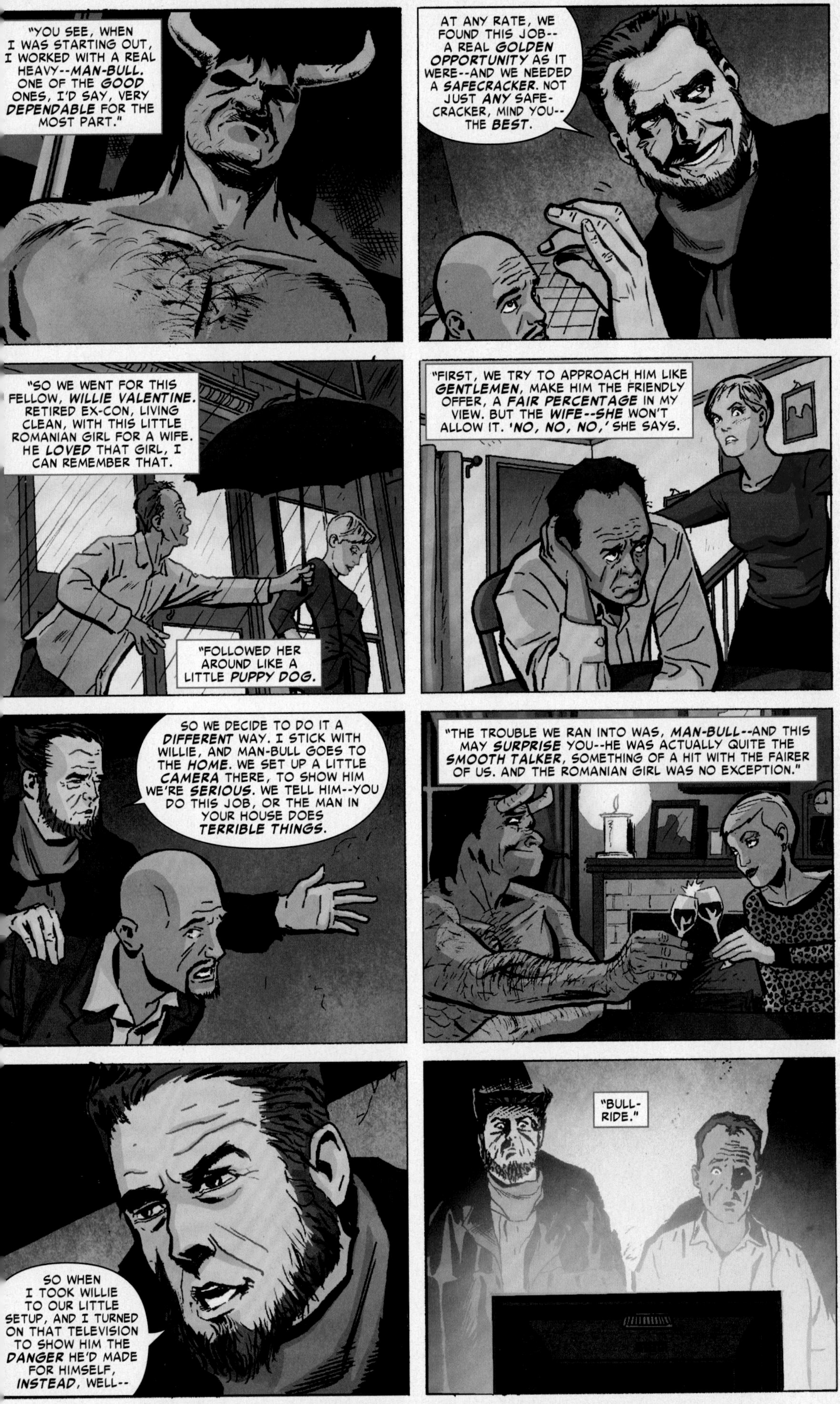
"YOU SEE, WHEN I WAS STARTING OUT, I WORKED WITH A REAL HEAVY--MAN-BULL. ONE OF THE GOOD ONES, I'D SAY, VERY DEPENDABLE FOR THE MOST PART."
AT ANY RATE, WE FOUND THIS JOB-- A REAL GOLDEN OPPORTUNITY AS IT WERE--AND WE NEEDED A SAFECRACKER. NOT JUST ANY SAFE-CRACKER, MIND YOU-- THE BEST.
"SO WE WENT FOR THIS FELLOW, WILLIE VALENTINE. RETIRED EX-CON, LIVING CLEAN, WITH THIS LITTLE ROMANIAN GIRL FOR A WIFE. HE LOVED THAT GIRL, I CAN REMEMBER THAT.
"FOLLOWED HER AROUND LIKE A LITTLE PUPPY DOG.
"FIRST, WE TRY TO APPROACH HIM LIKE GENTLEMEN, MAKE HIM THE FRIENDLY OFFER, A FAIR PERCENTAGE IN MY VIEW. BUT THE WIFE--SHE WON'T ALLOW IT. 'NO, NO, NO,' SHE SAYS.
SO WE DECIDE TO DO IT A DIFFERENT WAY. I STICK WITH WILLIE, AND MAN-BULL GOES TO THE HOME. WE SET UP A LITTLE CAMERA THERE, TO SHOW HIM WE'RE SERIOUS. WE TELL HIM--YOU DO THIS JOB, OR THE MAN IN YOUR HOUSE DOES TERRIBLE THINGS.
"THE TROUBLE WE RAN INTO WAS, MAN-BULL--AND THIS MAY SURPRISE YOU--HE WAS ACTUALLY QUITE THE SMOOTH TALKER, SOMETHING OF A HIT WITH THE FAIRER OF US. AND THE ROMANIAN GIRL WAS NO EXCEPTION."
SO WHEN I TOOK WILLIE TO OUR LITTLE SETUP, AND I TURNED ON THAT TELEVISION TO SHOW HIM THE DANGER HE'D MADE FOR HIMSELF, INSTEAD, WELL--
"BULL-RIDE."

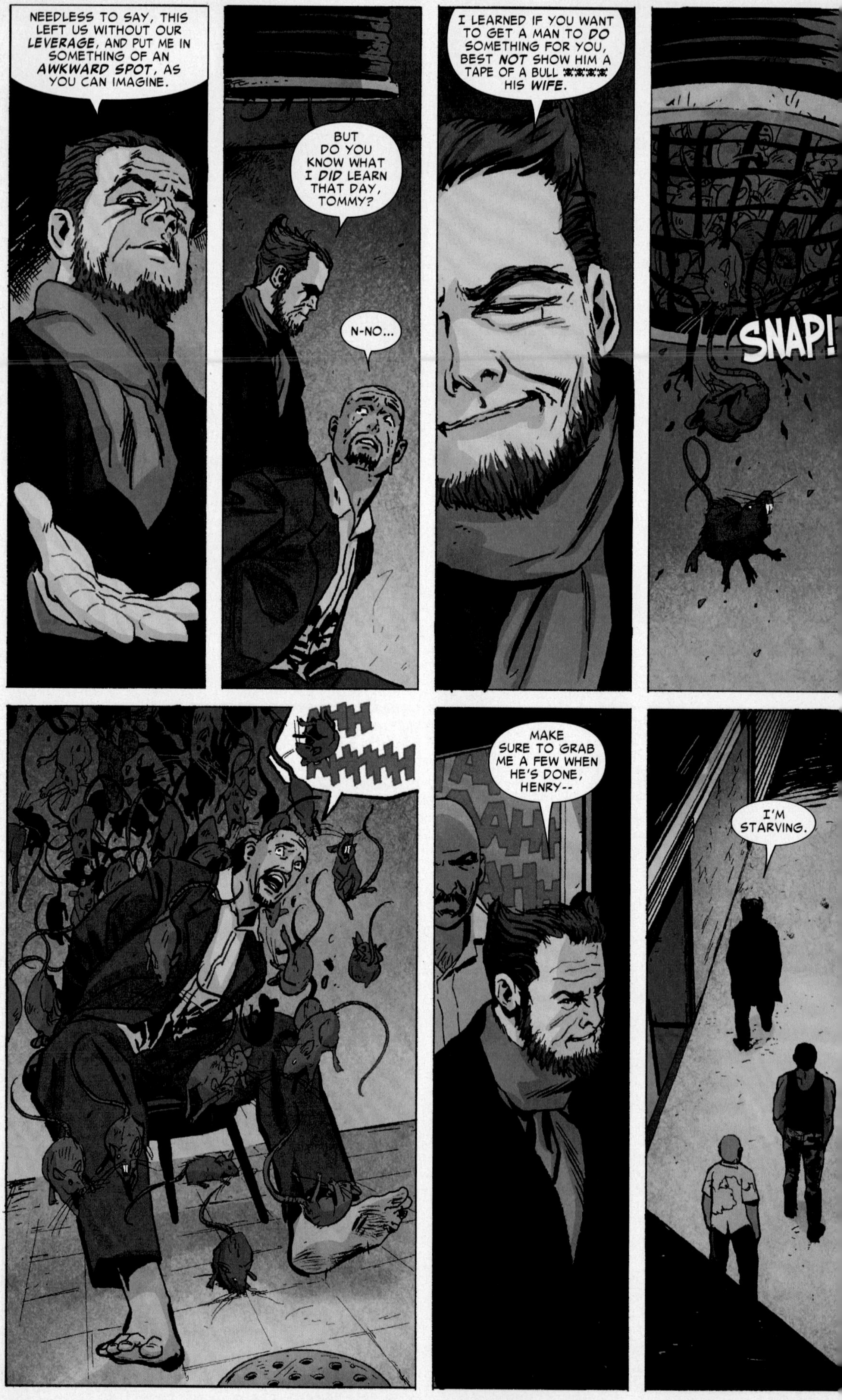
NEEDLESS TO SAY, THIS LEFT US WITHOUT OUR LEVERAGE, AND PUT ME IN SOMETHING OF AN AWKWARD SPOT, AS YOU CAN IMAGINE.
BUT DO YOU KNOW WHAT I DID LEARN THAT DAY, TOMMY?
N-NO...
I LEARNED IF YOU WANT TO GET A MAN TO DO SOMETHING FOR YOU, BEST NOT SHOW HIM A TAPE OF A BULL ☠✖☠ HIS WIFE.
SNAP!
AHH AHHHHH
MAKE SURE TO GRAB ME A FEW WHEN HE'S DONE, HENRY--
I'M STARVING.

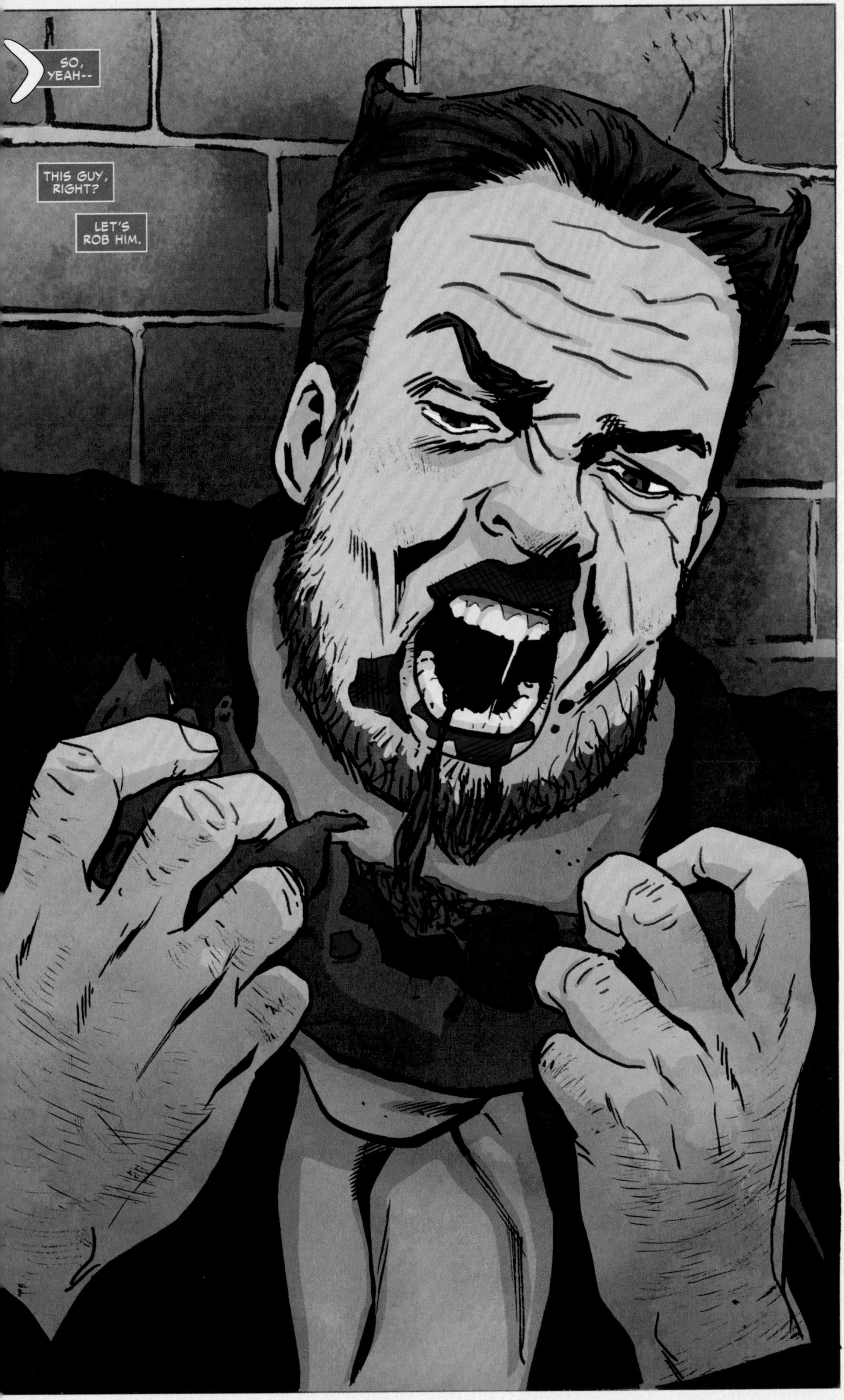
SO, YEAH--
THIS GUY, RIGHT?
LET'S ROB HIM.

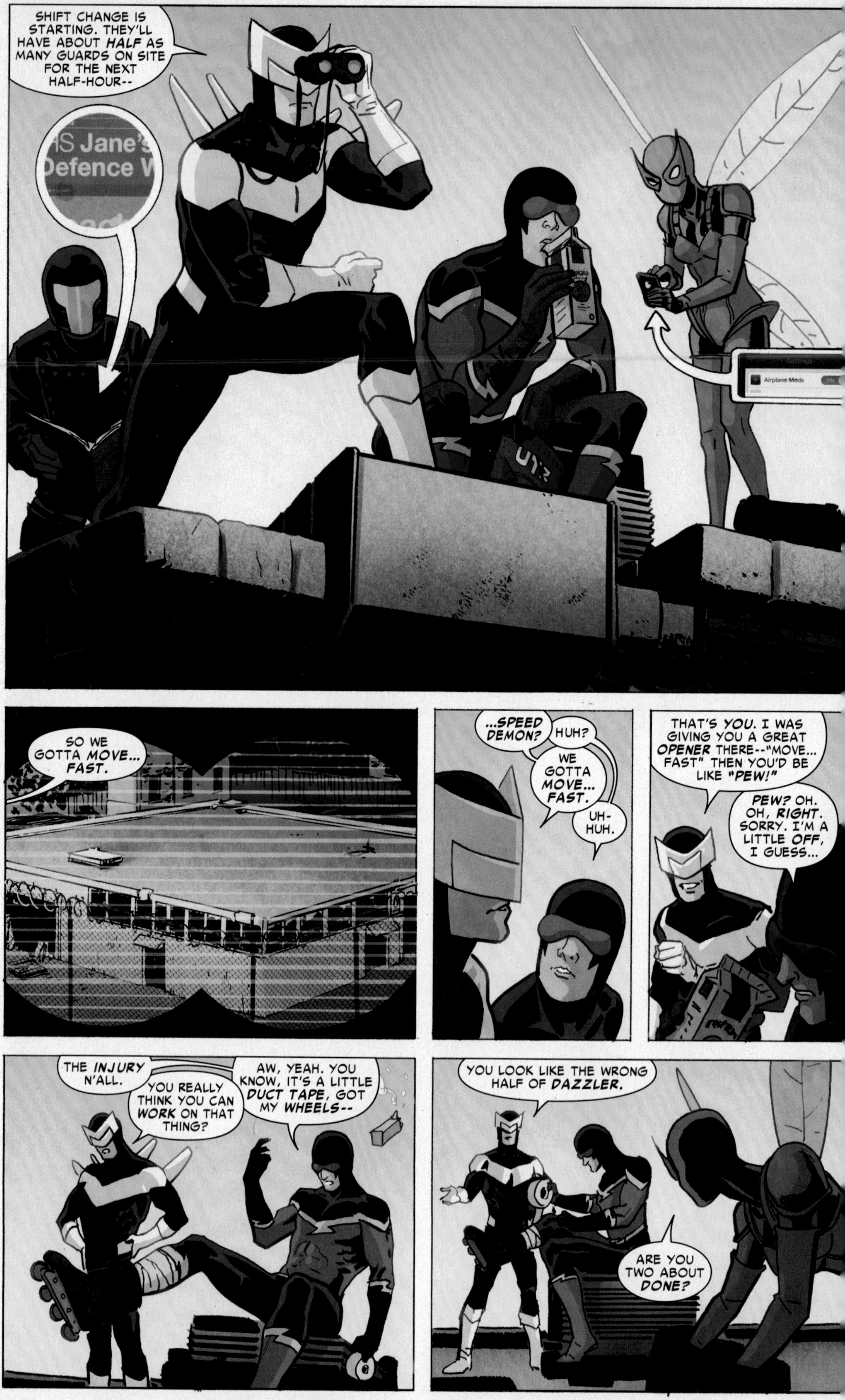

SHIFT CHANGE IS STARTING. THEY'LL HAVE ABOUT HALF AS MANY GUARDS ON SITE FOR THE NEXT HALF-HOUR--
Jane's Defence W
Airplane Mode
ON
SO WE GOTTA MOVE... FAST.
...SPEED DEMON?
HUH?
WE GOTTA MOVE... FAST.
UH-HUH.
THAT'S YOU. I WAS GIVING YOU A GREAT OPENER THERE--"MOVE... FAST" THEN YOU'D BE LIKE "PEW!"
PEW? OH. OH, RIGHT. SORRY. I'M A LITTLE OFF, I GUESS...
THE INJURY N'ALL.
YOU REALLY THINK YOU CAN WORK ON THAT THING?
AW, YEAH. YOU KNOW, IT'S A LITTLE DUCT TAPE, GOT MY WHEELS--
YOU LOOK LIKE THE WRONG HALF OF DAZZLER.
ARE YOU TWO ABOUT DONE?

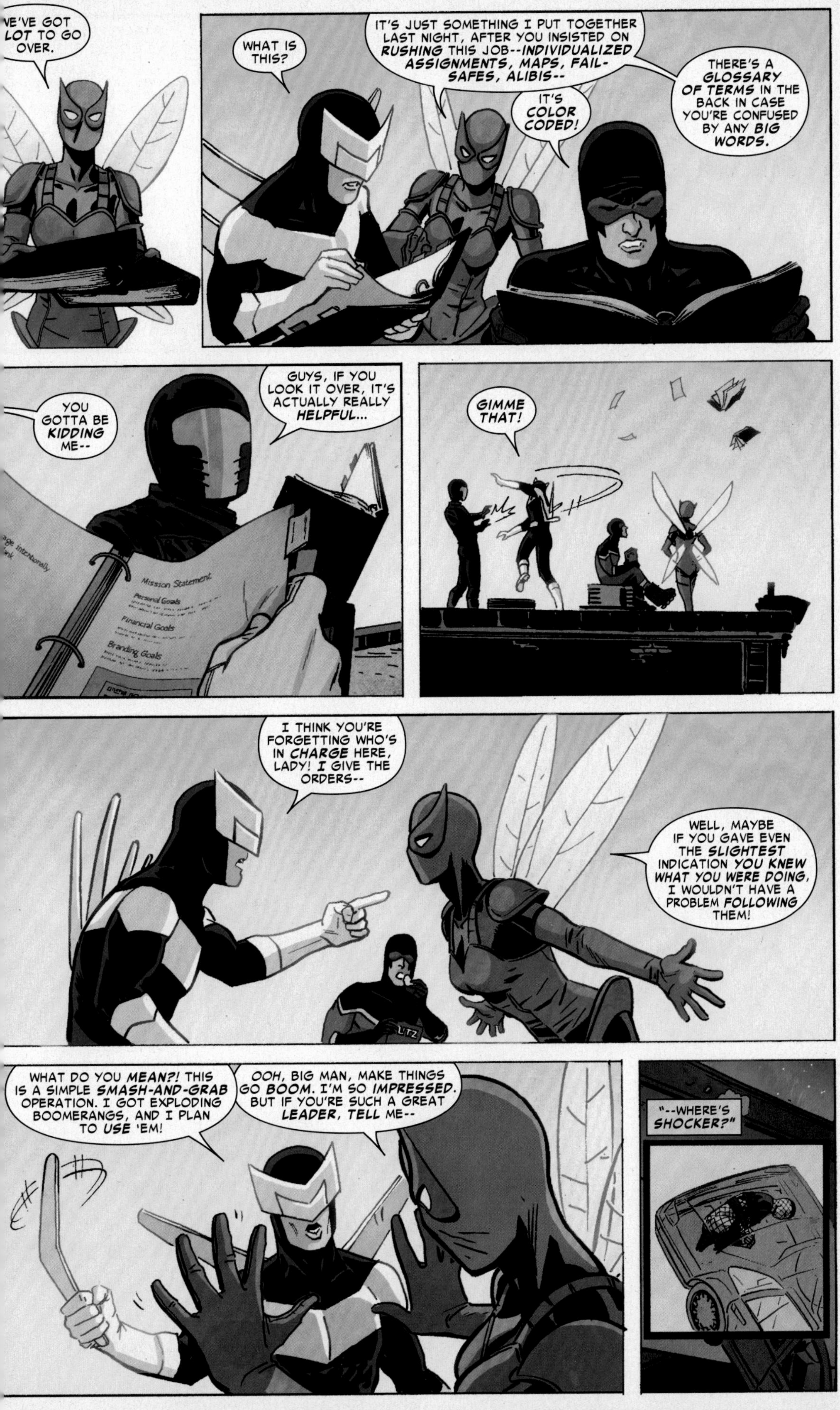

WE'VE GOT A LOT TO GO OVER.
WHAT IS THIS?
IT'S JUST SOMETHING I PUT TOGETHER LAST NIGHT, AFTER YOU INSISTED ON RUSHING THIS JOB--INDIVIDUALIZED ASSIGNMENTS, MAPS, FAIL-SAFES, ALIBIS--
IT'S COLOR CODED!
THERE'S A GLOSSARY OF TERMS IN THE BACK IN CASE YOU'RE CONFUSED BY ANY BIG WORDS.
YOU GOTTA BE KIDDING ME--
GUYS, IF YOU LOOK IT OVER, IT'S ACTUALLY REALLY HELPFUL...
Mission Statement
Personal Goals
Financial Goals
Branding Goals
GIMME THAT!
I THINK YOU'RE FORGETTING WHO'S IN CHARGE HERE, LADY! I GIVE THE ORDERS--
WELL, MAYBE IF YOU GAVE EVEN THE SLIGHTEST INDICATION YOU KNEW WHAT YOU WERE DOING, I WOULDN'T HAVE A PROBLEM FOLLOWING THEM!
WHAT DO YOU MEAN?! THIS IS A SIMPLE SMASH-AND-GRAB OPERATION. I GOT EXPLODING BOOMERANGS, AND I PLAN TO USE 'EM!
OOH, BIG MAN, MAKE THINGS GO BOOM. I'M SO IMPRESSED. BUT IF YOU'RE SUCH A GREAT LEADER, TELL ME--
"--WHERE'S SHOCKER?"

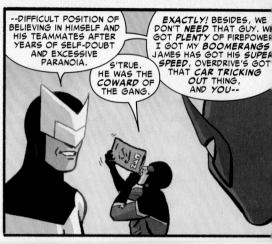

HERMAN? COME ON, I *TOLD* YOU, HE *CHICKENED OUT* LIKE ALWAYS.

OR, HE JUST DIDN'T HAVE CONFIDENCE IN YOUR *NON*-PLAN.

OR, I PUT HIM IN THE--

--DIFFICULT POSITION OF BELIEVING IN HIMSELF AND HIS TEAMMATES AFTER YEARS OF SELF-DOUBT AND EXCESSIVE PARANOIA.

S'TRUE. HE WAS THE *COWARD* OF THE GANG.

EXACTLY! BESIDES, WE DON'T *NEED* THAT GUY. W GOT *PLENTY* OF FIREPOWER I GOT MY *BOOMERANGS* JAMES HAS GOT HIS *SUPER SPEED*, OVERDRIVE'S GOT THAT *CAR TRICKING OUT* THING, AND *YOU*--

WELL, MAYBE YOU SHOULD JUST GO DOWN THERE AND *ANNOY* THE *HELL* OUT OF THOSE GUYS, TOO. MAYBE GIVE 'EM SOME *PAPERWORK* TO LOOK OVER.

NO? OKAY THEN. IF WE'RE *DONE* HERE, LIKE I SAID BEFORE--

WE GOTTA *MOVE*...

...*FAST*.

PEW

AWESOME.

KLAK

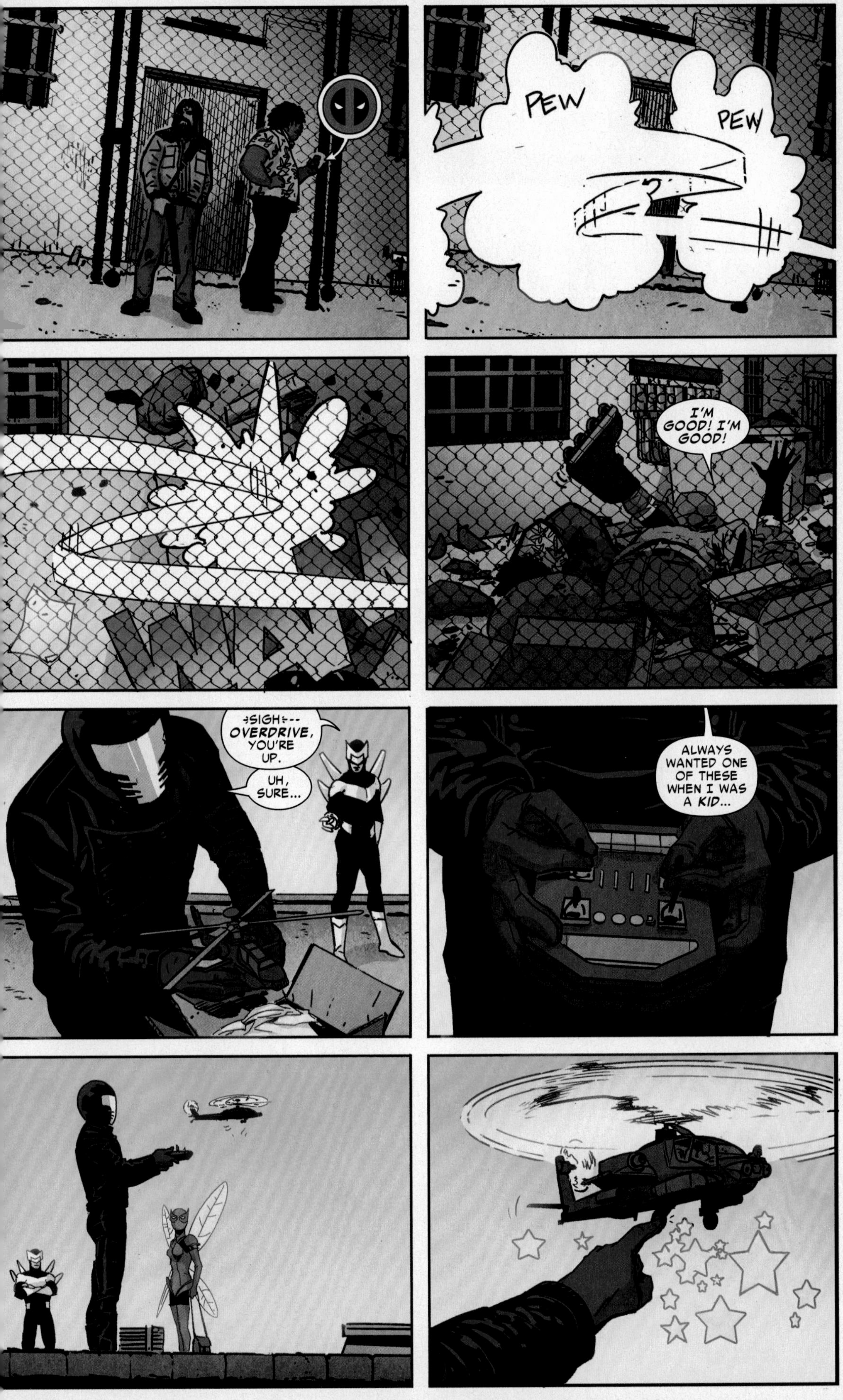
PEW
PEW
I'M GOOD! I'M GOOD!
+SIGH+-- OVERDRIVE, YOU'RE UP.
UH, SURE...
ALWAYS WANTED ONE OF THESE WHEN I WAS A KID...

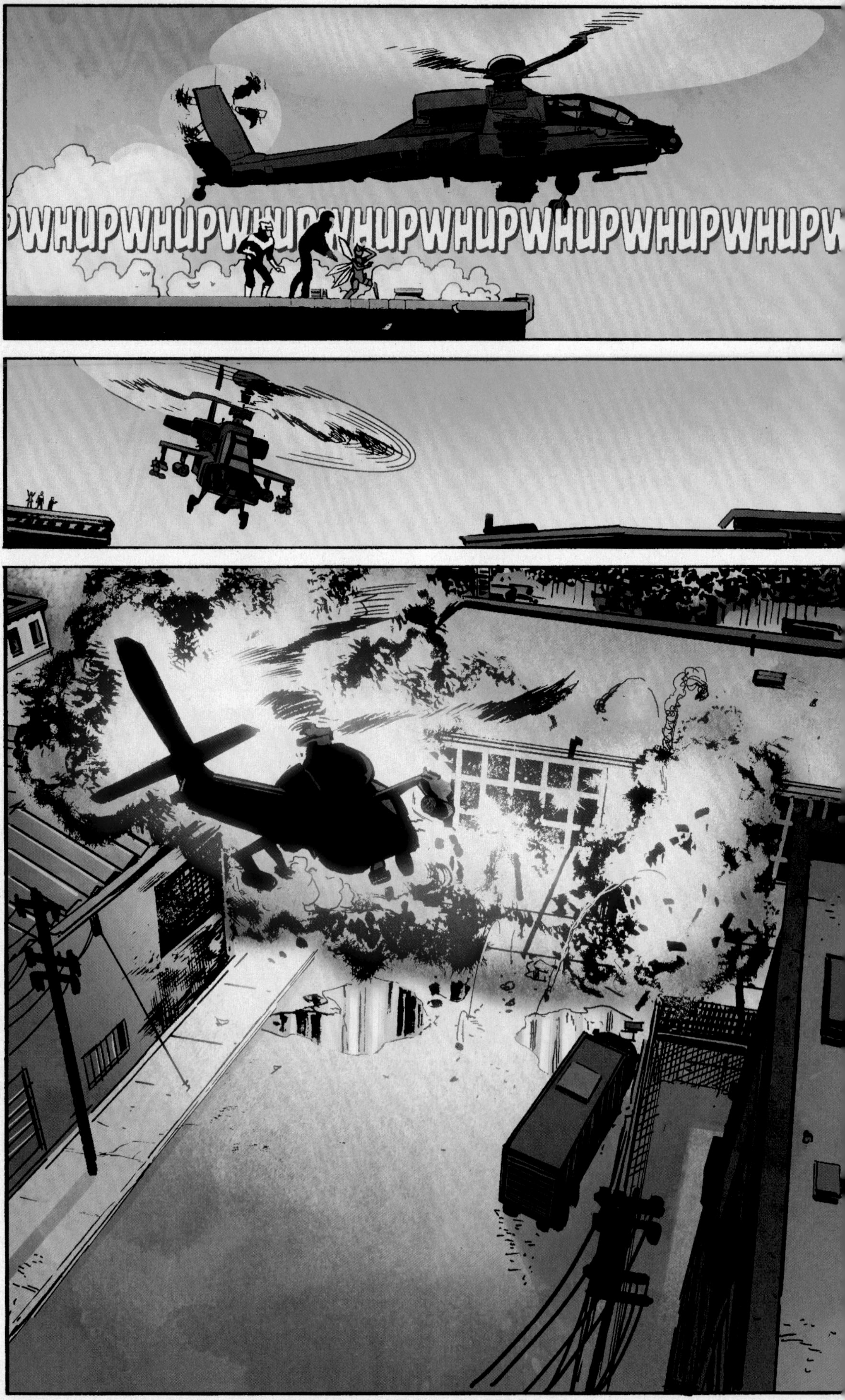
PWHUPWHUPWHUPWHUPWHUPWHUPWHUPWHUPW

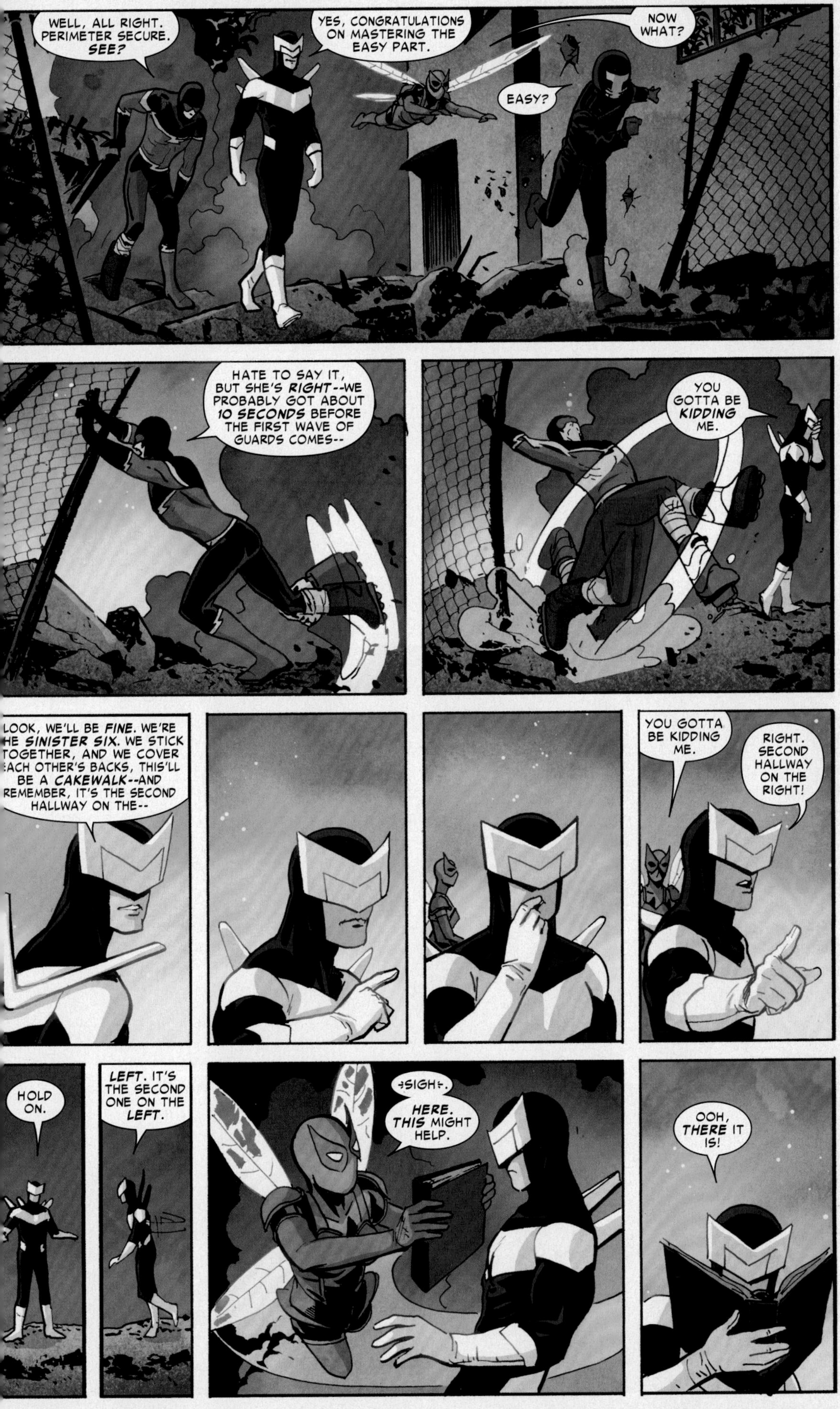
WELL, ALL RIGHT. PERIMETER SECURE. SEE?
YES, CONGRATULATIONS ON MASTERING THE EASY PART.
NOW WHAT?
EASY?
HATE TO SAY IT, BUT SHE'S RIGHT--WE PROBABLY GOT ABOUT 10 SECONDS BEFORE THE FIRST WAVE OF GUARDS COMES--
YOU GOTTA BE KIDDING ME.
LOOK, WE'LL BE FINE. WE'RE HE SINISTER SIX. WE STICK TOGETHER, AND WE COVER EACH OTHER'S BACKS, THIS'LL BE A CAKEWALK--AND REMEMBER, IT'S THE SECOND HALLWAY ON THE--
YOU GOTTA BE KIDDING ME.
RIGHT. SECOND HALLWAY ON THE RIGHT!
HOLD ON.
LEFT. IT'S THE SECOND ONE ON THE LEFT.
SIGH.
HERE. THIS MIGHT HELP.
OOH, THERE IT IS!

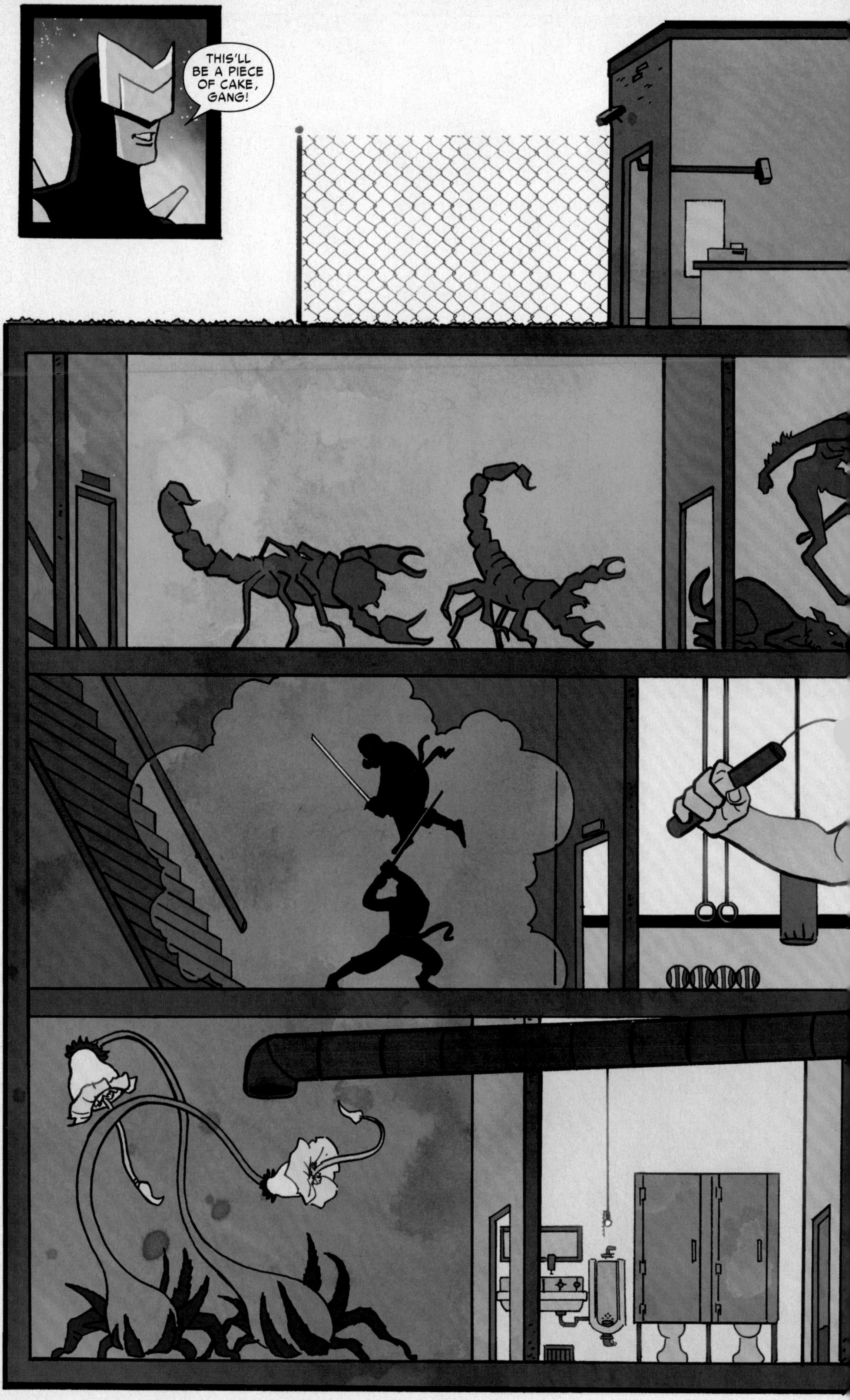
THIS'LL BE A PIECE OF CAKE, GANG!

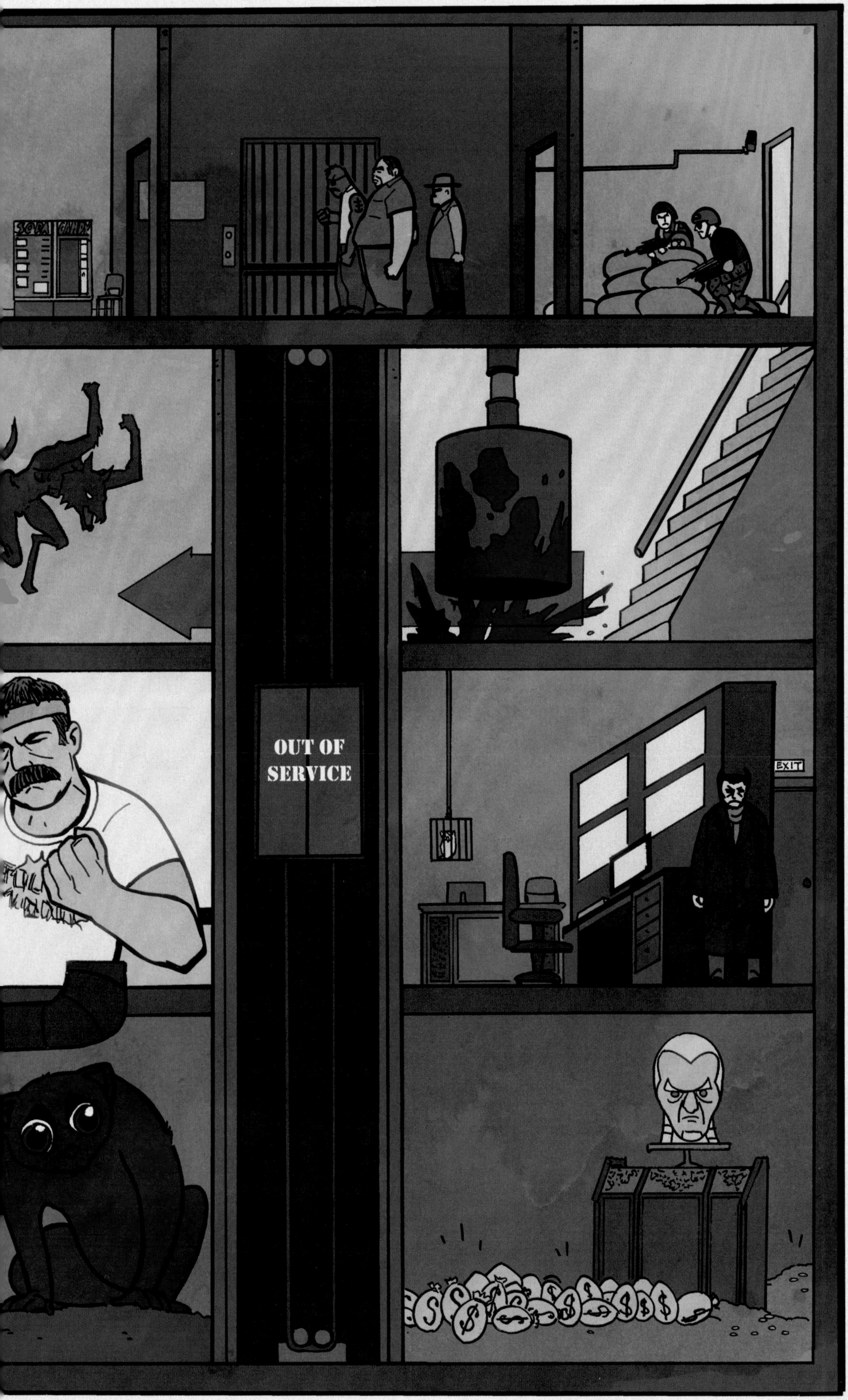
SODA
CANDY
OUT OF SERVICE
EXIT

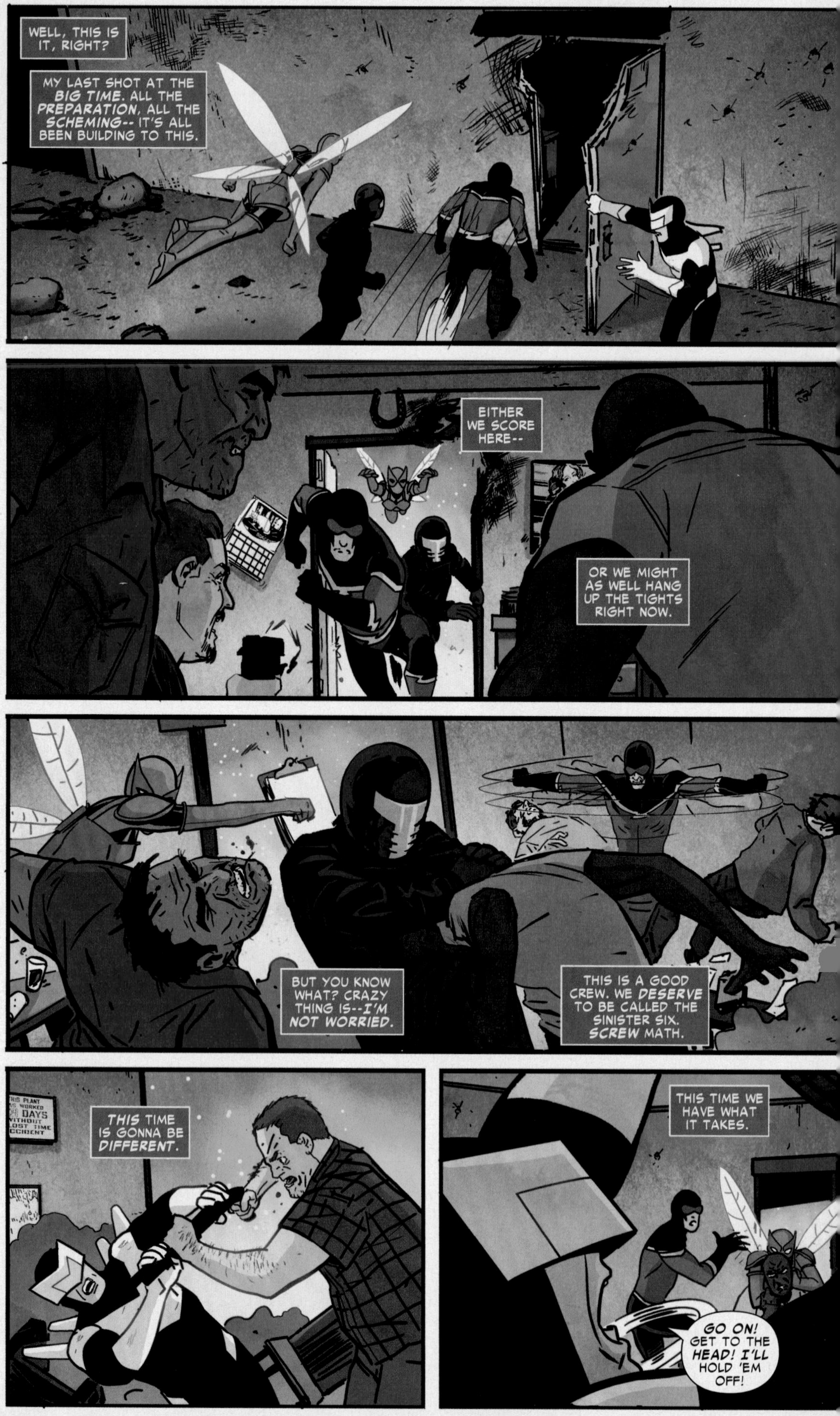
WELL, THIS IS IT, RIGHT?
MY LAST SHOT AT THE *BIG TIME*. ALL THE *PREPARATION*, ALL THE *SCHEMING*-- IT'S ALL BEEN BUILDING TO THIS.
EITHER WE SCORE HERE--
OR WE MIGHT AS WELL HANG UP THE TIGHTS RIGHT NOW.
BUT YOU KNOW WHAT? CRAZY THING IS--*I'M NOT WORRIED*.
THIS IS A GOOD CREW. WE *DESERVE* TO BE CALLED THE SINISTER SIX. *SCREW* MATH.
THIS TIME IS GONNA BE *DIFFERENT*.
THIS TIME WE HAVE WHAT IT TAKES.
GO ON! GET TO THE *HEAD*! I'LL HOLD 'EM OFF!

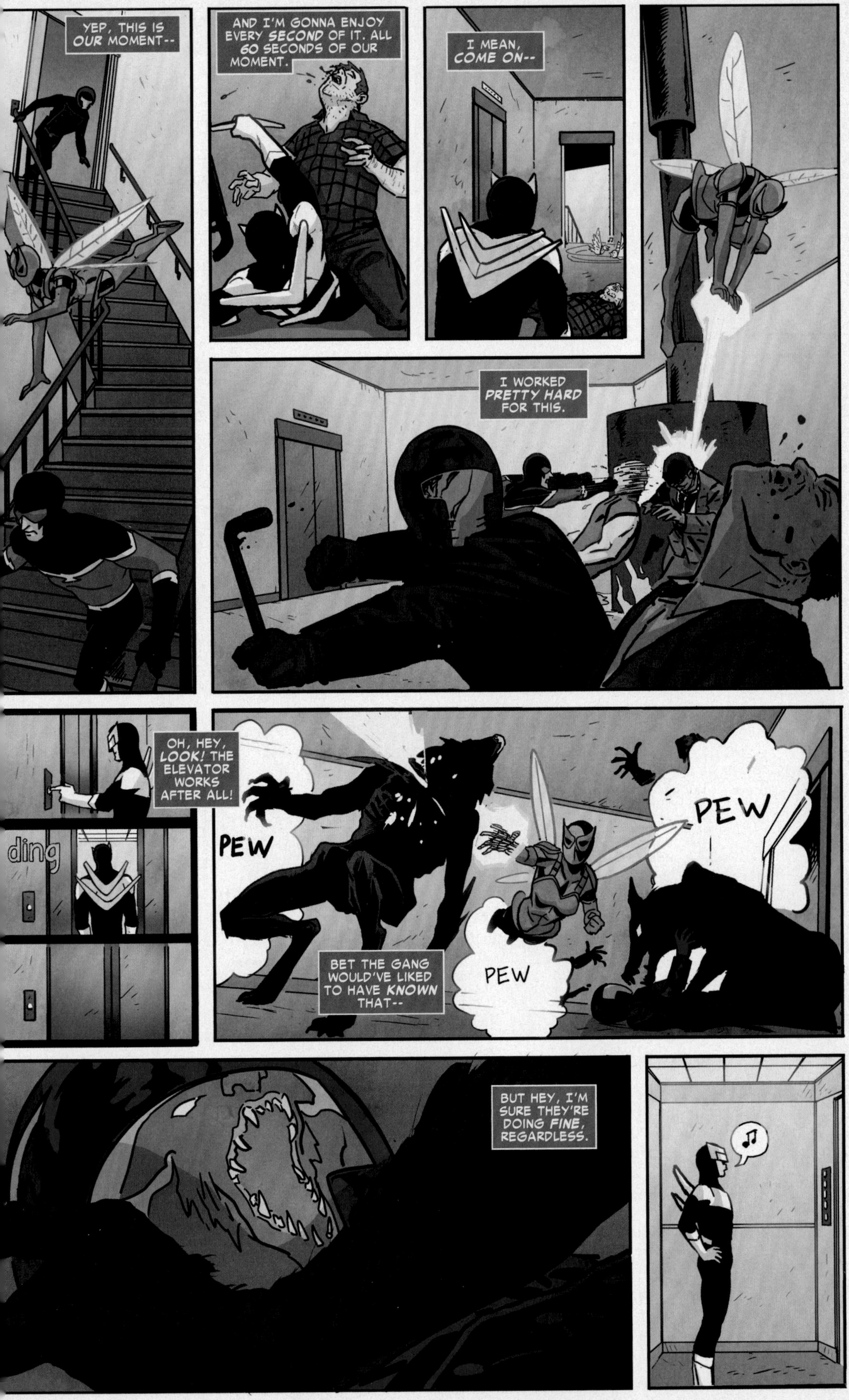
YEP, THIS IS OUR MOMENT--
AND I'M GONNA ENJOY EVERY SECOND OF IT. ALL 60 SECONDS OF OUR MOMENT.
I MEAN, COME ON--
I WORKED PRETTY HARD FOR THIS.
OH, HEY, LOOK! THE ELEVATOR WORKS AFTER ALL!
ding
PEW
PEW
BET THE GANG WOULD'VE LIKED TO HAVE KNOWN THAT--
PEW
BUT HEY, I'M SURE THEY'RE DOING FINE, REGARDLESS.
♪

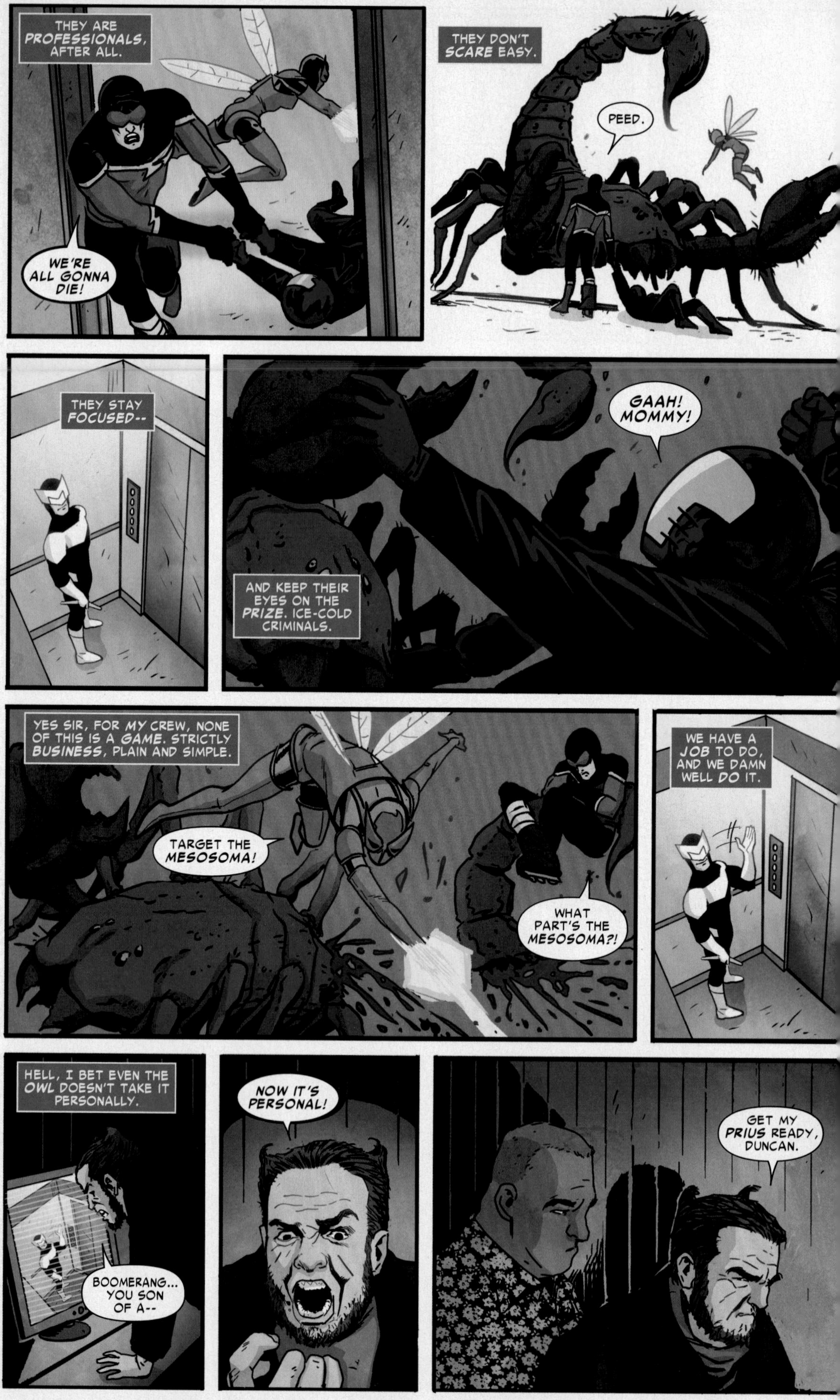
THEY ARE PROFESSIONALS, AFTER ALL.
WE'RE ALL GONNA DIE!
THEY DON'T SCARE EASY.
PEED.
THEY STAY FOCUSED--
GAAH! MOMMY!
AND KEEP THEIR EYES ON THE PRIZE. ICE-COLD CRIMINALS.
YES SIR, FOR MY CREW, NONE OF THIS IS A GAME. STRICTLY BUSINESS, PLAIN AND SIMPLE.
TARGET THE MESOSOMA!
WHAT PART'S THE MESOSOMA?!
WE HAVE A JOB TO DO, AND WE DAMN WELL DO IT.
HELL, I BET EVEN THE OWL DOESN'T TAKE IT PERSONALLY.
BOOMERANG... YOU SON OF A--
NOW IT'S PERSONAL!
GET MY PRIUS READY, DUNCAN.

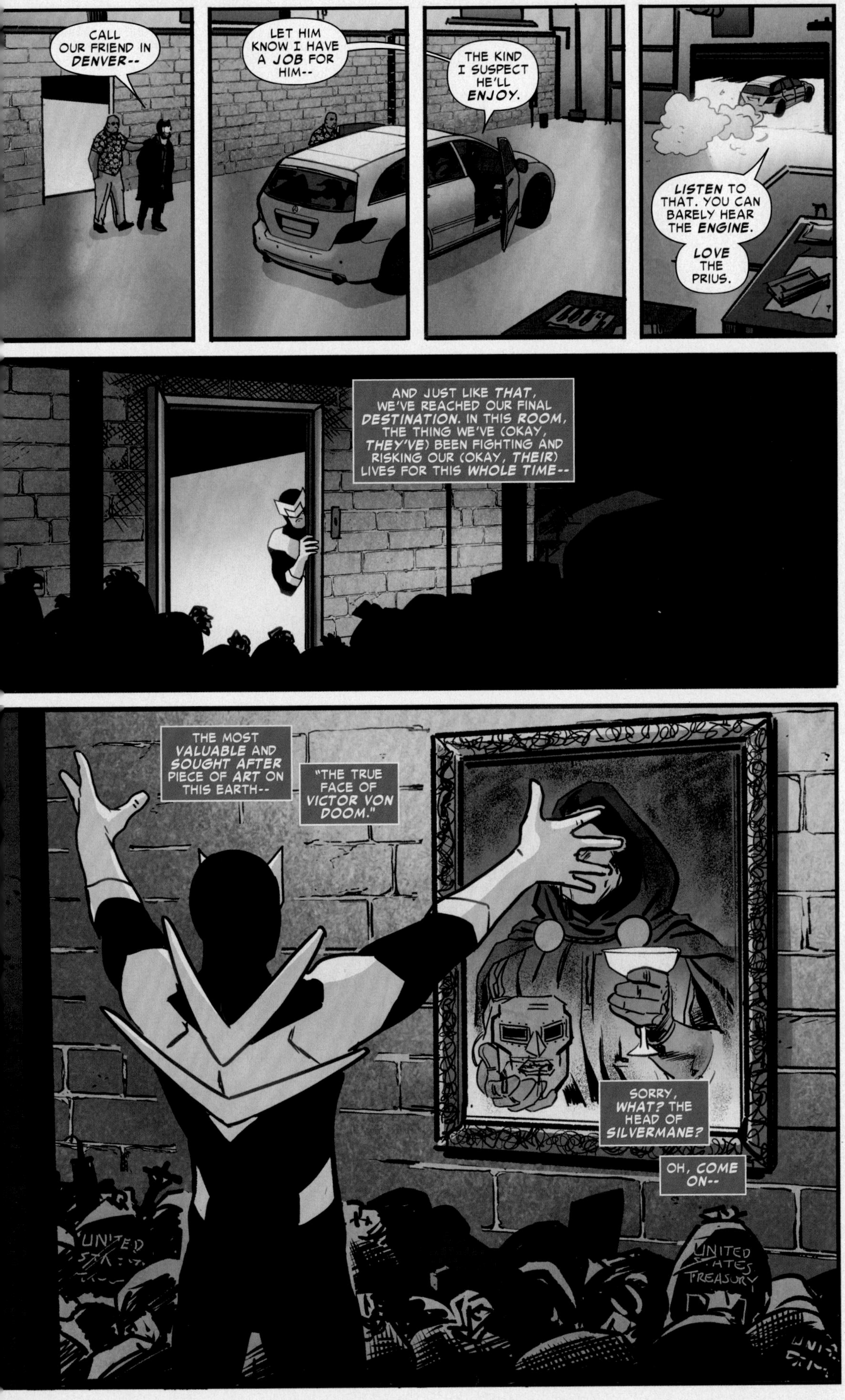
CALL OUR FRIEND IN DENVER--
LET HIM KNOW I HAVE A JOB FOR HIM--
THE KIND I SUSPECT HE'LL ENJOY.
LISTEN TO THAT. YOU CAN BARELY HEAR THE ENGINE.
LOVE THE PRIUS.
AND JUST LIKE THAT, WE'VE REACHED OUR FINAL DESTINATION. IN THIS ROOM, THE THING WE'VE (OKAY, THEY'VE) BEEN FIGHTING AND RISKING OUR (OKAY, THEIR) LIVES FOR THIS WHOLE TIME--
THE MOST VALUABLE AND SOUGHT AFTER PIECE OF ART ON THIS EARTH--
"THE TRUE FACE OF VICTOR VON DOOM."
SORRY, WHAT? THE HEAD OF SILVERMANE?
OH, COME ON--
UNITED STATES TREASURY

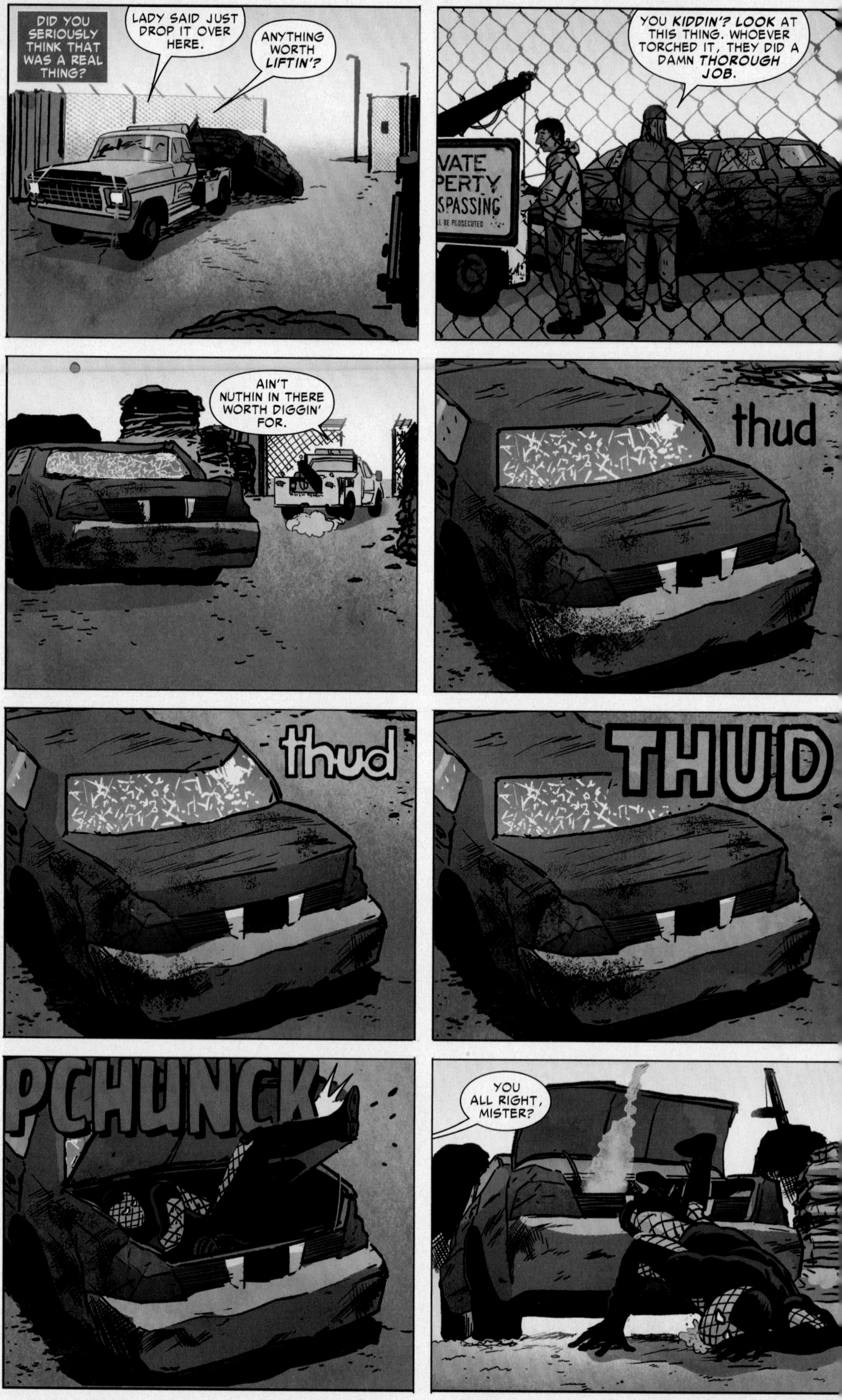
DID YOU SERIOUSLY THINK THAT WAS A REAL THING?
LADY SAID JUST DROP IT OVER HERE.
ANYTHING WORTH LIFTIN'?
YOU KIDDIN'? LOOK AT THIS THING. WHOEVER TORCHED IT, THEY DID A DAMN THOROUGH JOB.
VATE
PERTY
SPASSING
AIN'T NUTHIN IN THERE WORTH DIGGIN' FOR.
thud
thud
THUD
PCHUNCK
YOU ALL RIGHT, MISTER?

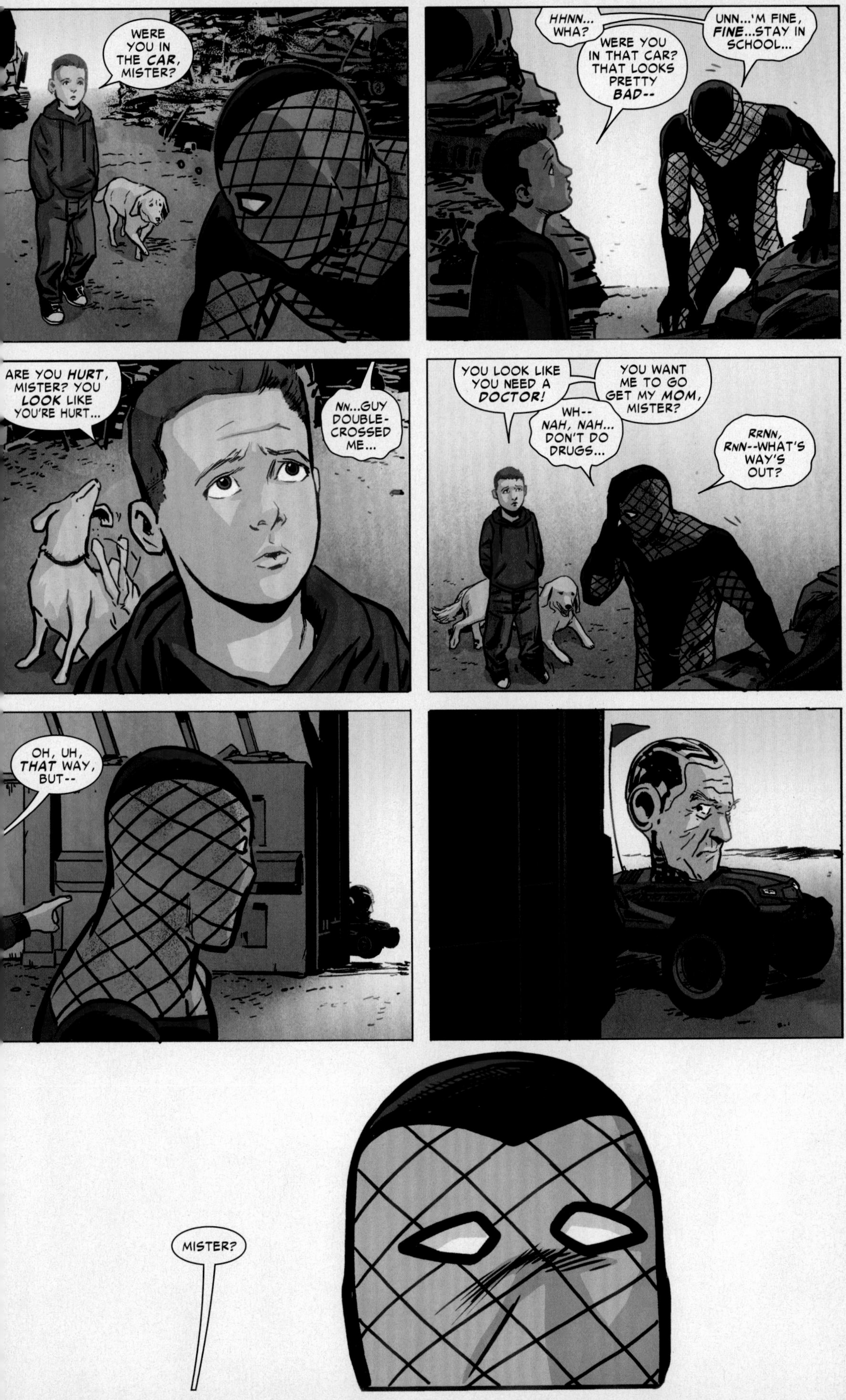
WERE YOU IN THE CAR, MISTER?
HHNN... WHA?
UNN...'M FINE, FINE...STAY IN SCHOOL...
WERE YOU IN THAT CAR? THAT LOOKS PRETTY BAD--
ARE YOU HURT, MISTER? YOU LOOK LIKE YOU'RE HURT...
NN...GUY DOUBLE-CROSSED ME...
YOU LOOK LIKE YOU NEED A DOCTOR!
YOU WANT ME TO GO GET MY MOM, MISTER?
WH-- NAH, NAH... DON'T DO DRUGS...
RRNN, RNN--WHAT'S WAY'S OUT?
OH, UH, THAT WAY, BUT--
MISTER?

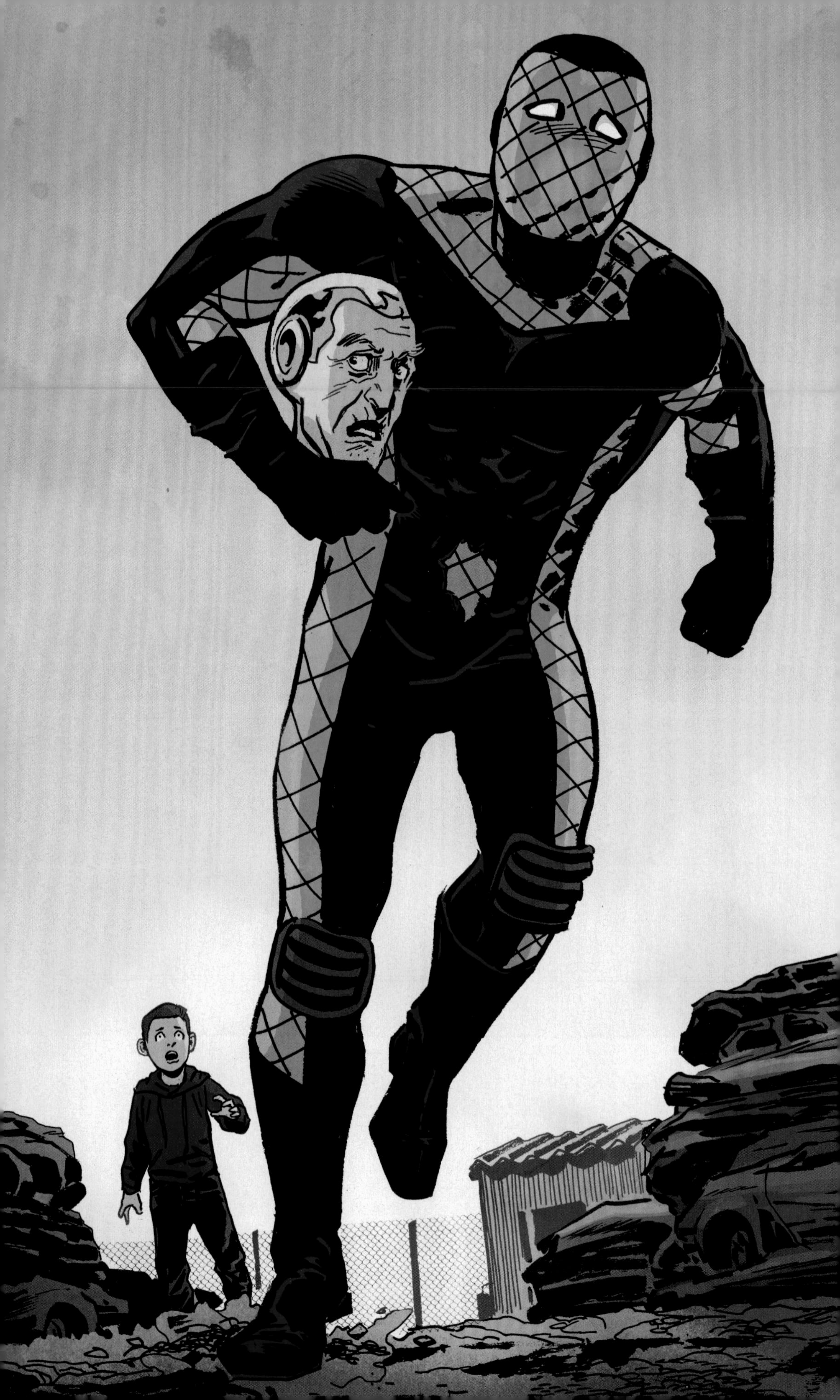

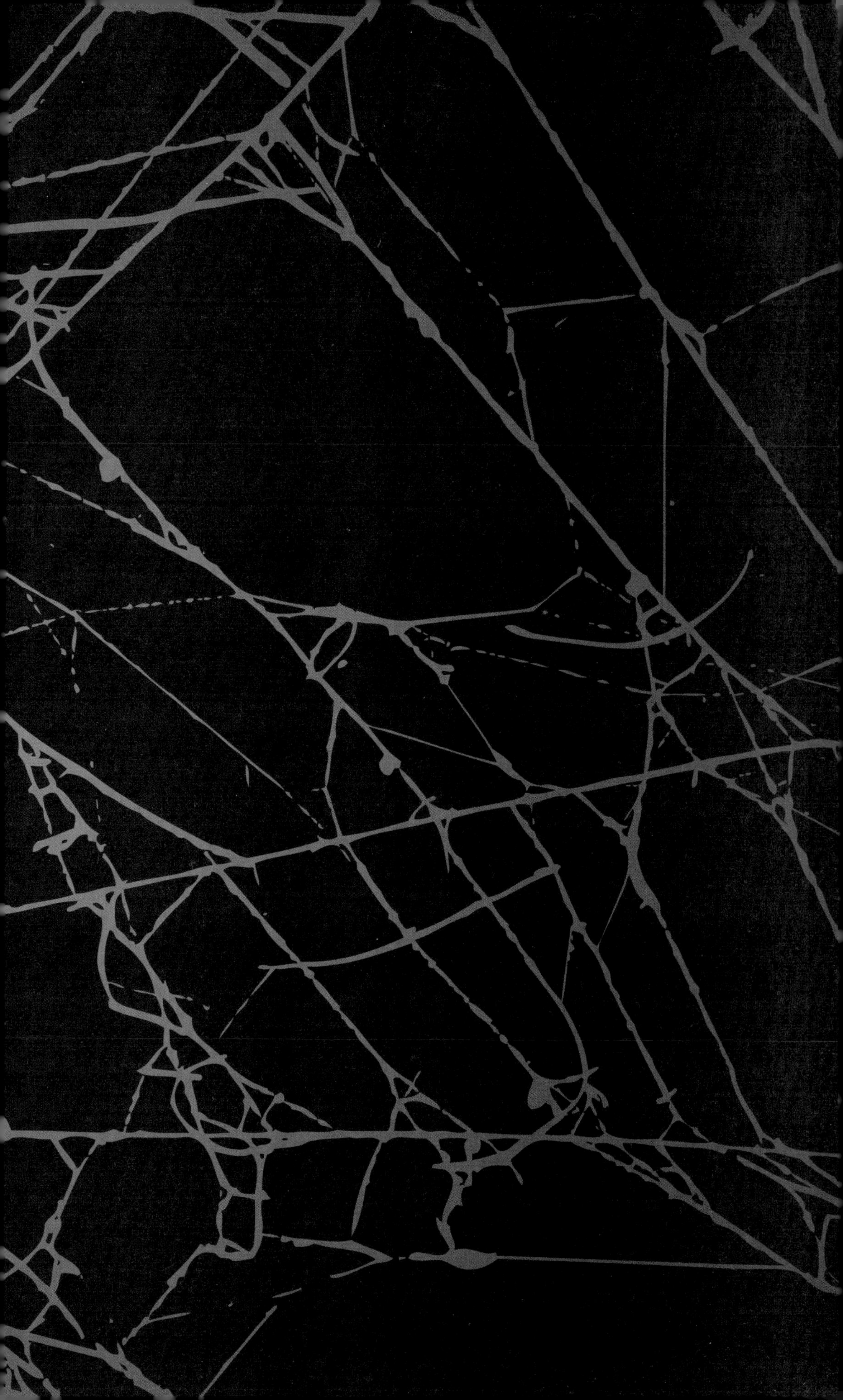

6

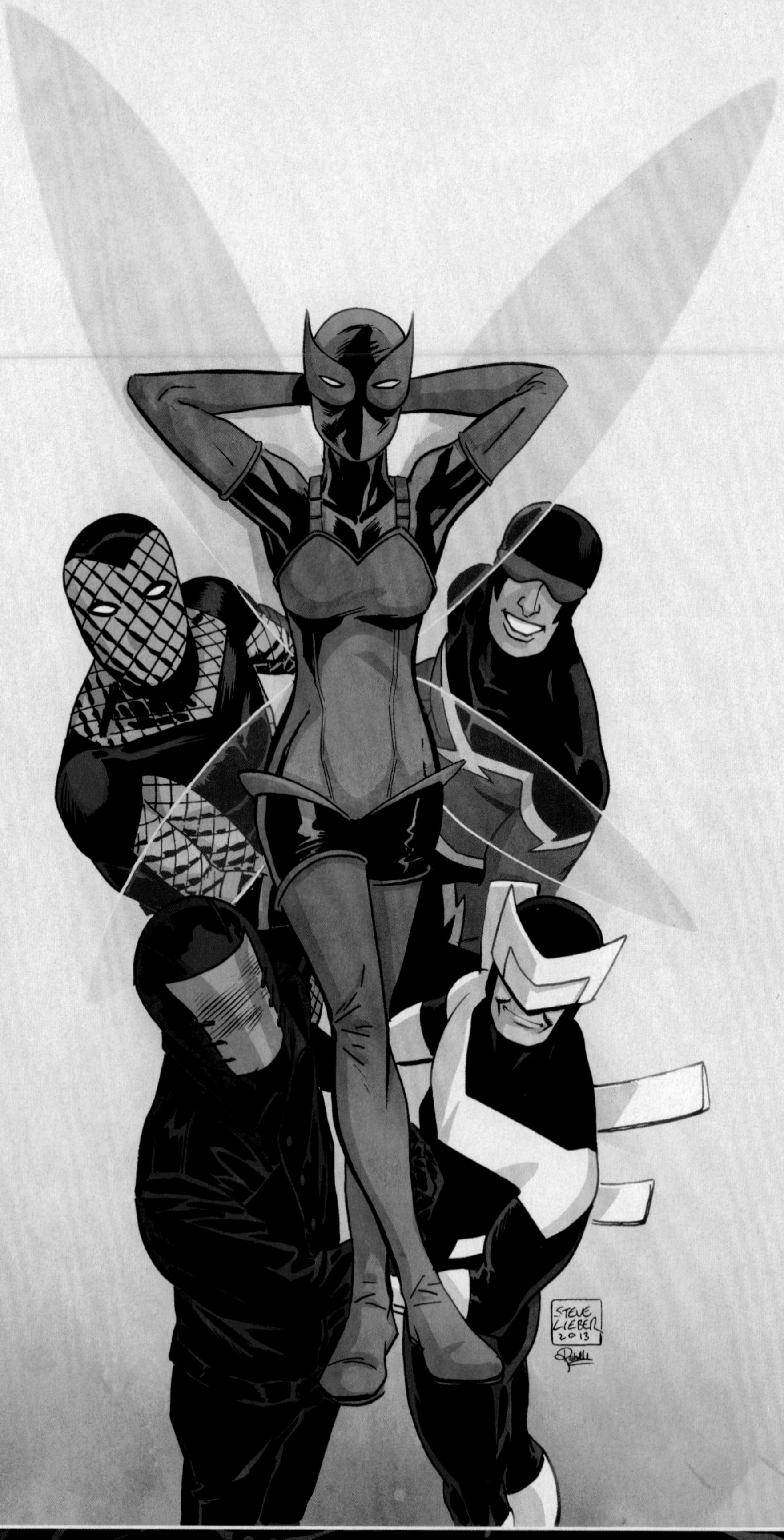
STEVE
LIEBER
2013

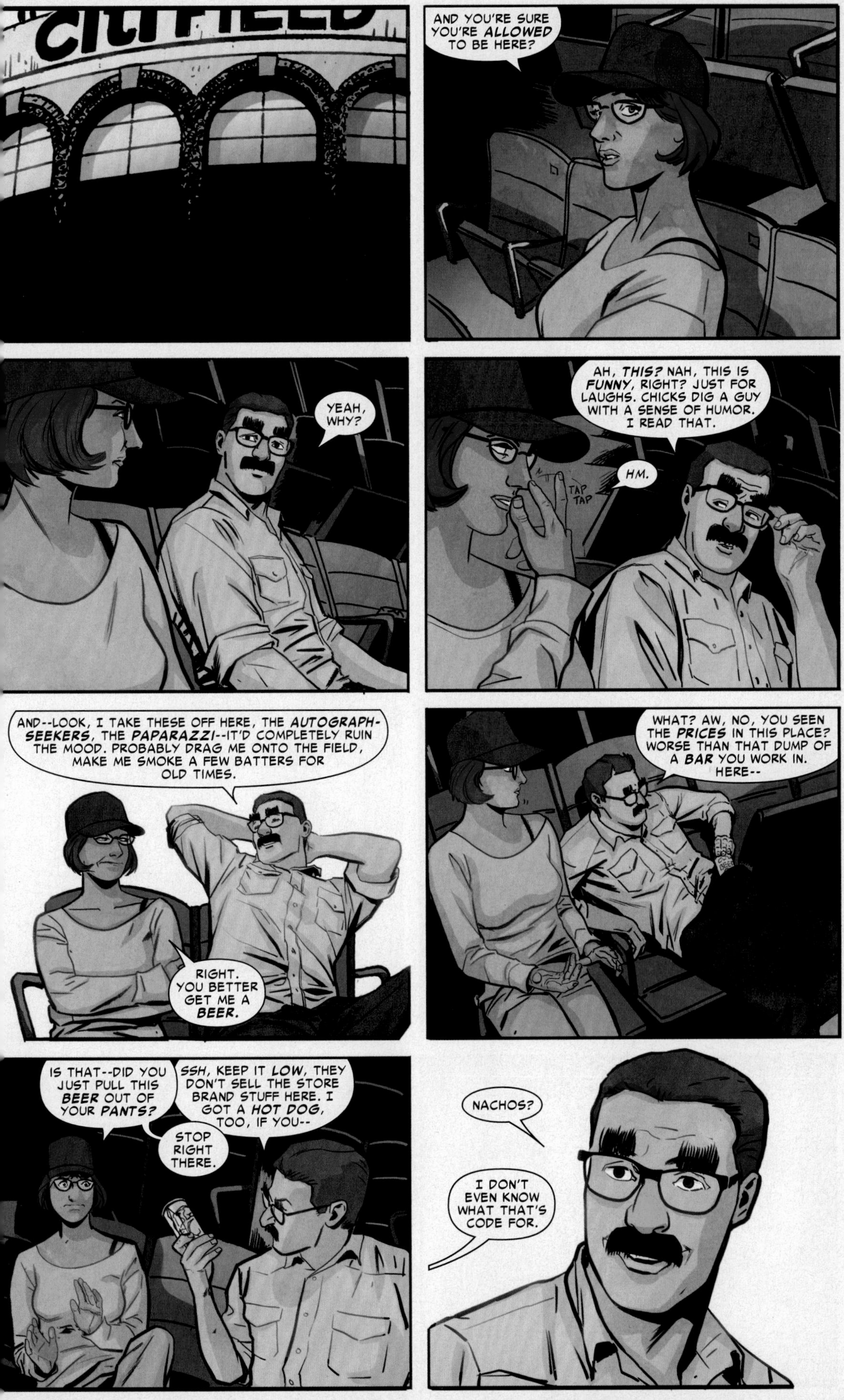
CITI FIELD
AND YOU'RE SURE YOU'RE ALLOWED TO BE HERE?
YEAH, WHY?
AH, THIS? NAH, THIS IS FUNNY, RIGHT? JUST FOR LAUGHS. CHICKS DIG A GUY WITH A SENSE OF HUMOR. I READ THAT.
TAP TAP
HM.
AND--LOOK, I TAKE THESE OFF HERE, THE AUTOGRAPH-SEEKERS, THE PAPARAZZI--IT'D COMPLETELY RUIN THE MOOD. PROBABLY DRAG ME ONTO THE FIELD, MAKE ME SMOKE A FEW BATTERS FOR OLD TIMES.
RIGHT. YOU BETTER GET ME A BEER.
WHAT? AW, NO, YOU SEEN THE PRICES IN THIS PLACE? WORSE THAN THAT DUMP OF A BAR YOU WORK IN. HERE--
IS THAT--DID YOU JUST PULL THIS BEER OUT OF YOUR PANTS?
SSH, KEEP IT LOW, THEY DON'T SELL THE STORE BRAND STUFF HERE. I GOT A HOT DOG, TOO, IF YOU--
STOP RIGHT THERE.
NACHOS?
I DON'T EVEN KNOW WHAT THAT'S CODE FOR.

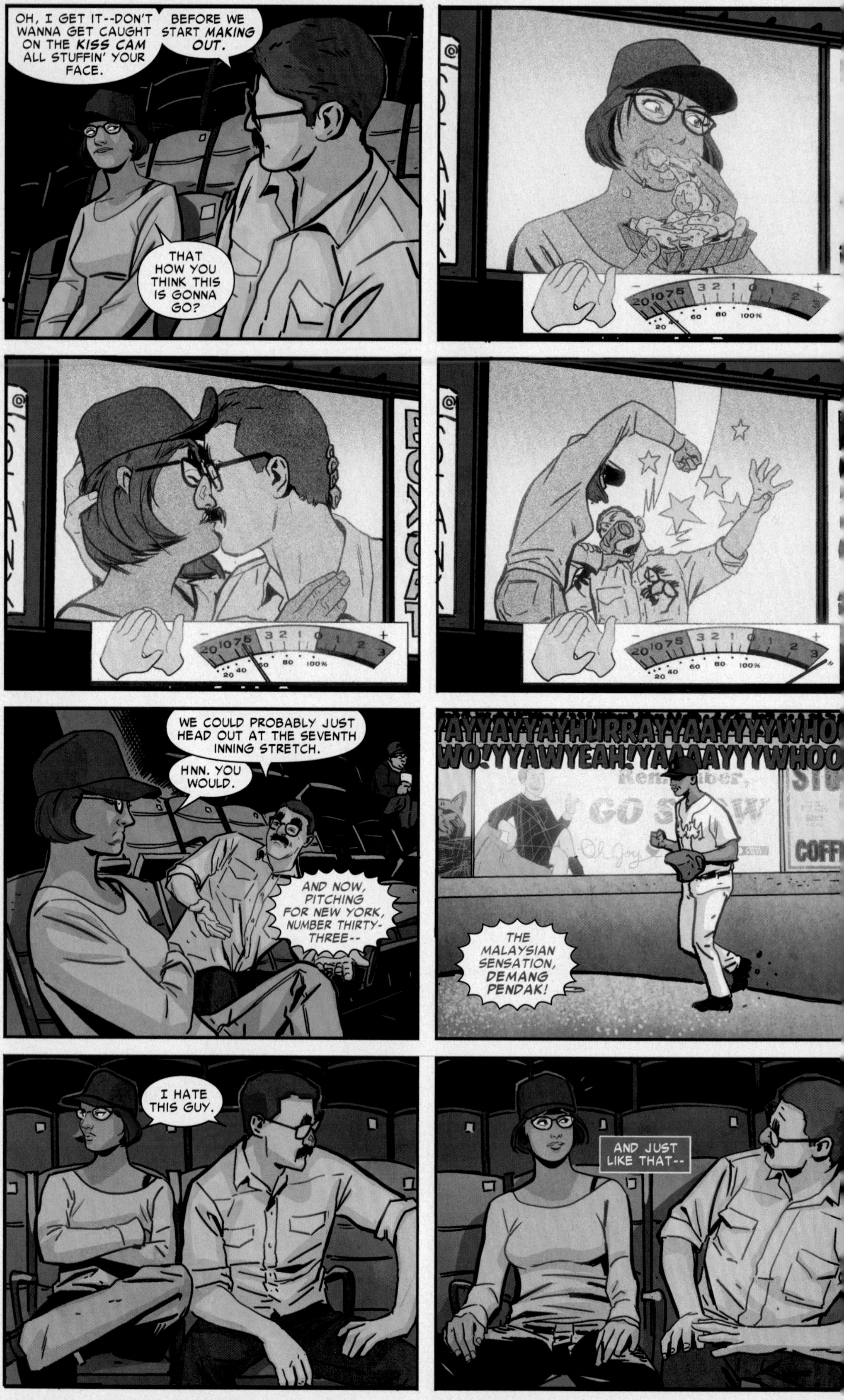
OH, I GET IT--DON'T WANNA GET CAUGHT ON THE KISS CAM ALL STUFFIN' YOUR FACE.
BEFORE WE START MAKING OUT.
THAT HOW YOU THINK THIS IS GONNA GO?
WE COULD PROBABLY JUST HEAD OUT AT THE SEVENTH INNING STRETCH.
HNN. YOU WOULD.
AND NOW, PITCHING FOR NEW YORK, NUMBER THIRTY-THREE--
YAYYAYYAYHURRAYYAAYYYYWHOO
WO!YYAWYEAH!YAAAAYYYWHOO
THE MALAYSIAN SENSATION, DEMANG PENDAK!
I HATE THIS GUY.
AND JUST LIKE THAT--

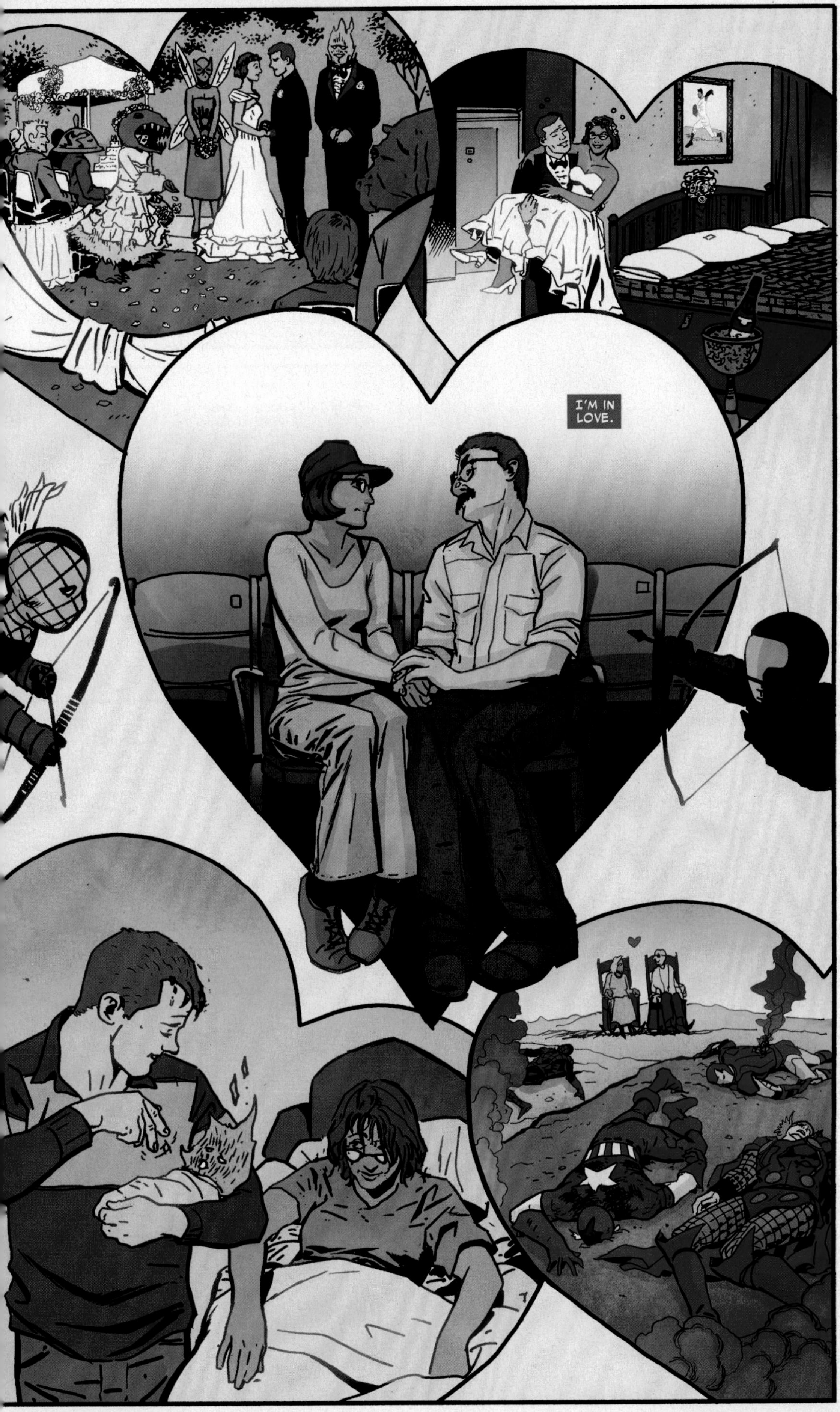
I'M IN LOVE.

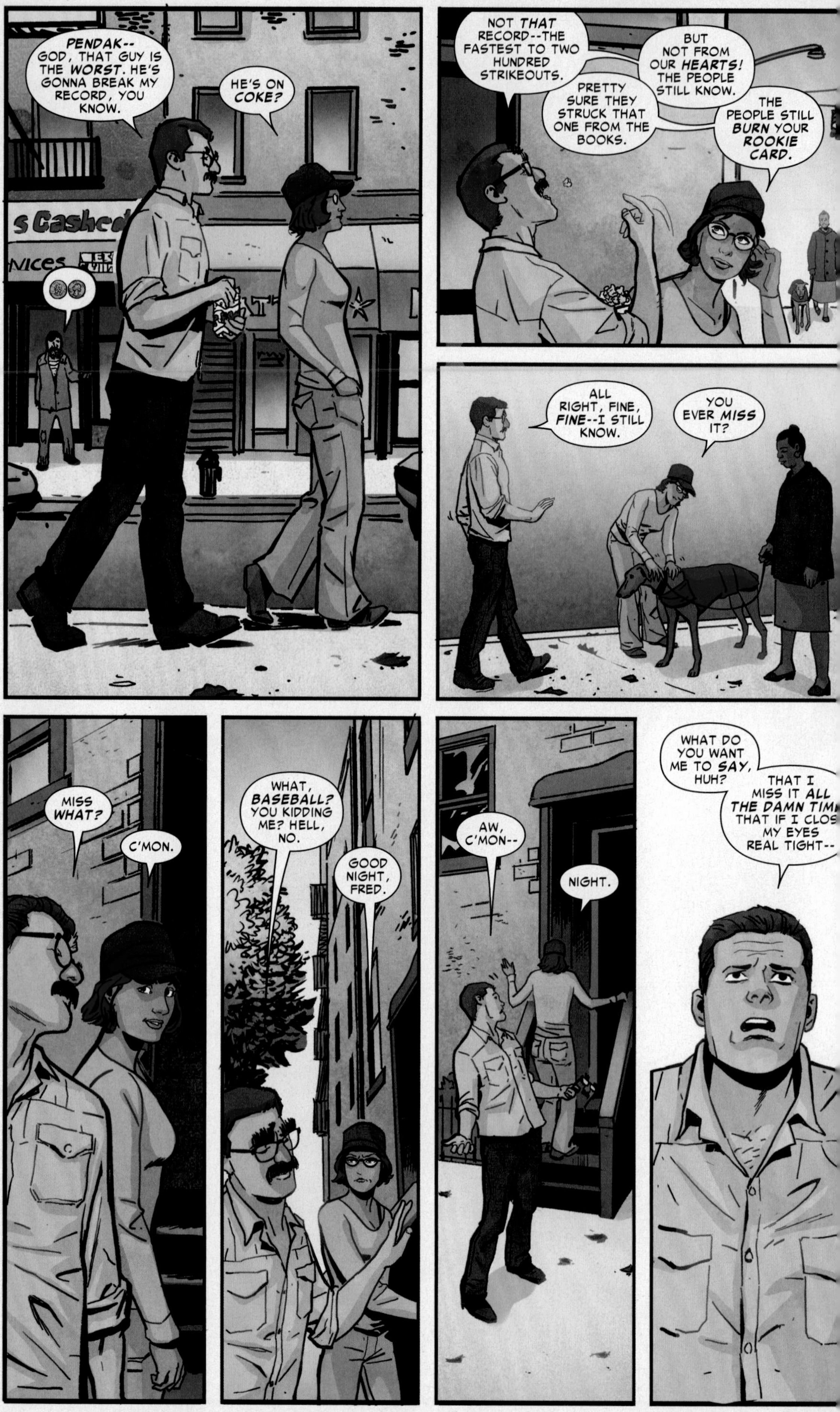

PENDAK-- GOD, THAT GUY IS THE WORST. HE'S GONNA BREAK MY RECORD, YOU KNOW.
HE'S ON COKE?
s Cashed
NICES
NOT THAT RECORD--THE FASTEST TO TWO HUNDRED STRIKEOUTS.
PRETTY SURE THEY STRUCK THAT ONE FROM THE BOOKS.
BUT NOT FROM OUR HEARTS! THE PEOPLE STILL KNOW.
THE PEOPLE STILL BURN YOUR ROOKIE CARD.
ALL RIGHT, FINE, FINE--I STILL KNOW.
YOU EVER MISS IT?
MISS WHAT?
C'MON.
WHAT, BASEBALL? YOU KIDDING ME? HELL, NO.
GOOD NIGHT, FRED.
AW, C'MON--
NIGHT.
WHAT DO YOU WANT ME TO SAY, HUH?
THAT I MISS IT ALL THE DAMN TIM THAT IF I CLOS MY EYES REAL TIGHT--

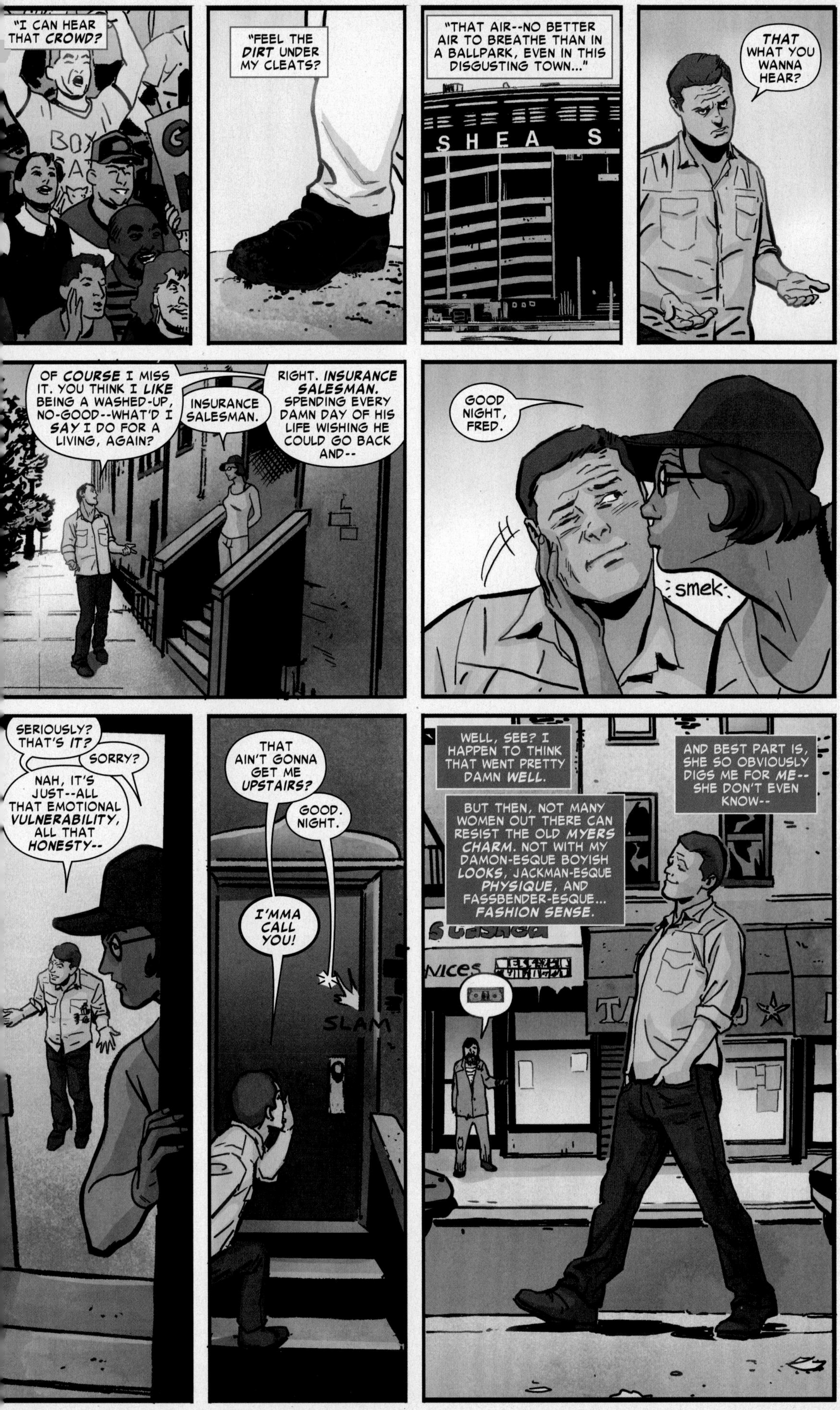
"I CAN HEAR THAT CROWD?
"FEEL THE DIRT UNDER MY CLEATS?
"THAT AIR--NO BETTER AIR TO BREATHE THAN IN A BALLPARK, EVEN IN THIS DISGUSTING TOWN..."
SHEA S
THAT WHAT YOU WANNA HEAR?
OF COURSE I MISS IT. YOU THINK I LIKE BEING A WASHED-UP, NO-GOOD--WHAT'D I SAY I DO FOR A LIVING, AGAIN?
INSURANCE SALESMAN.
RIGHT. INSURANCE SALESMAN. SPENDING EVERY DAMN DAY OF HIS LIFE WISHING HE COULD GO BACK AND--
GOOD NIGHT, FRED.
smek
SERIOUSLY? THAT'S IT?
SORRY?
NAH, IT'S JUST--ALL THAT EMOTIONAL VULNERABILITY, ALL THAT HONESTY--
THAT AIN'T GONNA GET ME UPSTAIRS?
GOOD. NIGHT.
I'MMA CALL YOU!
SLAM
WELL, SEE? I HAPPEN TO THINK THAT WENT PRETTY DAMN WELL.
BUT THEN, NOT MANY WOMEN OUT THERE CAN RESIST THE OLD MYERS CHARM. NOT WITH MY DAMON-ESQUE BOYISH LOOKS, JACKMAN-ESQUE PHYSIQUE, AND FASSBENDER-ESQUE... FASHION SENSE.
AND BEST PART IS, SHE SO OBVIOUSLY DIGS ME FOR ME--SHE DON'T EVEN KNOW--

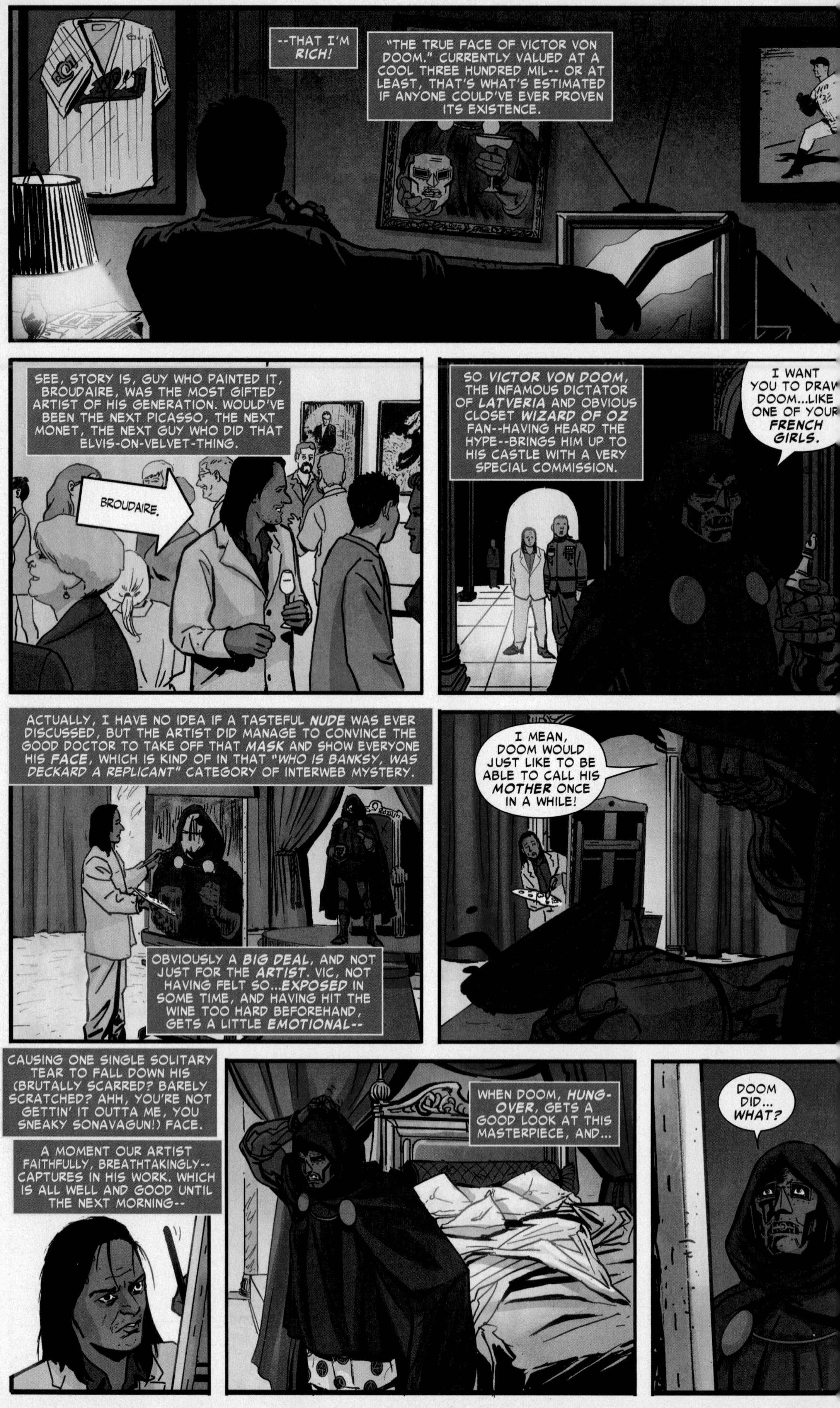
--THAT I'M RICH!
"THE TRUE FACE OF VICTOR VON DOOM." CURRENTLY VALUED AT A COOL THREE HUNDRED MIL-- OR AT LEAST, THAT'S WHAT'S ESTIMATED IF ANYONE COULD'VE EVER PROVEN ITS EXISTENCE.
SEE, STORY IS, GUY WHO PAINTED IT, BROUDAIRE, WAS THE MOST GIFTED ARTIST OF HIS GENERATION. WOULD'VE BEEN THE NEXT PICASSO, THE NEXT MONET, THE NEXT GUY WHO DID THAT ELVIS-ON-VELVET-THING.
BROUDAIRE.
SO VICTOR VON DOOM, THE INFAMOUS DICTATOR OF LATVERIA AND OBVIOUS CLOSET WIZARD OF OZ FAN--HAVING HEARD THE HYPE--BRINGS HIM UP TO HIS CASTLE WITH A VERY SPECIAL COMMISSION.
I WANT YOU TO DRAW DOOM...LIKE ONE OF YOUR FRENCH GIRLS.
ACTUALLY, I HAVE NO IDEA IF A TASTEFUL NUDE WAS EVER DISCUSSED, BUT THE ARTIST DID MANAGE TO CONVINCE THE GOOD DOCTOR TO TAKE OFF THAT MASK AND SHOW EVERYONE HIS FACE, WHICH IS KIND OF IN THAT "WHO IS BANKSY, WAS DECKARD A REPLICANT" CATEGORY OF INTERWEB MYSTERY.
OBVIOUSLY A BIG DEAL, AND NOT JUST FOR THE ARTIST. VIC, NOT HAVING FELT SO...EXPOSED IN SOME TIME, AND HAVING HIT THE WINE TOO HARD BEFOREHAND, GETS A LITTLE EMOTIONAL--
I MEAN, DOOM WOULD JUST LIKE TO BE ABLE TO CALL HIS MOTHER ONCE IN A WHILE!
CAUSING ONE SINGLE SOLITARY TEAR TO FALL DOWN HIS (BRUTALLY SCARRED? BARELY SCRATCHED? AHH, YOU'RE NOT GETTIN' IT OUTTA ME, YOU SNEAKY SONAVAGUN!) FACE.
A MOMENT OUR ARTIST FAITHFULLY, BREATHTAKINGLY--CAPTURES IN HIS WORK. WHICH IS ALL WELL AND GOOD UNTIL THE NEXT MORNING--
WHEN DOOM, HUNG-OVER, GETS A GOOD LOOK AT THIS MASTERPIECE, AND...
DOOM DID... WHAT?

THE ARTIST GETS THE *DEATH RAY* TREATMENT-- WHICH IS ACTUALLY GREAT NEWS FOR HIS *GALLERY SALES*, TURNS OUT--

BROUHAHA.

DOOM FINDS YOU *PRETENTIOUS* AND *OVER-RATED!*

BUT THE PAINTING ITSELF...DESPITE HIS *RAGE*, DOOM JUST *CAN'T* BRING HIMSELF TO *DESTROY* IT.

SO INSTEAD HE LOCKS IT AWAY DEEP IN HIS *DUNGEON*, WHERE IT REMAINED FOR *YEARS*...

UNTIL IT WAS LIBERATED BY THIEVES DURING THE *KRISTOFF* REGIME.

FROM THERE, IT CHANGES HANDS A COUPLE TIMES, THERE'S SOME *DOUBLE CROSSES* AND SHADY *DEALS*, WHATEVER, TOTALLY NOT IMPORTANT--BEFORE FINALLY, IT LANDS IN *ANOTHER* DUNGEON--THE *OWL'S*.

NOW, THROUGH ALL THIS, THE PAINTING'S LEGEND ONLY *GROWS*. NO ONE'S EVEN *SEEN* THE THING, NO ONE KNOWS *WHERE* IT IS-- AND ALL THAT JUST MAKES 'EM WANT IT *MORE*.

AND NOW I AM GONNA *GIVE IT TO THEM!**

*AT FULL PRICE.

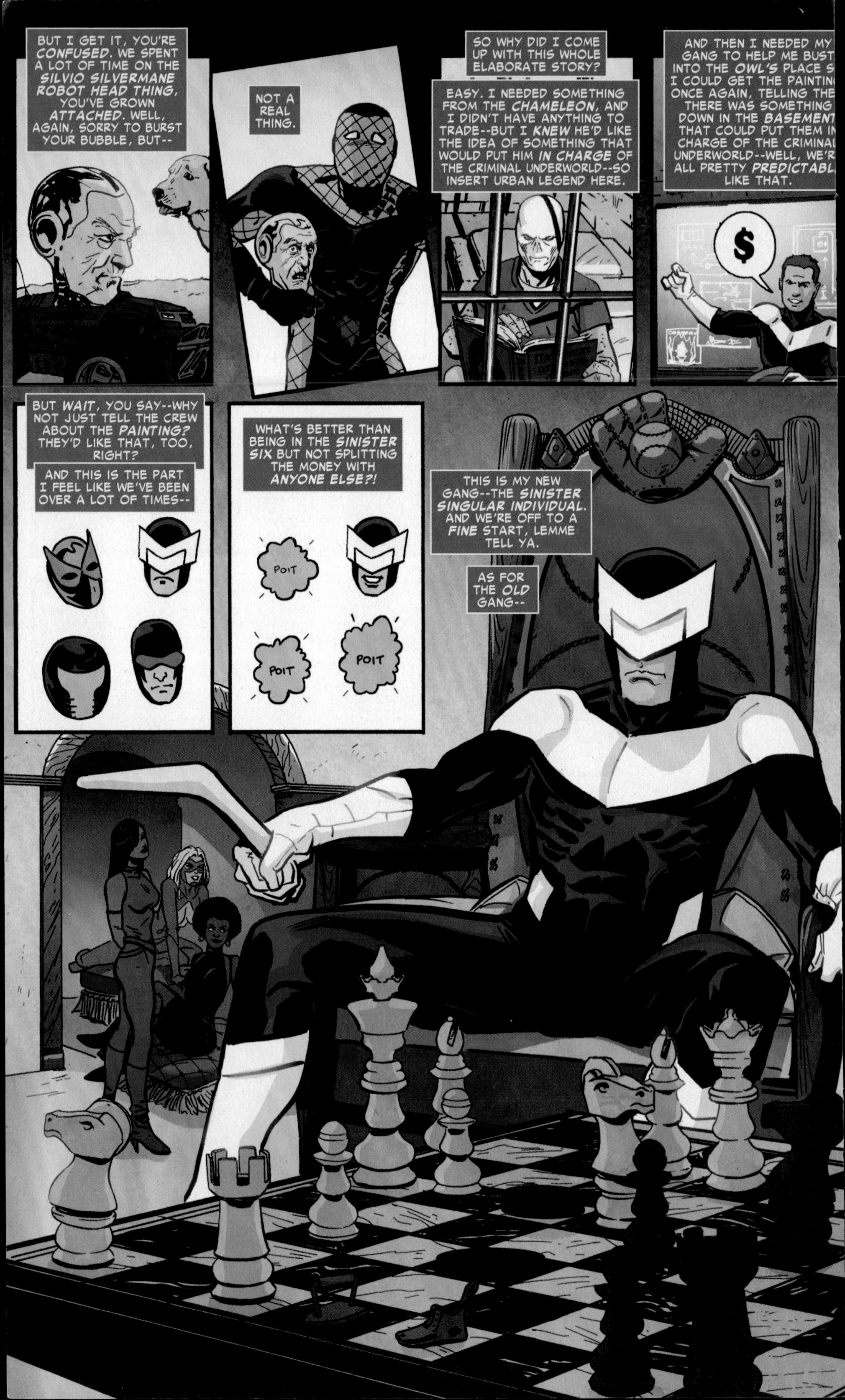

BUT I GET IT, YOU'RE CONFUSED. WE SPENT A LOT OF TIME ON THE SILVIO SILVERMANE ROBOT HEAD THING, YOU'VE GROWN ATTACHED. WELL, AGAIN, SORRY TO BURST YOUR BUBBLE, BUT--
NOT A REAL THING.
SO WHY DID I COME UP WITH THIS WHOLE ELABORATE STORY?
EASY. I NEEDED SOMETHING FROM THE CHAMELEON, AND I DIDN'T HAVE ANYTHING TO TRADE--BUT I KNEW HE'D LIKE THE IDEA OF SOMETHING THAT WOULD PUT HIM IN CHARGE OF THE CRIMINAL UNDERWORLD--SO INSERT URBAN LEGEND HERE.
AND THEN I NEEDED MY GANG TO HELP ME BUST INTO THE OWL'S PLACE S I COULD GET THE PAINTIN ONCE AGAIN, TELLING THE THERE WAS SOMETHING DOWN IN THE BASEMENT THAT COULD PUT THEM IN CHARGE OF THE CRIMINAL UNDERWORLD--WELL, WE'R ALL PRETTY PREDICTABL LIKE THAT.
$
BUT WAIT, YOU SAY--WHY NOT JUST TELL THE CREW ABOUT THE PAINTING? THEY'D LIKE THAT, TOO, RIGHT?
AND THIS IS THE PART I FEEL LIKE WE'VE BEEN OVER A LOT OF TIMES--
WHAT'S BETTER THAN BEING IN THE SINISTER SIX BUT NOT SPLITTING THE MONEY WITH ANYONE ELSE?!
POIT
POIT
POIT
THIS IS MY NEW GANG--THE SINISTER SINGULAR INDIVIDUAL. AND WE'RE OFF TO A FINE START, LEMME TELL YA.
AS FOR THE OLD GANG--

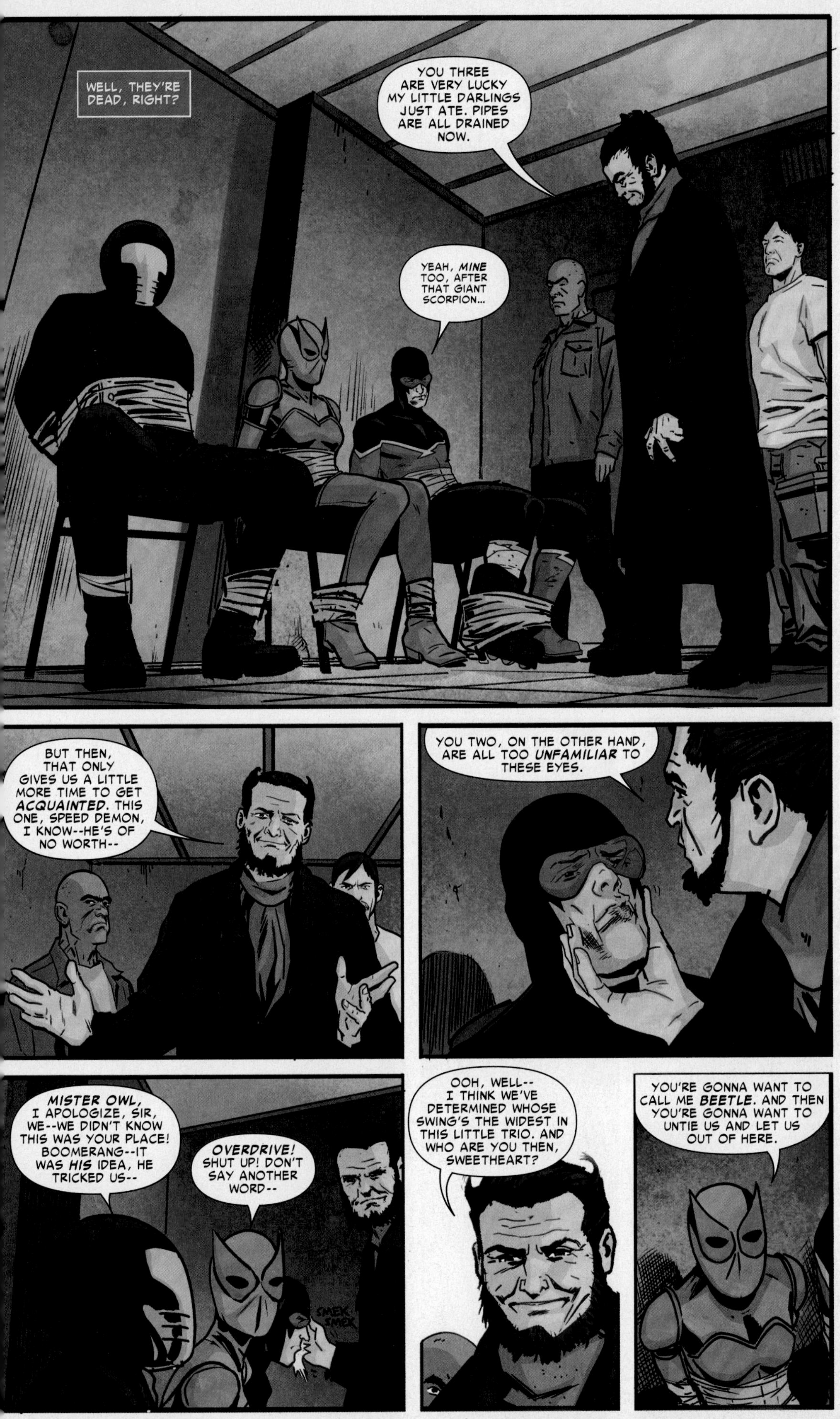
WELL, THEY'RE DEAD, RIGHT?
YOU THREE ARE VERY LUCKY MY LITTLE DARLINGS JUST ATE. PIPES ARE ALL DRAINED NOW.
YEAH, MINE TOO, AFTER THAT GIANT SCORPION...
BUT THEN, THAT ONLY GIVES US A LITTLE MORE TIME TO GET ACQUAINTED. THIS ONE, SPEED DEMON, I KNOW--HE'S OF NO WORTH--
YOU TWO, ON THE OTHER HAND, ARE ALL TOO UNFAMILIAR TO THESE EYES.
MISTER OWL, I APOLOGIZE, SIR, WE--WE DIDN'T KNOW THIS WAS YOUR PLACE! BOOMERANG--IT WAS HIS IDEA, HE TRICKED US--
OVERDRIVE! SHUT UP! DON'T SAY ANOTHER WORD--
SMEK SMEK
OOH, WELL-- I THINK WE'VE DETERMINED WHOSE SWING'S THE WIDEST IN THIS LITTLE TRIO. AND WHO ARE YOU THEN, SWEETHEART?
YOU'RE GONNA WANT TO CALL ME BEETLE. AND THEN YOU'RE GONNA WANT TO UNTIE US AND LET US OUT OF HERE.

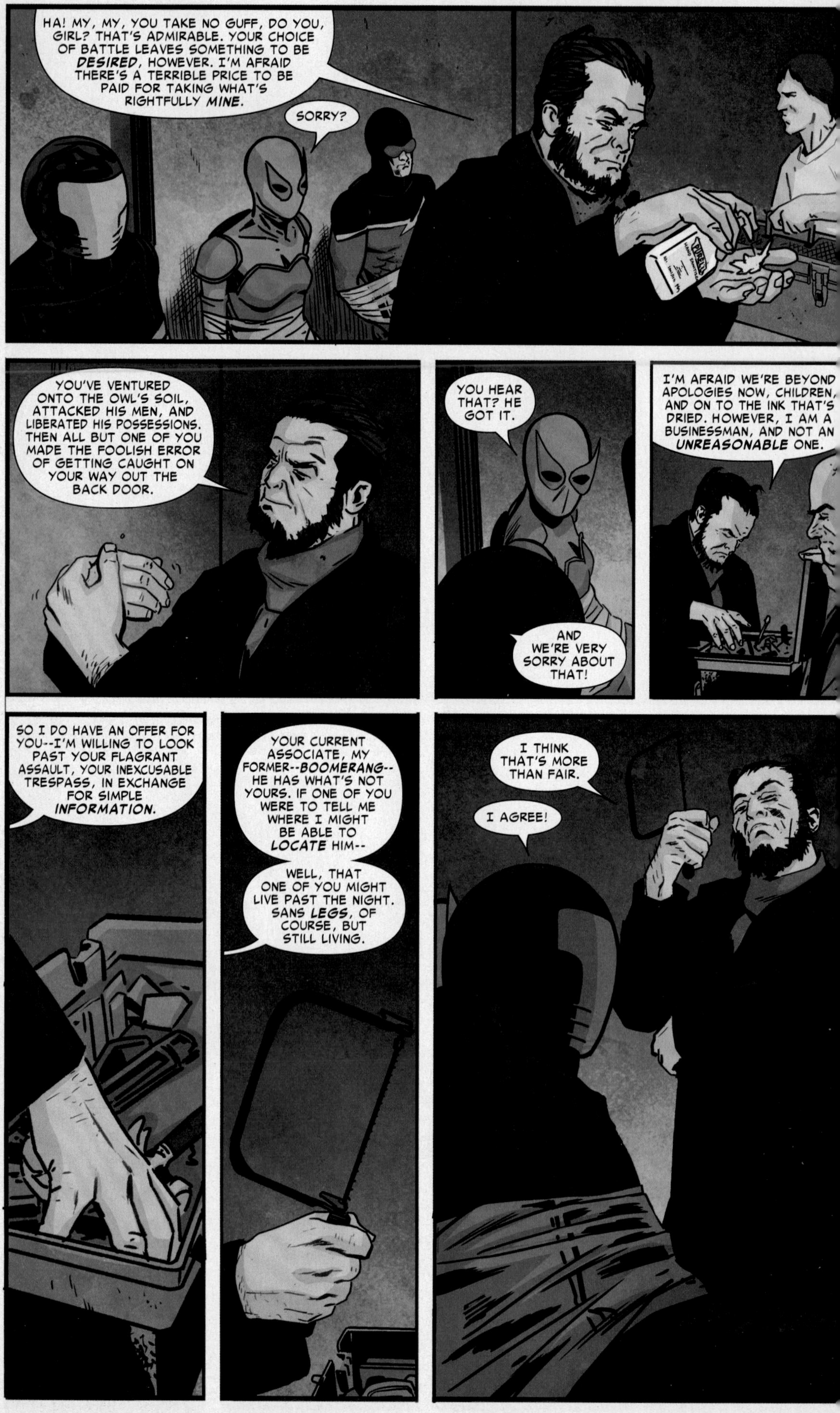
HA! MY, MY, YOU TAKE NO GUFF, DO YOU, GIRL? THAT'S ADMIRABLE. YOUR CHOICE OF BATTLE LEAVES SOMETHING TO BE DESIRED, HOWEVER. I'M AFRAID THERE'S A TERRIBLE PRICE TO BE PAID FOR TAKING WHAT'S RIGHTFULLY MINE.
SORRY?
YOU'VE VENTURED ONTO THE OWL'S SOIL, ATTACKED HIS MEN, AND LIBERATED HIS POSSESSIONS. THEN ALL BUT ONE OF YOU MADE THE FOOLISH ERROR OF GETTING CAUGHT ON YOUR WAY OUT THE BACK DOOR.
YOU HEAR THAT? HE GOT IT.
AND WE'RE VERY SORRY ABOUT THAT!
I'M AFRAID WE'RE BEYOND APOLOGIES NOW, CHILDREN, AND ON TO THE INK THAT'S DRIED. HOWEVER, I AM A BUSINESSMAN, AND NOT AN UNREASONABLE ONE.
SO I DO HAVE AN OFFER FOR YOU--I'M WILLING TO LOOK PAST YOUR FLAGRANT ASSAULT, YOUR INEXCUSABLE TRESPASS, IN EXCHANGE FOR SIMPLE INFORMATION.
YOUR CURRENT ASSOCIATE, MY FORMER--BOOMERANG--HE HAS WHAT'S NOT YOURS. IF ONE OF YOU WERE TO TELL ME WHERE I MIGHT BE ABLE TO LOCATE HIM--
WELL, THAT ONE OF YOU MIGHT LIVE PAST THE NIGHT. SANS LEGS, OF COURSE, BUT STILL LIVING.
I THINK THAT'S MORE THAN FAIR.
I AGREE!

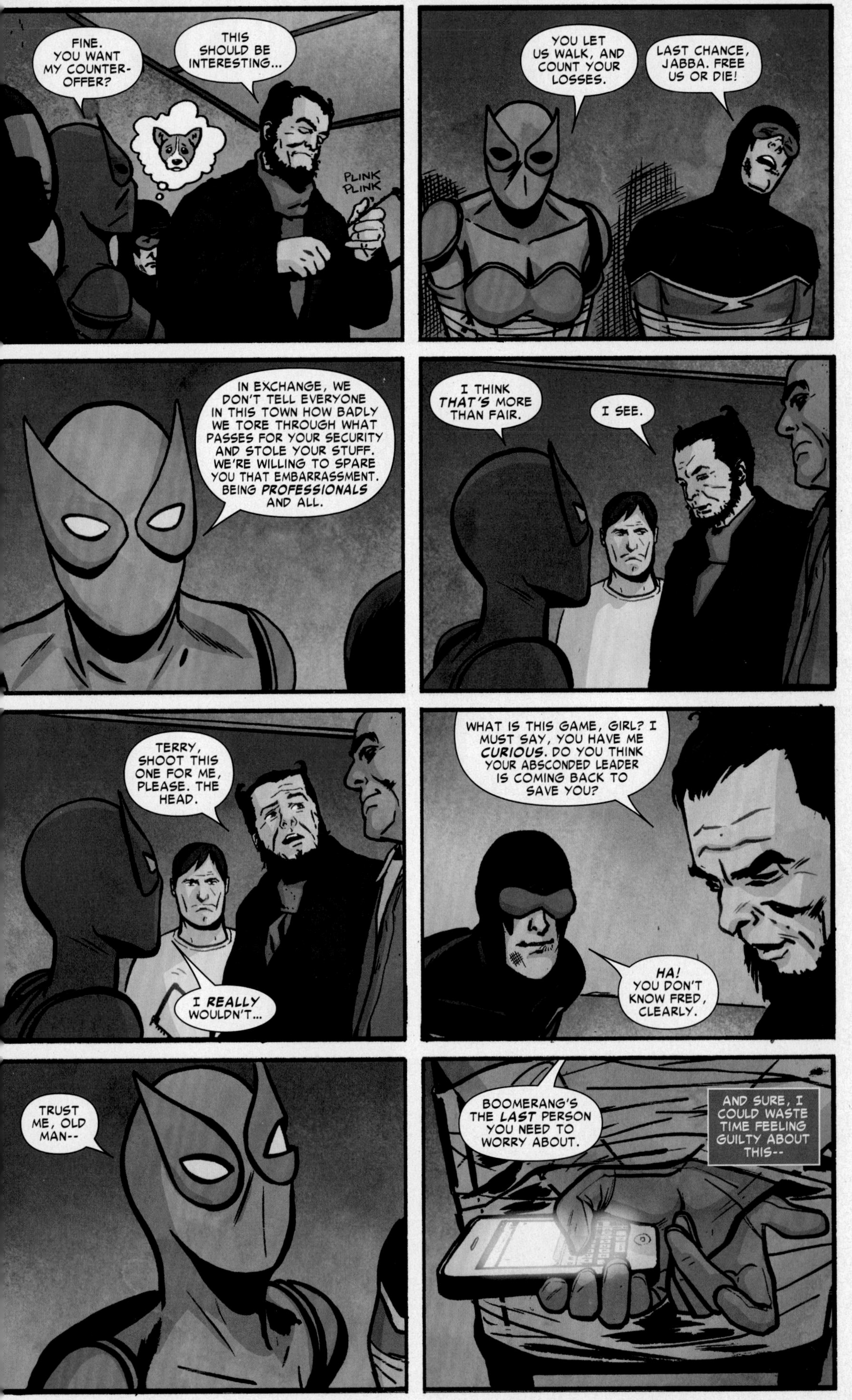
FINE. YOU WANT MY COUNTER-OFFER?
THIS SHOULD BE INTERESTING...
PLINK PLINK
YOU LET US WALK, AND COUNT YOUR LOSSES.
LAST CHANCE, JABBA. FREE US OR DIE!
IN EXCHANGE, WE DON'T TELL EVERYONE IN THIS TOWN HOW BADLY WE TORE THROUGH WHAT PASSES FOR YOUR SECURITY AND STOLE YOUR STUFF. WE'RE WILLING TO SPARE YOU THAT EMBARRASSMENT. BEING PROFESSIONALS AND ALL.
I THINK THAT'S MORE THAN FAIR.
I SEE.
TERRY, SHOOT THIS ONE FOR ME, PLEASE. THE HEAD.
I REALLY WOULDN'T...
WHAT IS THIS GAME, GIRL? I MUST SAY, YOU HAVE ME CURIOUS. DO YOU THINK YOUR ABSCONDED LEADER IS COMING BACK TO SAVE YOU?
HA! YOU DON'T KNOW FRED, CLEARLY.
TRUST ME, OLD MAN--
BOOMERANG'S THE LAST PERSON YOU NEED TO WORRY ABOUT.
AND SURE, I COULD WASTE TIME FEELING GUILTY ABOUT THIS--

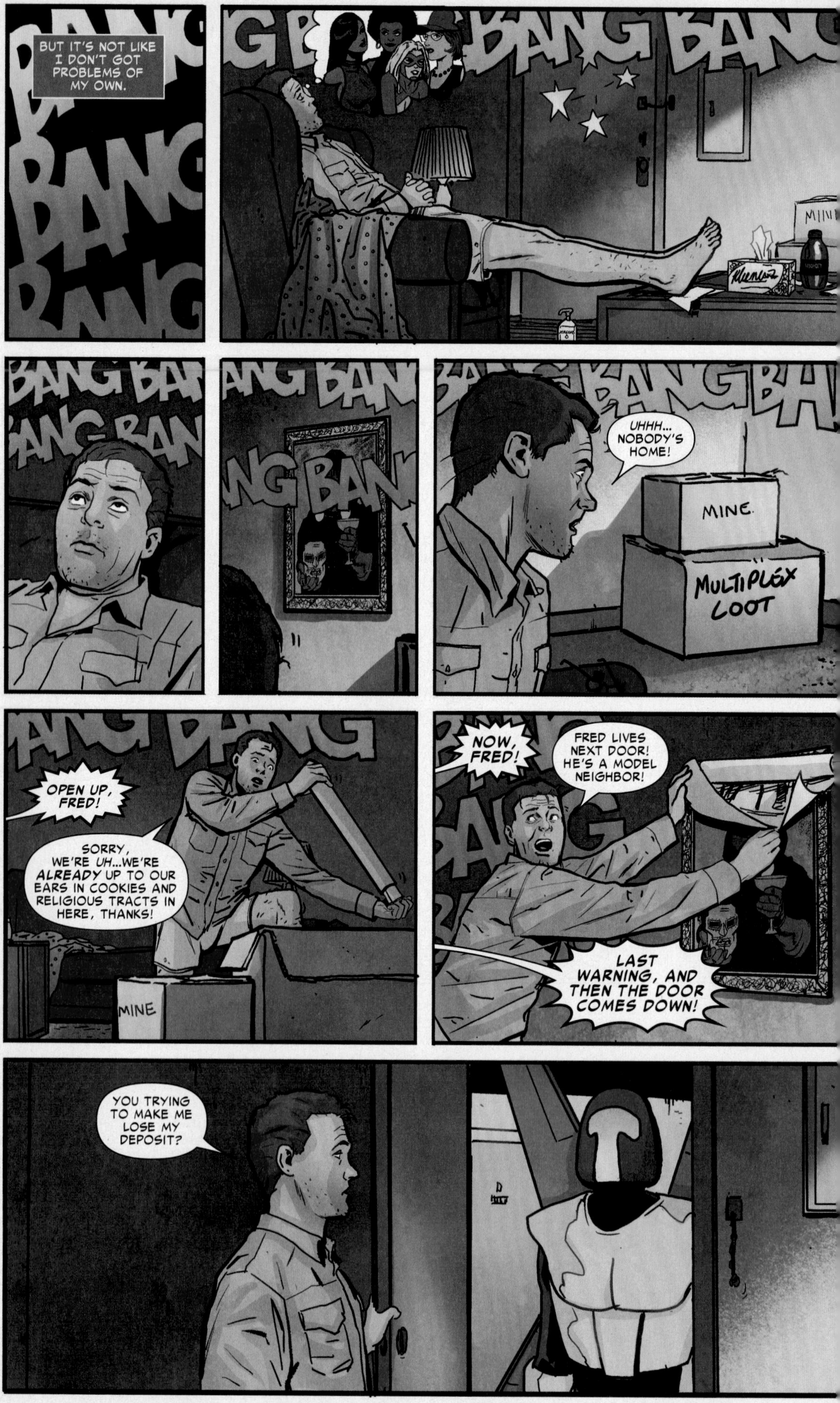

BUT IT'S NOT LIKE I DON'T GOT PROBLEMS OF MY OWN.
BANG BANG BANG BANG
BANG BANG BANG
UHHH... NOBODY'S HOME!
MINE.
MULTIPLEX LOOT
OPEN UP, FRED!
SORRY, WE'RE UH...WE'RE ALREADY UP TO OUR EARS IN COOKIES AND RELIGIOUS TRACTS IN HERE, THANKS!
MINE
NOW, FRED!
FRED LIVES NEXT DOOR! HE'S A MODEL NEIGHBOR!
LAST WARNING, AND THEN THE DOOR COMES DOWN!
YOU TRYING TO MAKE ME LOSE MY DEPOSIT?

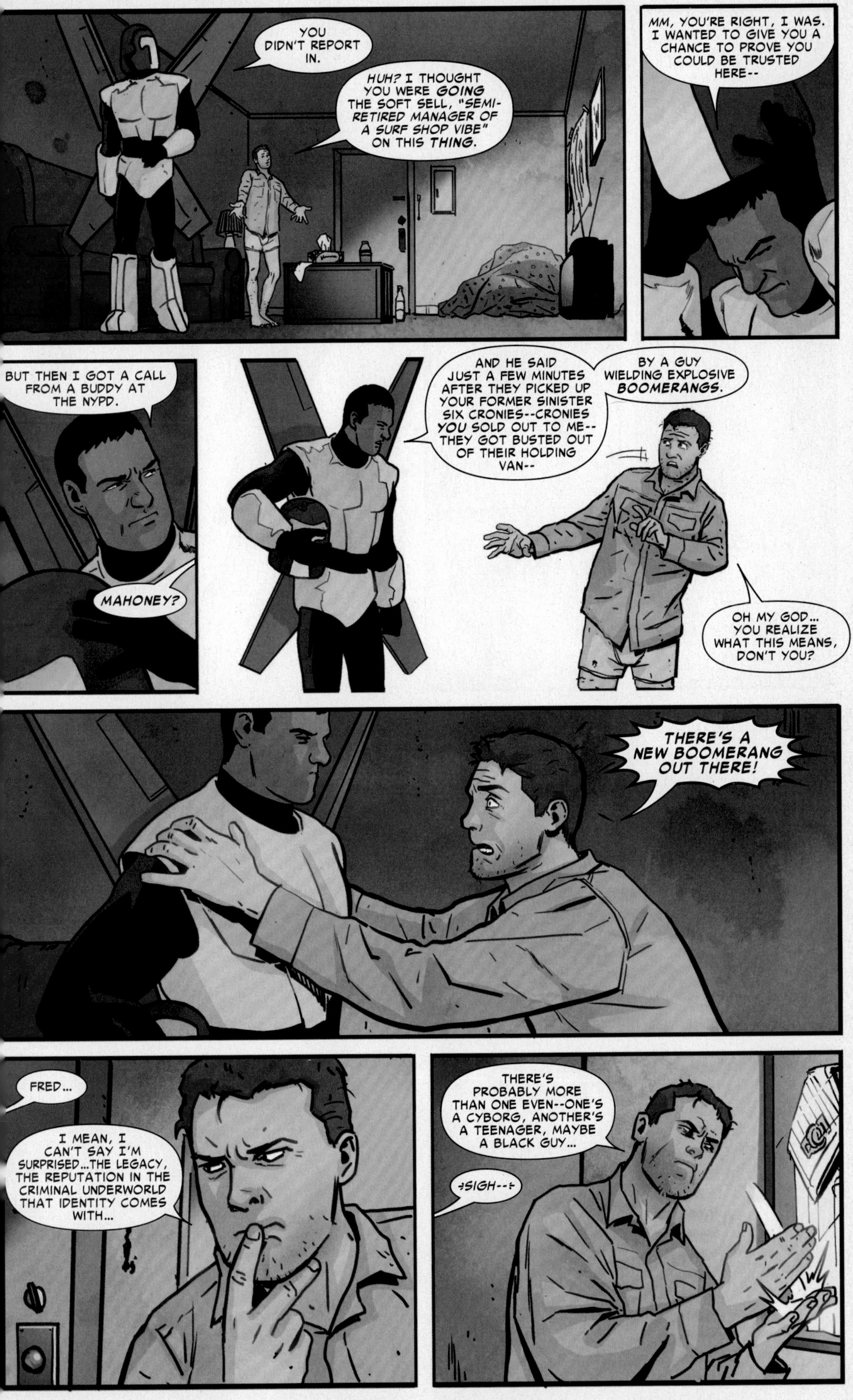
YOU DIDN'T REPORT IN.
HUH? I THOUGHT YOU WERE GOING THE SOFT SELL, "SEMI-RETIRED MANAGER OF A SURF SHOP VIBE" ON THIS THING.
MM, YOU'RE RIGHT, I WAS. I WANTED TO GIVE YOU A CHANCE TO PROVE YOU COULD BE TRUSTED HERE--
BUT THEN I GOT A CALL FROM A BUDDY AT THE NYPD.
MAHONEY?
AND HE SAID JUST A FEW MINUTES AFTER THEY PICKED UP YOUR FORMER SINISTER SIX CRONIES--CRONIES YOU SOLD OUT TO ME--THEY GOT BUSTED OUT OF THEIR HOLDING VAN--
BY A GUY WIELDING EXPLOSIVE BOOMERANGS.
OH MY GOD... YOU REALIZE WHAT THIS MEANS, DON'T YOU?
THERE'S A NEW BOOMERANG OUT THERE!
FRED...
I MEAN, I CAN'T SAY I'M SURPRISED...THE LEGACY, THE REPUTATION IN THE CRIMINAL UNDERWORLD THAT IDENTITY COMES WITH...
THERE'S PROBABLY MORE THAN ONE EVEN--ONE'S A CYBORG, ANOTHER'S A TEENAGER, MAYBE A BLACK GUY...
-SIGH--

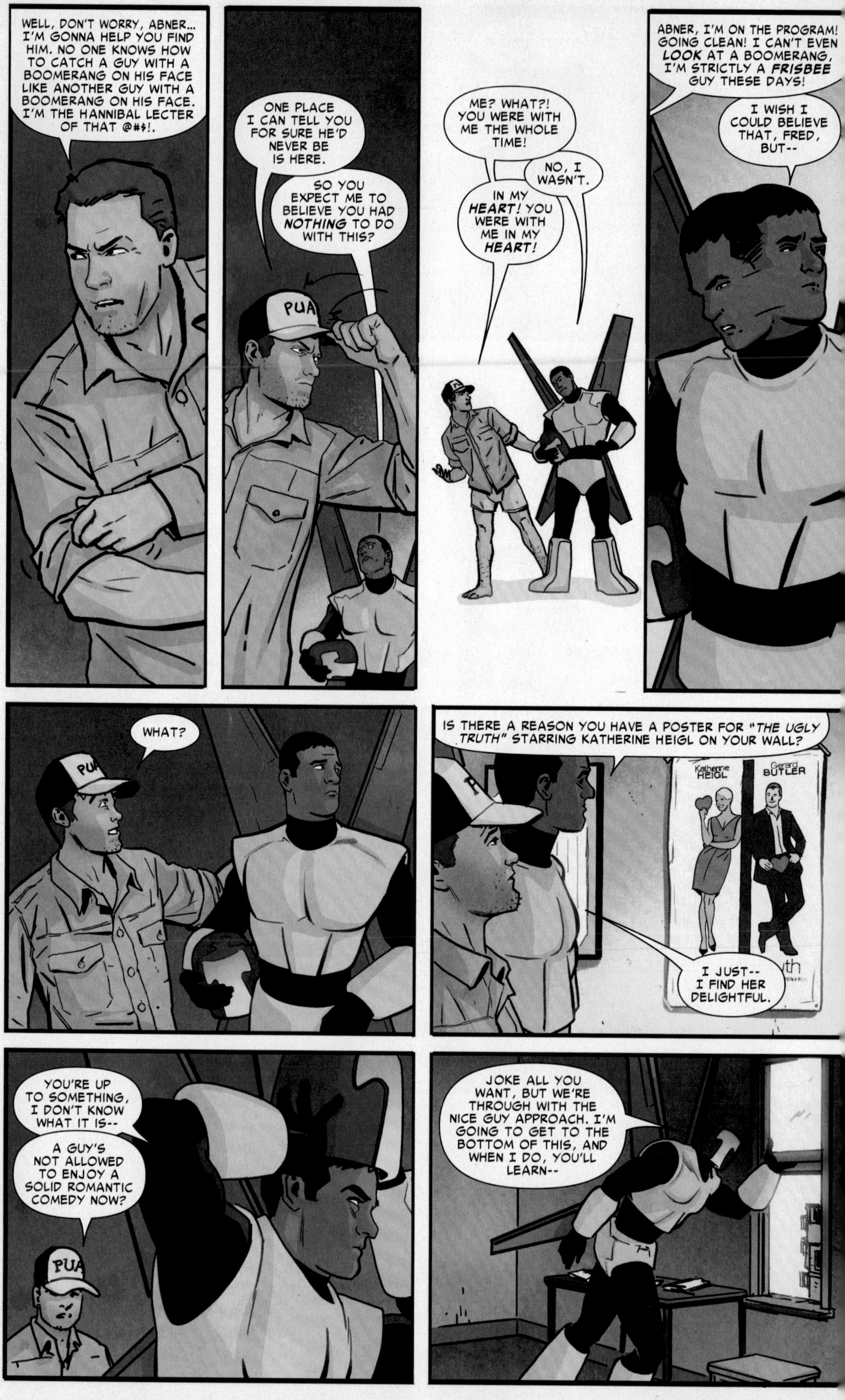
WELL, DON'T WORRY, ABNER... I'M GONNA HELP YOU FIND HIM. NO ONE KNOWS HOW TO CATCH A GUY WITH A BOOMERANG ON HIS FACE LIKE ANOTHER GUY WITH A BOOMERANG ON HIS FACE. I'M THE HANNIBAL LECTER OF THAT @#$!.
ONE PLACE I CAN TELL YOU FOR SURE HE'D NEVER BE IS HERE.
SO YOU EXPECT ME TO BELIEVE YOU HAD NOTHING TO DO WITH THIS?
PUA
ME? WHAT?! YOU WERE WITH ME THE WHOLE TIME!
NO, I WASN'T.
IN MY HEART! YOU WERE WITH ME IN MY HEART!
ABNER, I'M ON THE PROGRAM! GOING CLEAN! I CAN'T EVEN LOOK AT A BOOMERANG, I'M STRICTLY A FRISBEE GUY THESE DAYS!
I WISH I COULD BELIEVE THAT, FRED, BUT--
WHAT?
PUA
IS THERE A REASON YOU HAVE A POSTER FOR "THE UGLY TRUTH" STARRING KATHERINE HEIGL ON YOUR WALL?
Katherine HEIGL
Gerard BUTLER
I JUST-- I FIND HER DELIGHTFUL.
YOU'RE UP TO SOMETHING, I DON'T KNOW WHAT IT IS--
A GUY'S NOT ALLOWED TO ENJOY A SOLID ROMANTIC COMEDY NOW?
PUA
JOKE ALL YOU WANT, BUT WE'RE THROUGH WITH THE NICE GUY APPROACH. I'M GOING TO GET TO THE BOTTOM OF THIS, AND WHEN I DO, YOU'LL LEARN--

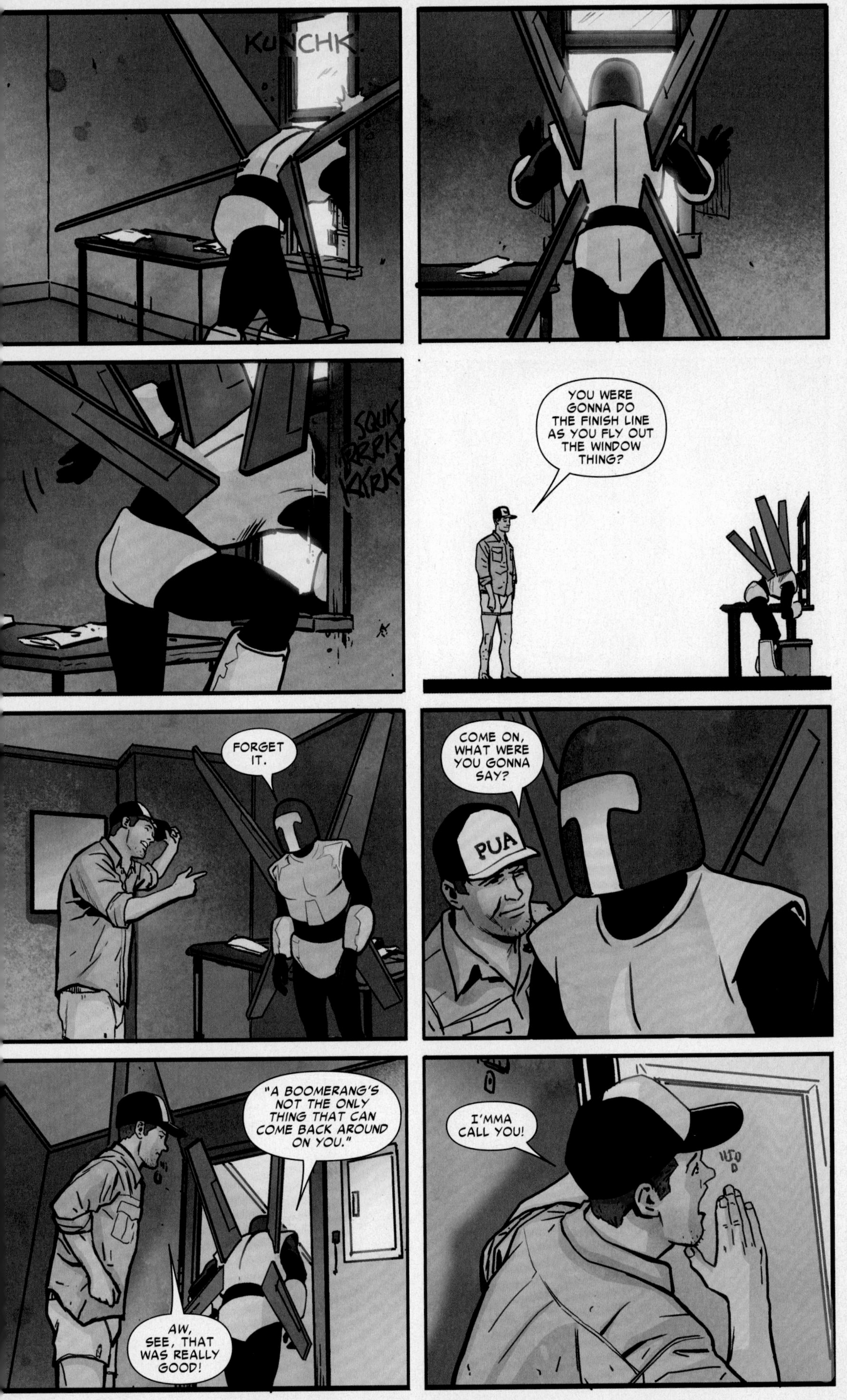
KUNCHK
SQUK
RRRK
KRRK
YOU WERE GONNA DO THE FINISH LINE AS YOU FLY OUT THE WINDOW THING?
FORGET IT.
COME ON, WHAT WERE YOU GONNA SAY?
PUA
"A BOOMERANG'S NOT THE ONLY THING THAT CAN COME BACK AROUND ON YOU."
AW, SEE, THAT WAS REALLY GOOD!
I'MMA CALL YOU!

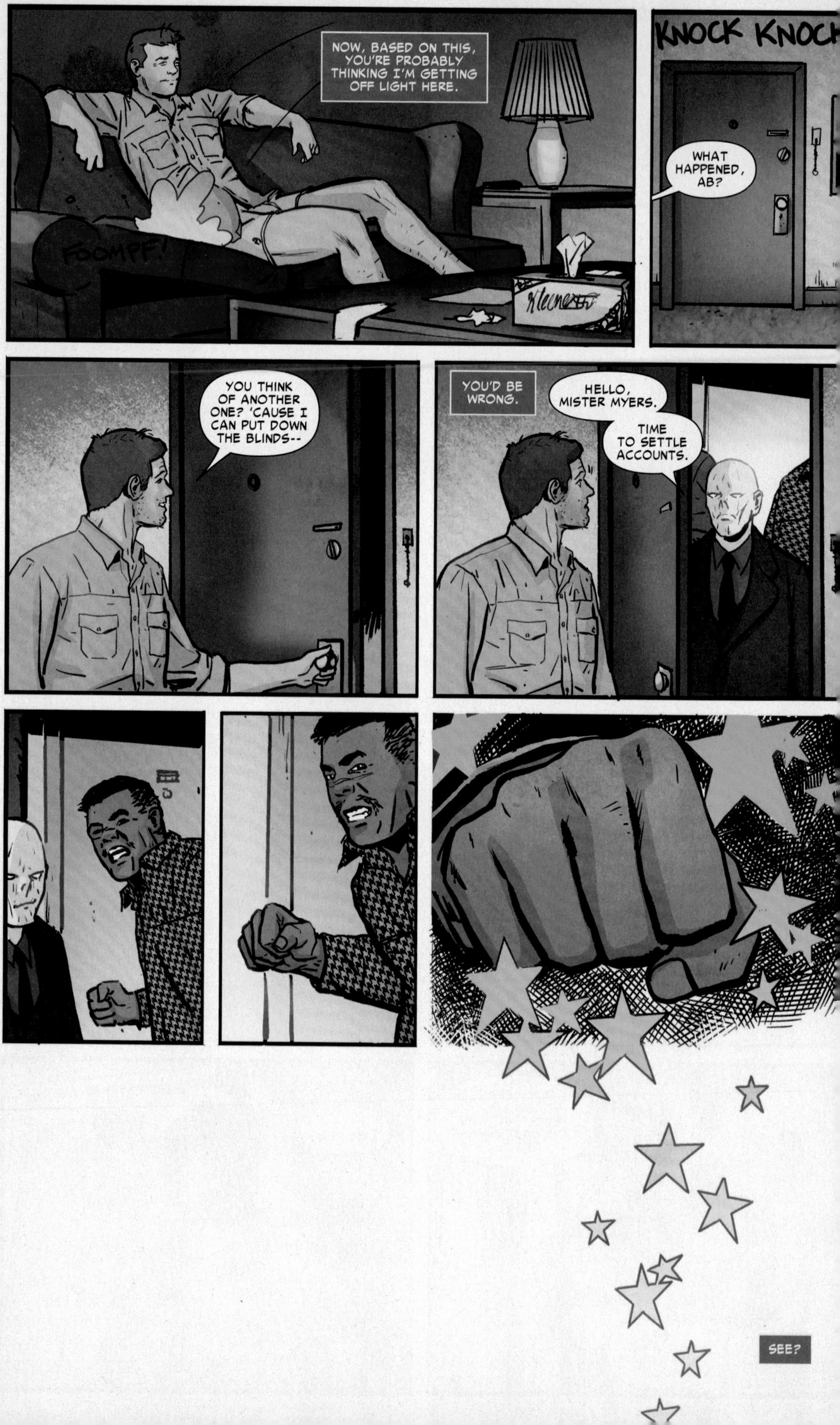
NOW, BASED ON THIS, YOU'RE PROBABLY THINKING I'M GETTING OFF LIGHT HERE.
FOOMPF!
KNOCK KNOCK
WHAT HAPPENED, AB?
YOU THINK OF ANOTHER ONE? 'CAUSE I CAN PUT DOWN THE BLINDS--
YOU'D BE WRONG.
HELLO, MISTER MYERS.
TIME TO SETTLE ACCOUNTS.
SEE?

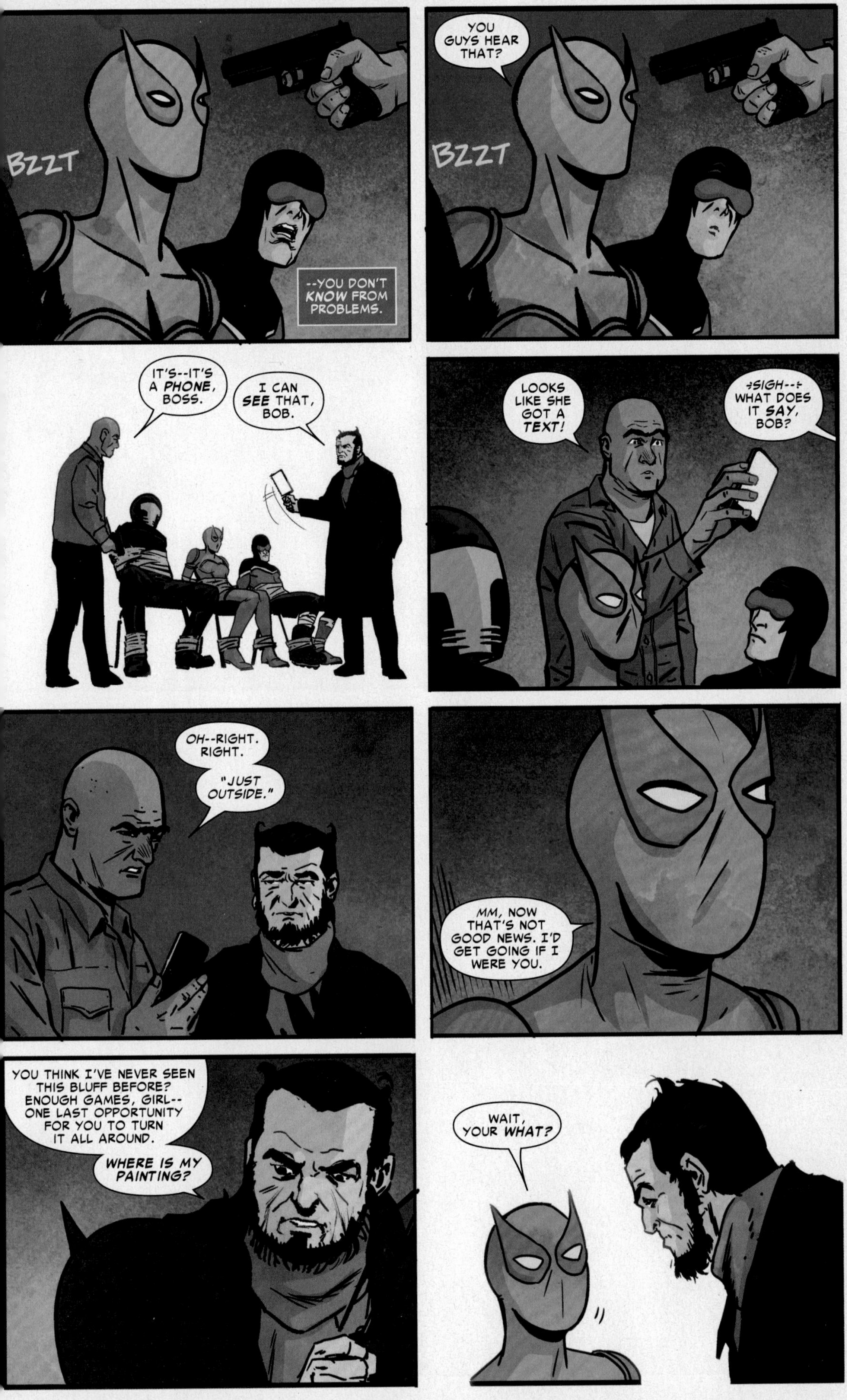

BZZT
--YOU DON'T KNOW FROM PROBLEMS.
YOU GUYS HEAR THAT?
BZZT
IT'S--IT'S A PHONE, BOSS.
I CAN SEE THAT, BOB.
LOOKS LIKE SHE GOT A TEXT!
-SIGH-- WHAT DOES IT SAY, BOB?
OH--RIGHT. RIGHT.
"JUST OUTSIDE."
MM, NOW THAT'S NOT GOOD NEWS. I'D GET GOING IF I WERE YOU.
YOU THINK I'VE NEVER SEEN THIS BLUFF BEFORE? ENOUGH GAMES, GIRL-- ONE LAST OPPORTUNITY FOR YOU TO TURN IT ALL AROUND.
WHERE IS MY PAINTING?
WAIT, YOUR WHAT?

BLAM BLAM

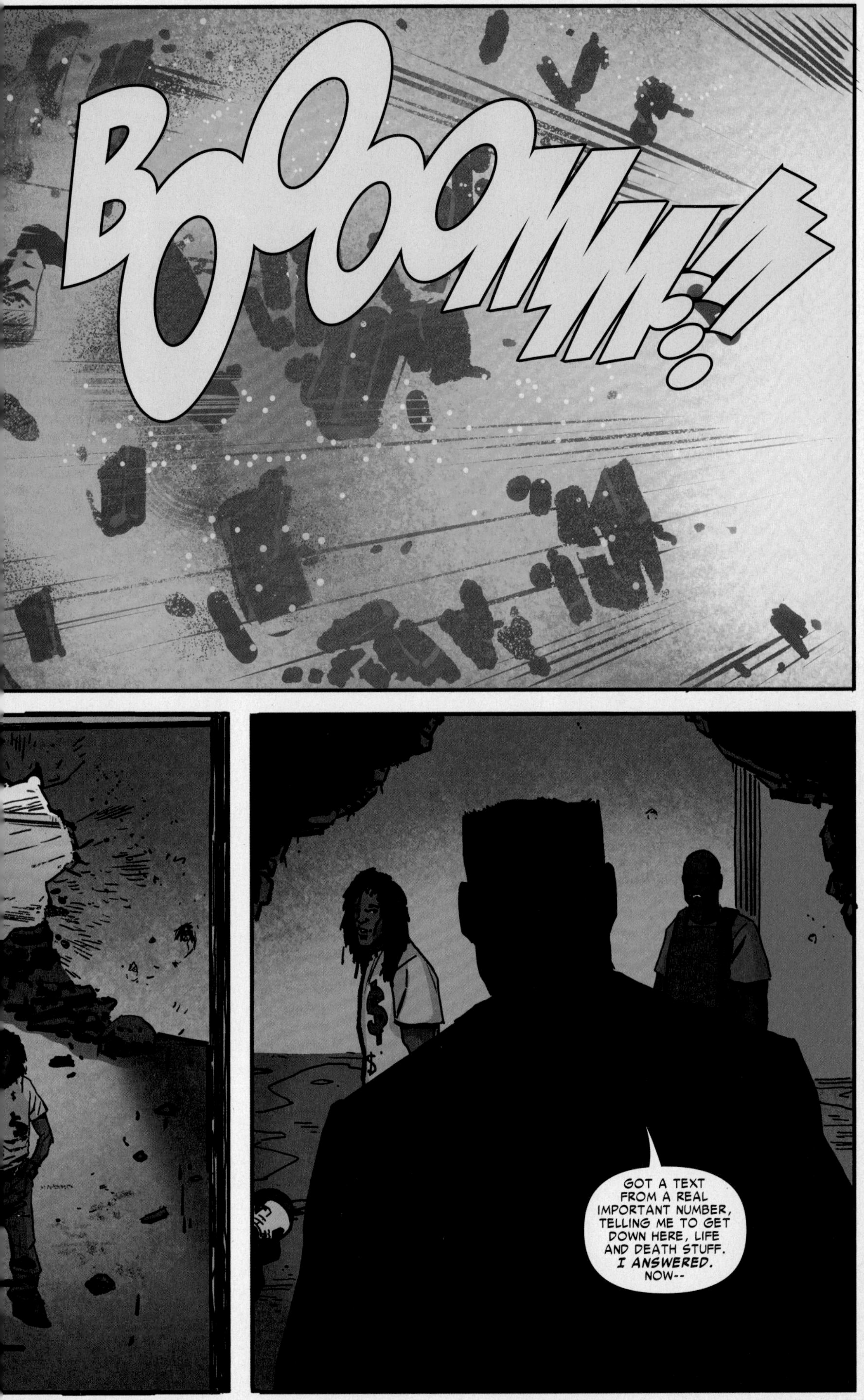
BOOOMM!!
GOT A TEXT FROM A REAL IMPORTANT NUMBER, TELLING ME TO GET DOWN HERE, LIFE AND DEATH STUFF. *I ANSWERED.* NOW--

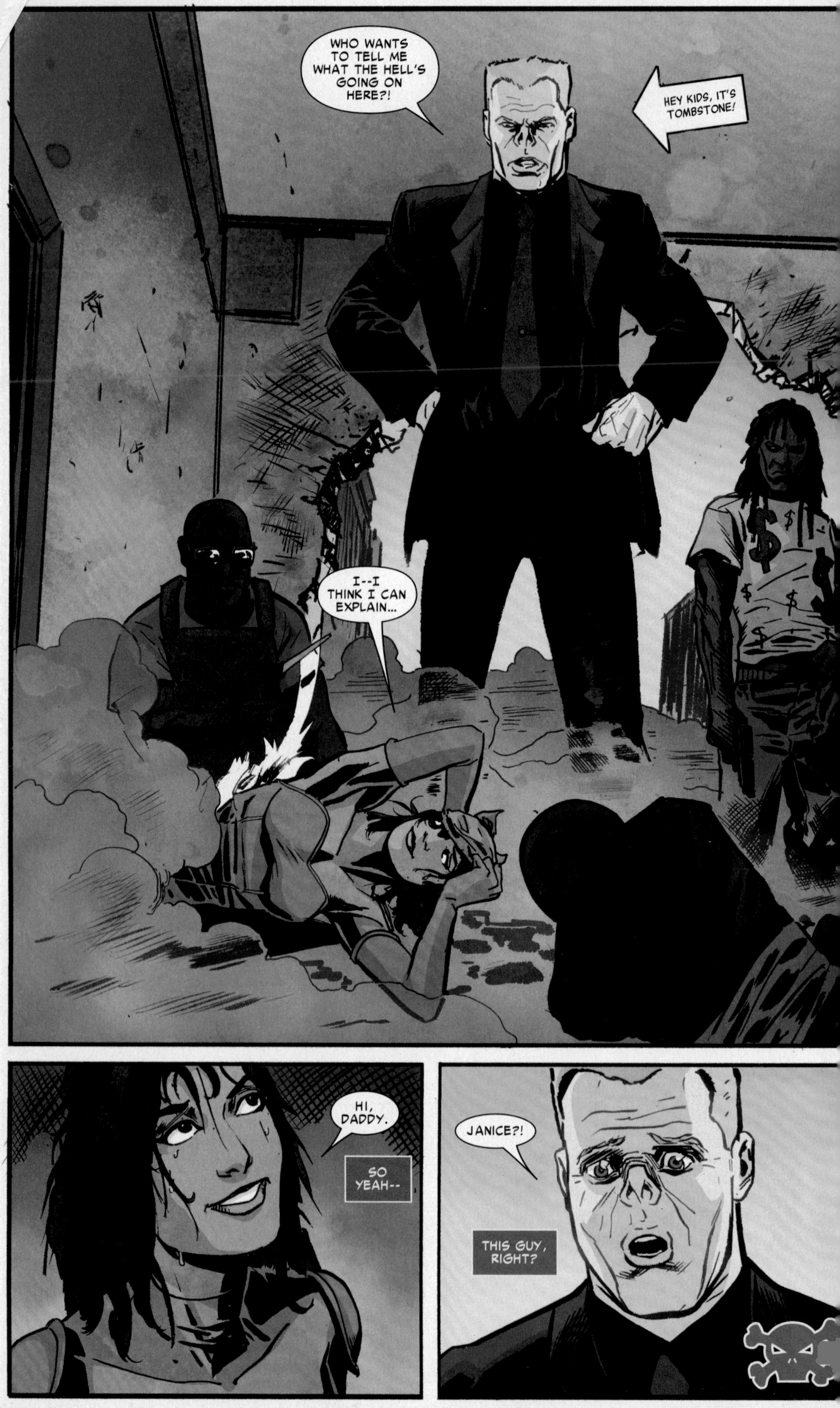
WHO WANTS TO TELL ME WHAT THE HELL'S GOING ON HERE?!
HEY KIDS, IT'S TOMBSTONE!
I--I THINK I CAN EXPLAIN...
HI, DADDY.
SO YEAH--
JANICE?!
THIS GUY, RIGHT?

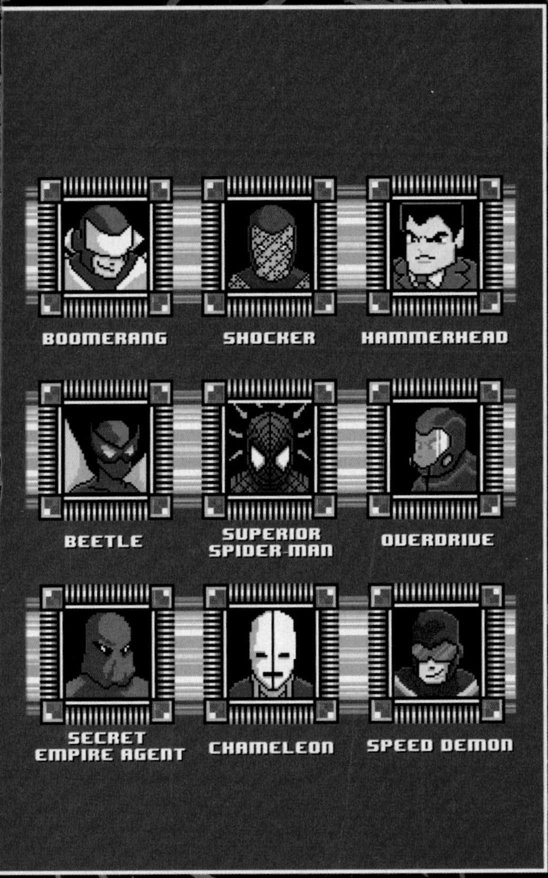
BOOMERANG
SHOCKER
HAMMERHEAD
BEETLE
SUPERIOR SPIDER-MAN
OVERDRIVE
SECRET EMPIRE AGENT
CHAMELEON
SPEED DEMON

#1 8-BIT VARIANT
BY MATTHEW C. WAITE

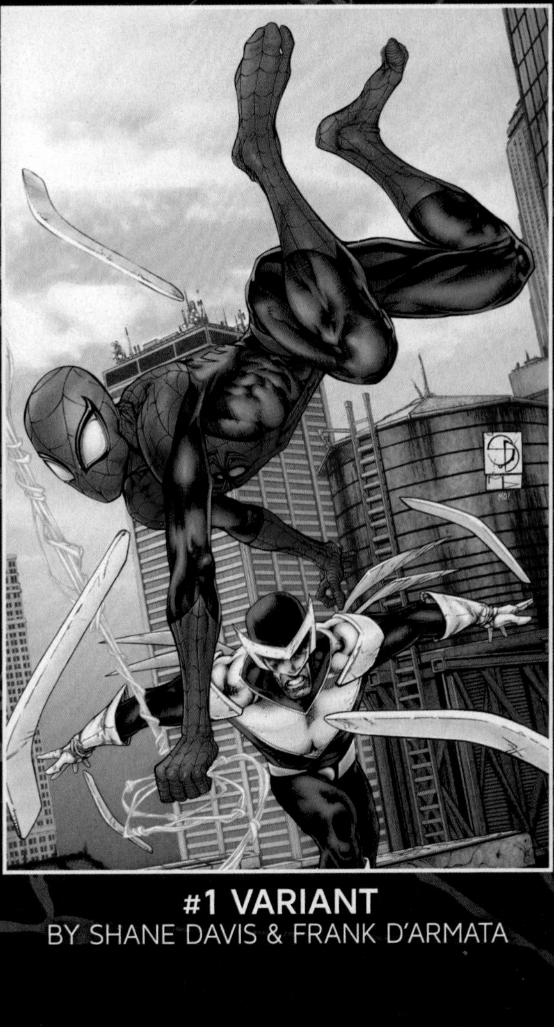

#1 VARIANT
BY SHANE DAVIS & FRANK D'ARMATA

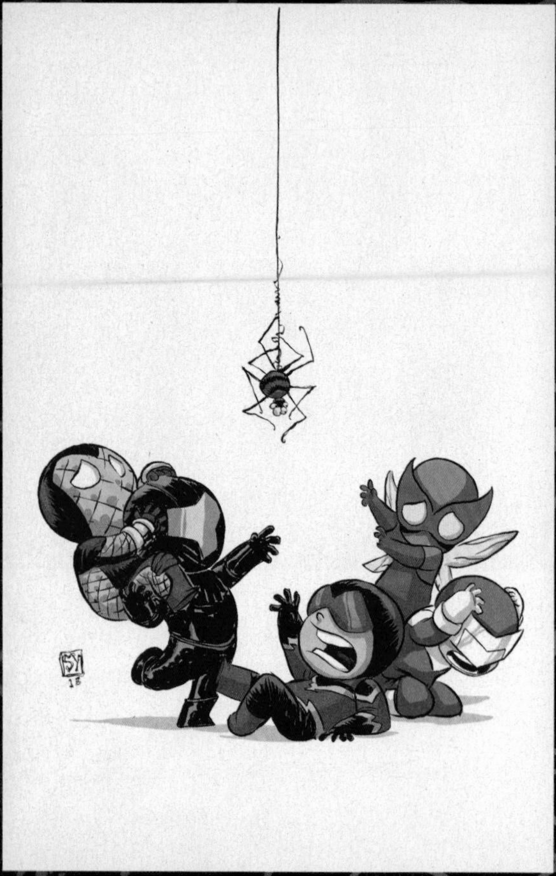

#1 VARIANT
BY SKOTTIE YOUNG

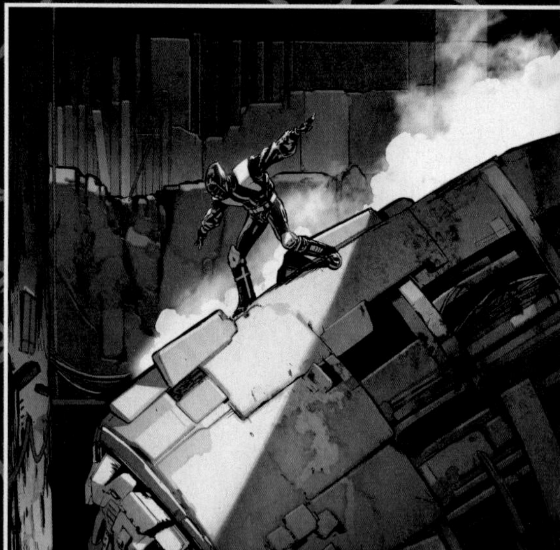

#2 VARIANT
BY PHIL JIMENEZ & MARTE GRACIA

#3 VARIANT
BY MARK BAGLEY, MARK MORALES
& CHRIS SOTOMAYOR

#4 VARIANT
BY DECLAN SHALVEY & JORDIE BELLAIRE

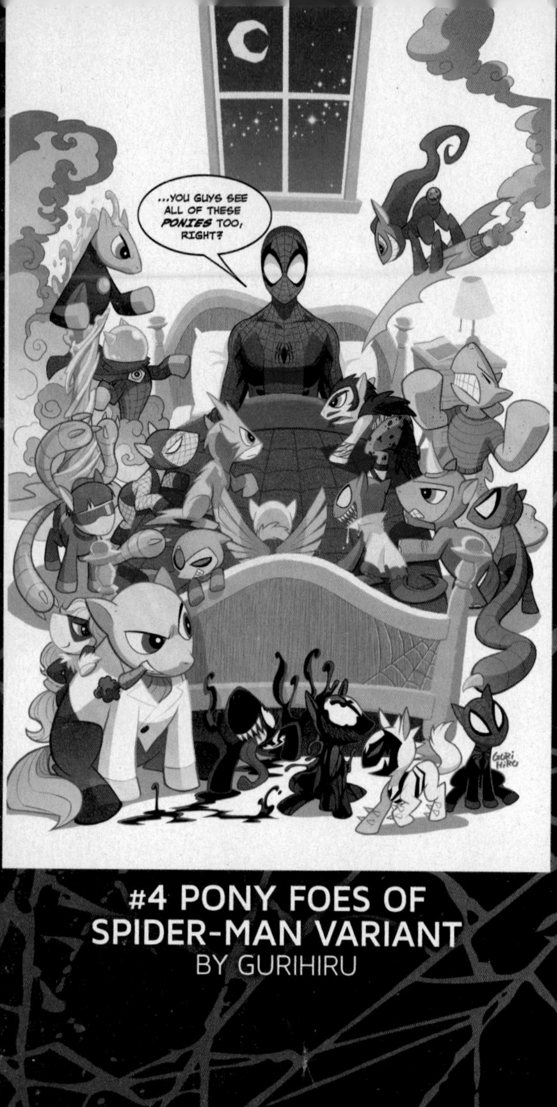
...YOU GUYS SEE ALL OF THESE PONIES TOO, RIGHT?
GURIHIRU

#4 PONY FOES OF SPIDER-MAN VARIANT
BY GURIHIRU

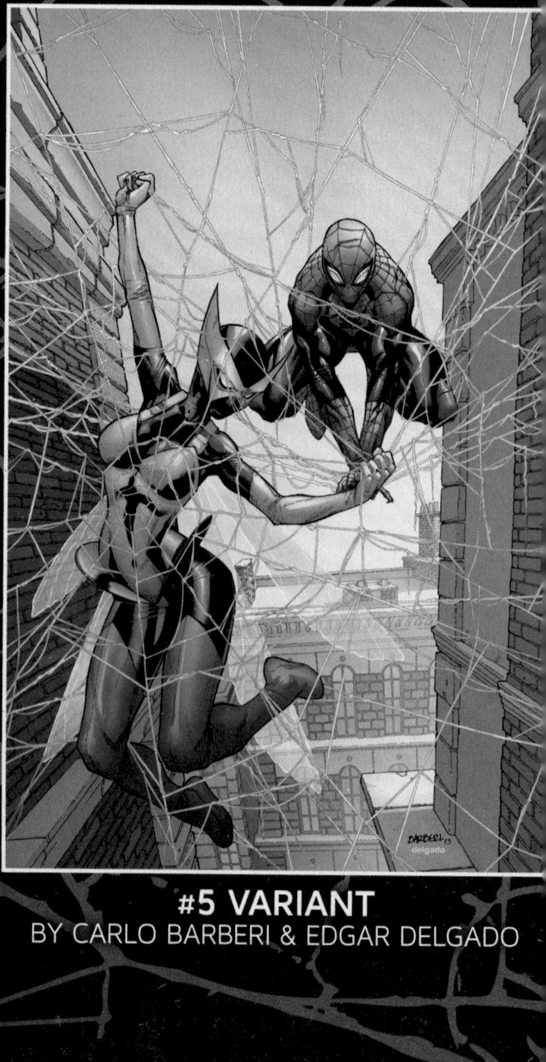

#5 VARIANT
BY CARLO BARBERI & EDGAR DELGADO